Penguin Books

YOUR
MEMORY

Alan Baddeley is Director of the British Medical
Research Council's Applied Psychology Unit in
Cambridge, Professor of Cognitive Psychology
at Cambridge University and a Fellow of
Churchill College. He is a member of the
Academia Europea and a Fellow of the Royal
Society. His books include *The Psychology of
Memory* (1976), *Working Memory* (1986) and
Human Memory: Theory and Practice (1990),
one of the most comprehensive and readable
specialist texts on the subject in print today. He
is also joint editor of *Attention and Performance,
IX* (1981), *Research Directions in Cognitive
Science: A European Perspective, Vol. 1 Cognitive
Psychology* (1989) and *Human Factors in
Hazardous Situations* (1990). He has published
over 200 papers concerned with human memory
problems and performance under stress, and has
contributed chapters to many books intended
for a non-specialist audience. In recent years his
principal research interests have been in short-
term working memory and its links with
language, and in understanding the breakdown
of memory that unfortunately often occurs in
brain-damaged patients.

Dedication

To Roland, Gavin and Bart

YOUR MEMORY

A USER'S GUIDE

ALAN BADDELEY

Penguin Books

PENGUIN BOOKS

Published by the Penguin Group
Penguin Books Ltd, 27 Wrights Lane, London W8 5TZ, England
Penguin Books USA Inc., 375 Hudson Street, New York, New York 10014, USA
Penguin Books Australia Ltd, Ringwood, Victoria, Australia
Penguin Books Canada Ltd, 10 Alcorn Avenue, Toronto, Ontario, Canada M4V 3B2
Penguin Books (NZ) Ltd, 182-190 Wairau Road, Auckland 10, New Zealand

Penguin Books Ltd, Registered Offices: Harmondsworth, Middlesex, England

First published by Sidgwick and Jackson 1982
Published in Pelican Books 1983
Reprinted in Penguin Books 1992
This edition first published by Prion, an imprint of Multimedia Books Ltd 1993
Published in Penguin Books 1994
10 9 8 7 6 5 4 3 2 1

Contents

Preface

This second edition of Your Memory *owes its existence to Len Berkowitz, a social psychologist visiting Cambridge from the University of Wisconsin, who regretted the fact that the first edition was no longer available in the United States. He urged me, directly and through various of his publishing friends, to reissue it. I had initially no intention of rewriting the book, but on re-examination it became clear that a good deal had happened, both in the field of memory research in general and in my own interests, in the ten years since it was first published. Multimedia, the original publisher, was enthusiastic about the idea of a revision, and the book that follows is the result.*

Your Memory *is a guide to the whole terrain of human memory, to the general lie of the land as well as its most salient features. It also visits many exotic and curious by-ways. We all possess memories, and one way to understand them is to use them under controlled conditions. As before, I have included numerous brief demonstrations that I hope you, the reader, will try out as a prelude to appreciating the more formal experiments that make up the backbone of the book.*

As with any guide, there is always the problem of where to begin. A historian would begin with long-term learning, the first aspect of memory to be studied scientifically, and leave until later the more recent and complex field of short-term and working memory. Logically, however, it makes more sense to parallel the operation of the memory system itself, beginning with short-term and working memory and then moving on to long-term learning and forgetting. This is the approach that I have adopted, accepting the risk of presenting more complex and recent developments first. However, if you prefer a somewhat gentler introduction to the subject I suggest you postpone Chapters 2 and 3 until you have read the chapters that deal with long-term memory.

The most obvious change in the study of human memory over the last decade has been a determined move out of the laboratory and into the everyday world.

Ten years ago I had to search hard to find good real-world examples of work illustrating principles that were being investigated in the laboratory. This time round I had a wide range of intriguing new studies to choose from, including a number of topics suggested by Stephen Ceci of Cornell University.

Social preoccupations have also changed. Work on eyewitness testimony, principally centered on laboratory studies ten years ago, has begun to influence the law, with the result that there are now many psychologists active in the legal system. Their work has led to the development of new techniques for interviewing witnesses and those accused of crime. In recent years child abuse has become a subject of great public concern. As described in Chapter 7, eliciting 'true' memories from both children and adults in child abuse cases is extremely difficult. Here too psychologists are making a significant contribution.

This new edition has also given me the opportunity to review aspects of memory development in childhood and memory changes associated with aging, contrasting the graceful decline that accompanies healthy aging with the more baleful deterioration seen in Alzheimer's disease.

My own principal area of interest, working memory, has developed considerably in the last ten years. We now know a good deal more about the role of working memory in language acquisition in children and in second language learning in adults. This has come about partly through the study of memory breakdown in brain-damaged individuals — the mechanisms of normal memory are often revealed through their breakdown.

In preparing this second edition I have had the invaluable help of my secretary Julia Darling. I am also grateful to Lorraine Dickey at Multimedia, for seeing the book through the first stages of revision, and to Anne Cope for piloting it through the final editing and production process.

Alan Baddeley
Cambridge, May 1993

1 What is memory?

'I have a terrible memory.' How often have you heard that? In my own case, whenever I meet someone, and in casual conversation admit that I carry out research on memory, by far the most common response is 'You should do some work on me — my memory is awful!' So is mine — I even managed to forget to turn up to a radio phone-in on memory. I was reminded of my dreadful lapse by reading the radio section of the newspaper, and arrived at the studio just in time to be asked by the anchor man for 'a few tips on improving your memory!'

I also believe, however, that I have a good memory, and would argue, despite its occasionally embarrassing fallibility, that both my memory and yours exceed that of the best computer in terms of capacity, flexibility and durability. In the chapters that follow, I hope to persuade you to share my admiration.

Perhaps the best way to appreciate the importance of memory is to consider what it would be like to live without it, or rather without them, since memory is not a single organ like the heart or liver, but an alliance of systems that work together, allowing us to learn from the past and predict the future.

In recent years we have learnt a great deal from the study of memory impairment following brain damage. Almost any damage to the brain will lead to some slow-down in learning and some impairment in the speed with which we access old memories. Certain areas of the brain, however, are particularly crucial for memory. Serious damage to these can lead to dense amnesia, which can be a crippling handicap.

Consider the case of Clive Wearing, a talented musician and an expert on early music, who fell ill as a result of a viral infection. The *Herpes simplex* virus is carried by a large percentage of the population, typically having no worse effect than causing the occasional cold sore. On very rare occasions, however, the virus manages to overcome the brain's natural defenses and causes an inflammation known as encephalitis. This can lead to extensive brain damage, and until relatively recently was frequently fatal. Although the disease can now be treated, patients often suffer extensive brain damage which frequently leads to memory problems.

Clive Wearing is a particularly dramatic example of the terrible after-effects of encephalitis. He is so impaired that he cannot remember what happened more than minutes before, with the result that he is convinced that he has only just recovered consciousness. He keeps a diary which records this obsession — page upon page of records indicating the date, the time and the fact that consciousness has just been regained. When confronted with evidence of earlier apparent conscious awareness, by being shown a video of himself, for example, he becomes upset and denies the evidence, even after many

'Trace of memory', a watercolor by Elie Abrahami. The artist had depicted a lumber room of strange objects, with a blank 'no-go' area above and a sealed compartment below.

years of being in this condition. It is as if, faced with the enormity of a life limited to a horizon of a few seconds, he clings to the view that he has just recovered consciousness, with the implication that in the future all will be well.

Clive's world was very effectively portrayed in a television program by Jonathan Miller entitled "Prisoner of Consciousness'. Whenever his wife appears, Clive greets her with the joy appropriate to someone who has not seen

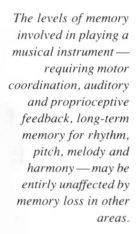

The levels of memory involved in playing a musical instrument — requiring motor coordination, auditory and proprioceptive feedback, long-term memory for rhythm, pitch, melody and harmony — may be entirely unaffected by memory loss in other areas.

a loved one for many months. She has only to leave the room for two or three minutes and return for the joy to be repeated, a process that is always full of emotion, and always expressed in the same way. Clive lives in a permanent present, unable to register change or to use the past to anticipate the future, a situation he once described as 'Hell on earth. It's like being dead — all the bloody time!'

Clive's memory for his past is less dramatically impaired than his ongoing memory. Nevertheless it is severely disrupted — he knows who he is, and can give you a broad outline of his earlier life, but with very little accurate detail. He was not certain, for instance, whether his current, second, wife and he were married or not. He could remember, given appropriate prompts, certain highlights of his life, such as singing for the Pope during a papal visit to London or directing the first performance of *Messiah* in London with authentic instruments and decor. He had written a book on the early composer Lassus, but could remember virtually nothing about him. His visual memory was also impaired — he had spent four years in Cambridge, but did not recognize a photograph of his old college. His general knowledge was similarly reduced — he had no idea, for example, who was the author of *Romeo and Juliet*.

There was, however, one area that was remarkably preserved, namely his musical skills. On one occasion his wife returned home to discover that his old choir was visiting him, and that he was conducting them just as he did in the old days. He could sight-read music and was able to accompany himself on the harp-sichord, playing quite complex music and singing with great skill and feeling. Alas, he appears to find the transition from music back to his desolate state of amnesia particularly disturbing, with the result that music does not seem to provide the kind of solace that one might have hoped.

Clive has been in this state since 1985. He is still convinced that he has just woken up. He still lives in a desolate, eternal present. He cannot enjoy books because he cannot follow their plots, and takes no interest in current affairs because, likewise, they are meaningless because he does not remember their context. If he goes out, he immediately becomes lost. He is indeed a prisoner limited to a brief island of consciousness in a sea of amnesia.

The tragic case of Clive Wearing demonstrates that memory is important, but what is memory?

The physical basis of memory

It is often assumed by non-psychologists, and indeed by a few psychologists, that psychological theories should have the final aim of giving a physiological account of psychological facts. This view, which is sometimes called reductionism, sees a continuous chain of explanation, extending down from psychology through physiology, biochemistry and biophysics, and so on right down to the subatomic particles studied by the physicist.

Suppose I were an architect and wanted to find out about London's St Paul's Cathedral. I could pursue my enquiries at many different levels. I could ask about the history of the building and how it came to be built following the Great Fire. I could ask about the style, and the influence of classical architecture on Sir Christopher Wren, who built it. I could ask about its function, and I could ask about the details of the material which went into its construction. The viewpoint that a study of memory must begin with its biochemistry would be somewhat analogous to advocating that anyone interested in St Paul's Cathedral should begin by studying the atomic structure of brick and stone. There is no doubt that such a study would be relevant, and indeed if the atomic structure of the bricks had been inappropriate, the cathedral would never have stood up. However, one could know everything about the atomic structure of brick and stone and yet know virtually nothing of interest about the cathedral. On the other hand, one could know a great deal about the cathedral without having any knowledge of the physico-chemical properties of brick and stone.

The structure of materials does of course at some point constrain the architect and obviously has an important bearing on the creation of a building. Similarly, in principle, a number of aspects of human memory could be importantly influenced by physiological or biochemical findings. However many of the claims for an understanding of the molecular basis of memory that were being made a few years ago have since been shown to be premature. The neurochemistry of memory is proving much more complex than was previously suspected. There is no doubt that progress is being made in this important area, and that one day there may be a very fruitful collaboration between the human experimental psychologist and the neurochemist. At present, however, there is little area of overlap, so I will give only a brief account of some of the work concerned with the neurophysiology of learning and memory.

The neurophysiology of learning and memory

Learning almost certainly involves a chain of electrophysiological and neuro-chemical changes in the brain. Such changes are currently very difficult to study in the human brain, but considerable progress is being made in understanding the processes involved in learning in less complex organisms. For example, Kandel has worked on the very simple marine organism *Aplysia*, which combines neuronal simplicity with a capacity for simple learning. It is capable, for example, of showing the phenomenon known as *habituation*. This is a process whereby a stimulus that initially evokes a response gradually comes to be ignored when it is repeated, in the absence of any positive or negative outcome. In the case of *Aplysia*, if one stimulates the siphon, both the siphon and the gill tend to be withdrawn initially; after repeated stimulation the withdrawal response stops, an effect that can last from minutes up to weeks. The withdrawal response involves electrical transmission across synapses, the special junctions between neurons, or nerve cells. Transmission across synapses depends on neurotransmitters, chemical messengers that allow one neuron to communicate with another. These in turn depend upon the release of calcium ions. The process of repeated stimulation gradually reduces the activity of the channels that release calcium ions, thus reducing the likelihood that sufficient calcium ions will be released to cause firing or onward transmission of a nerve impulse.

The opposite to habituation is *sensitization,* a process that occurs when an independent stimulus increases the probability of a response. Hearing a shot, for example, might make you sufficiently jumpy to be startled by the sound of a car door slamming subsequently. In the case of *Aplysia*, an unpleasant stimulus to the tail enhances the withdrawal response when the siphon is touched. This is caused by an increase in the amount of neurotransmitter substance released as a result of a greater influx of calcium ions into the terminal.

Aplysia is also capable of the form of learning known as *classical conditioning*. The best known example of classical conditioning was that observed in dogs by the Russian physiologist Pavlov, who showed that when the presentation of food was regularly associated with a bell, eventually the sound of the bell alone led to salivation. In the case of *Aplysia*, the equivalent to food is a strong stimulation to the tail, which causes the automatic response of withdrawing the gill and siphon. The equivalent of the bell is a mild touch of the siphon, which does not of itself lead to withdrawal. However, when the light touch is consistently followed by a strong tail stimulus, it eventually leads to withdrawal of the gill and siphon in the absence of the tail stimulus. This simple analog of learning can persist for several days. Kandel suggests that the underlying mechanism is similar to that of sensitization; the light touch to the siphon eventually leads, through association with the stronger tail stimulus, to an increase in the flow of calcium ions into the terminal, leading to firing and transmission of the nerve impulse across the synapse.

The underlying mechanism for more complex aspects of learning and memory remains in doubt. However, one possible mechanism is suggested by the effect known as *long-term potentiation* (LTP), a phenomenon first discovered by Bliss and Lomo in the 1970s. While working on the hippocampus of the rabbit (a part of the brain that appears to be heavily involved in learning and memory), they found that intense electrical stimulation of connected areas resulted in hippocampal cells responding more strongly to stimuli than they had done previously. This enhanced response lasted for days, weeks, and even longer, suggesting that it might be a mechanism for long-term learning.

Subsequent research has indicated that LTP depends upon the activity of the receptors on both sides of the synapse. When the pre-synaptic sending mechanism receives high-frequency stimulation, it releases the neurotransmitter glutamate. For LTP to occur, however, the post-synaptic or receiving neuron must also be operating at the appropriate level. The relevant post-synaptic receptors are sensitive to a substance known by the abbreviation NMDA (N-Methyl-D-Aspartate), and firing depends on having exactly the right balance of ions in the receptor channel. When both pre- and post-synaptic circumstances are right, the nature of the synapse changes, so that in future a much weaker pre-synaptic stimulus will cause the post-synaptic neuron to fire.

The fact that the cells associated with LTP are particularly numerous in the hippocampus, which is assumed to be crucially involved in learning and memory, provides some encouragement for believing that this may indeed be a basic

A PCB, or printed circuit board. Looks complex? The 11 million or so nerve cells (neurons) in the human brain, and the connections between them, can be imagined as a PCB of enormously greater three-dimensional complexity.

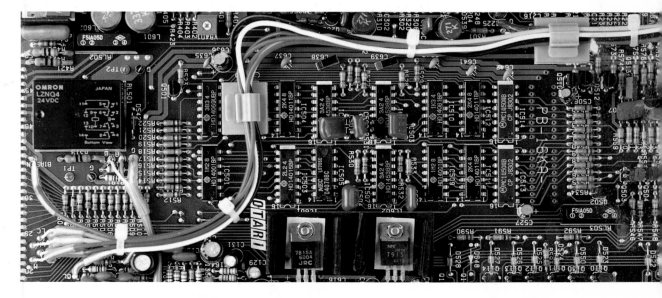

Donald Hebb, the Canadian psychologist whose ideas about the basis of learning, proposed in 1949, are still influential.

learning mechanism. In a classic book published in 1949 the Canadian psychologist Donald Hebb speculated that a mechanism such as this might underlie the process of learning. Since that time a number of computer-based learning models have been developed using Hebb's ideas.

How psychologists study memory

While some psychologists are involved in trying to understand the physiological basis of memory, this is not the most common approach and will play little part in the remainder of this account of human memory. If psychologists do not study memory by examining its physical or biochemical characteristics, how do they arrive at their findings? Do they simply ask people how they remember things? On the whole they do not. While it is unwise to ignore people's comments on how they learn or remember, experience has shown that this kind of information is an unreliable source of evidence.

Consider, for example, the question of visual imagery. In the nineteenth century Sir Francis Galton did a classic study which involved writing to a large number of eminent men and asking them to try to conjure up an image of their breakfast tables on the morning they received this unusual request. They were asked to comment at length on the richness, detail and vividness of the image they created, and enormously wide differences were observed, some respondents reporting that their remembered breakfast table was almost as vivid as their direct perception of it, others reporting no imagery at all. Subsequent work has confirmed that people differ extremely in the reported vividness of their imagery. Yet attempts to relate this to their memory abilities have proved universally disappointing. For example, Sir Frederick Bartlett had his subjects try to recall stories, and noted that although those who claimed to have vivid visual imagery were on the whole more confident in their powers of memory than those without such imagery, they were no more accurate in their recall. A much later study by three American investigators, di Vesta, Ingersoll and Sunshine, looked at the relationship between stated vividness of imagery, and a range of other tests. Memory performance was not related to vividness of imagery and indeed the only measure that did show relationship to imagery was a measure called 'social desirability', claimed to be an indicator of the extent to which subjects attempt to be obliging and give socially acceptable answers! Hence although large differences in the reported use of visual imagery exist, they do not seem to tell us very much about the functioning of human memory, whereas other methods based on performance rather than self-report have proved very fruitful, as we shall see.

If people's comments on their own memory are unreliable, how does one investigate memory? The answer is, by setting subjects various memory tasks and scoring how well or badly they do them. Sometimes experiments take advantage of participants' differential memory abilities, but more frequently they take advantage of the difficulties people have and the mistakes they make when asked to remember certain types of material. If I were to present you with a string of consonants, say *l r p f q h*, and ask you to repeat them back to me, you would probably get most of them right, but your occasional errors would be revealing; for example, you would tend to substitute *b* for *p* or *s* for *f,* the errors being similar in sound to the correct item. I would conclude from this, as Conrad and Hull did, that you used verbal or acoustic memory rather than visual memory in order to remember the letters.

Another way of exploring human memory is to use a method known as 'selective interference'. I might, for example, want to test the idea that people remember addresses or telephone numbers by repeating them under their breath. I could prevent such repetition and see if it impairs recall. Ask someone to articulate an irrelevant word such as 'the' while they are trying to rehearse or write down a telephone number and their performance drops dramatically.

The chapters that follow are concerned with human memory for a wide range of material, but you will no doubt notice rather a lot of work on memory for verbal material. The reasons for this are twofold. First, there is no doubt that verbal coding plays an extremely important part in human memory. Even when one is remembering visually presented items, or recalling actions or incidents, there is a strong tendency to supplement other aspects of memory by verbalizing, turning what may be initially purely a visual task into a combined visual and verbal one. The second reason for a predominance of verbal material is more practical. On the whole it is much easier to select and control verbal material than it is to manipulate visual, tactile or auditory stimuli. Suppose, for example, one wants to study the effects of the familiarity of the material one is using. Information exists on the frequency with which every word in the English language is used, allowing us to quantify the familiarity variable very simply. Similarly, data exist on the age at which people tend to first encounter particular words, on the tendency of a word to evoke a visual image, and so on, making verbal material by far the easiest to manipulate in experimental settings.

Another advantage of using words and letters as test materials is that they can be presented in the spoken or written mode, and can be recalled in either. With visual material, however, we are limited to one mode of presentation, and typically to testing by recognition, since it is hard for a subject to indicate visual recall other than by drawing, which has major limitations unless one is a talented draughtsman.

As will become clear from the chapters that follow, psychologists investigating memory are largely in the position of someone trying to understand the functioning of a machine without being able to look inside it. Consequently they have to rely on manipulating the tasks that the machine must carry out, and on carefully observing its behavior under various conditions. Such an approach demands considerable patience and ingenuity but, as I hope you will agree by the end of this book, it can produce important insights.

The nature of human memory

While the plight of Clive Wearing argues strongly for the general importance of memory, it does not tell us much about the detailed nature of the systems underlying human memory. Suppose we wanted to replace his faulty memory, what characteristics should our memory prosthesis provide?

Another way of asking the same question would be to take an evolutionary perspective and speculate on what memory functions might prove useful to an organism evolving in a complex and varied, but nevertheless structured, world. Let us assume that the organism has been given a number of sensory channels — vision, hearing, touch and smell, for example. Information from these various channels ought, in principle, to be related; objects such as trees can be seen and touched, and indeed heard as the wind rustles through their leaves. Appreciating this and creating some representation of an object is likely to require memory, at least of a temporary form, a short-term or working memory that will allow the organism to pull together information from a number of sources and integrate it into a coherent view of the surrounding world.

It would also be useful to build up, over time, some knowledge about the world. Given that the world is at least partly predictable, it would be advantageous to learn which foods are good and which cause illness, for example. In short, some form of long-term memory would also be useful. Such long-term learning can be of several different kinds, however, and each kind seems to obey different rules. Clive Wearing retains his skills as a musical performer, but his capacity to retrieve facts about the past (details of his musical achievements, the names of great composers) is grossly impaired.

Clues as to the structure of the complex alliance of systems that we call human memory are provided by other individuals with less dramatic memory problems, and of course by the study of the memory processes of normal people, as will become clear in later chapters. However, it might be helpful at this point to give a brief overview of the probable psychological structure of human memory, so as to provide a general framework within which the rest of the book can be interpreted.

The realization that memory can be fragmented into subcomponents is not a new one; it was proposed in the 1890s by the great American psychologist William James, and again by Donald Hebb in 1949. Experimental evidence for the fractionation of human memory has developed principally over the last 30 years. Until the 1960s many psychologists felt that it was unnecessary to assume more than one kind of memory, but by the early 1970s some form of distinction between long- and short-term memory was widely accepted. By the end of the decade both short- and long-term memory systems had been subdivided further.

While not everyone would be entirely happy with the structure I am going to propose, there is by now broad agreement that some such fractionation is useful. While I like to refer to separate *systems* and *subsystems*, other theorists might prefer to emphasize the different *processes* involved in remembering, rather than the underlying structures within which such processes operate. However we are likely to agree on virtually all of the information about human memory that I shall be presenting in this book. If there is disagreement, it is most likely to occur in areas where the evidence is too scanty to allow us to decide between a number of plausible alternatives.

Consider, for example, Clive Wearing's inability to remember what he has had for breakfast. Why does he have this problem? One possibility is that the experience of having breakfast never registers in his brain; in other words no memory trace is laid down. A second possibility is that a trace is laid down, but fades away very rapidly. A third possibility is that the memory trace is there, but cannot be accessed or retrieved. The memory trace may be like a book in a library with no catalog system. As we shall see later, deciding which, if any, of these scenarios is responsible for an observed memory failure is extremely difficult. Nevertheless it is important and potentially helpful to bear in mind that any adequate memory system must be capable of registering information presented, storing that information over time, and retrieving it when required.

How many kinds of memory?

Intense controversy during the 1960s led to a whole range of memory models of a broadly similar form. They tended to assume three kinds of memory — sensory memory, short-term memory and long-term memory — and are well represented by the model proposed by Richard Atkinson and Richard Shiffrin. Because it was both typical and influential, this model acquired the nickname the *modal model*. In this model it is assumed that information comes in from the environment

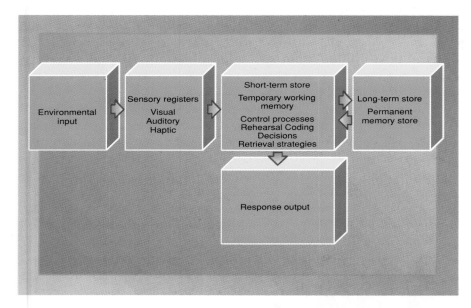

The flow of information through the memory system, as conceptualized by Atkinson and Shiffrin.

through a parallel series of brief sensory memory stores and goes into a common short-term store. This is assumed to act as a working memory, capable of manipulating information and relating it to long-term storage. Indeed the short-term store forms a crucial link in this model; without it, neither the learning of new material nor the recollection of old information is possible. We will consider each of these sub-components separately.

Sensory memory

When you go to the cinema you see what appears to be a continuous scene in which people apparently move quite normally. What is actually presented to your eyes is a series of frozen images interspersed with brief periods of darkness. In order to see a continuously moving image it is necessary for the brain's visual system to store the information from one frame until the arrival of the next. The visual store responsible for this is one of a whole series of sensory memory systems that are intimately involved in our perception of the world.

The eye 'remembers'. Although the glow has moved on, its image on the retina persists for a fraction of a second, allowing the single point of light to be seen as a circle.

Even within visual memory there are probably many components capable of storing visual information for a brief period of time. If you move the end of a brightly glowing cigarette in a darkened room you will find that a trace is left behind — you can write a letter of the alphabet and someone else will 'see' the letter. This effect was used to measure the duration of the visual sensory memory trace as long ago as 1740 by a Swedish investigator, Segner, who attached a glowing ember to a rotating wheel. When the wheel was rotated rapidly, a complete circle could be seen, since the trace left at the beginning of the circle was still glowing brightly by the time the ember returned to its starting point. If the wheel was moved slowly, only a partial circle would be seen, since the trace of the first part had faded by the time the ember returned to its starting point. By rotating the wheel at a speed which just allowed a complete circle to be drawn, and measuring the time taken for one revolution, Segner was able to estimate the duration of this brief sensory store. He found it to be approximately one-tenth of a second.

This phenomenon, known as 'persistence of vision', can be demonstrated even more simply. Spread out the fingers of your hand and pass them in front of your eyes. Do so slowly at first and you will notice that the scene seems unstable and tends to jump about. Now move your fingers to and fro rapidly. You will then see what appears to be the normal scene, although possibly a little blurred. In the rapid movement condition, the scene is interrupted only briefly, allowing the information registered by the retina to be refreshed before it fades away.

There are at least two, and probably more, components to sensory visual memory, or *iconic memory* as it is sometimes called. One of these appears to depend on the retina of the eye and is primarily influenced by the brightness of the stimulus presented. The second one occurs at a point in the brain after information from both retinas has been received and integrated. This component is much more sensitive to pattern than to brightness, and represents the operation of a system involved in shape recognition.

An analogous series of sensory memories occurs in hearing. If I were to present an extremely brief click in one corner of the room, you would be very good at deciding from which direction the click came. In order to do this, you would use the tiny difference in the time of arrival of the click at your two ears, performing a task analogous to the use of sonar to locate the position of a ship. However, in order to make use of this discrepancy in time of arrival of the click at the two ears, it is necessary to have a system that will store the first click until the arrival of the second, allowing this difference to be estimated extremely accurately. While one would not term this a memory system in the usual sense, it certainly is a system for storing and retrieving information, and as such can legitimately be described as a very brief sensory memory system.

The existence of a rather more durable auditory memory system can be shown as follows. Suppose I were to read out to you a series of nine-digit telephone numbers. The chances are that you would get most of the digits of each number right, but would tend to make errors. If I then switched to a system of presenting the numbers visually, one digit at a time, you would find that you made rather more errors, particularly towards the end of the sequence. The graph below shows a typical error pattern for nine-digit sequences both read and heard.

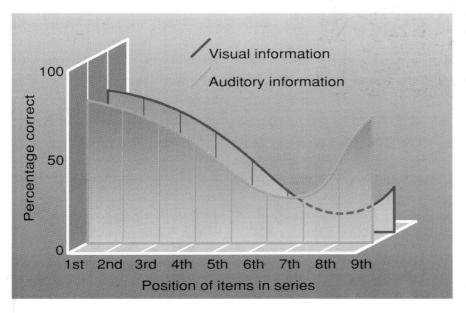

Auditory information lingers longer in sensory memory than visual information. This explains why the later words in a series of words are better remembered if they are heard rather than read.

The most striking feature of the graph on page 19 is the discrepancy between the two modes of presentation in the case of the last item presented. When this is spoken, it is almost always correctly recalled; when it is presented visually, errors are very numerous. The reason for this appears to be that when the sequence is spoken, the last item can still be recovered from a brief auditory memory, sometimes referred to as *echoic memory* since it is rather like an echo lingering on after the item has been spoken. The echo is limited to one or possibly two items. Consequently it can be wiped out by presenting a further irrelevant item afterwards. Echoic memory is left holding the irrelevant item instead of the last digit. Hence if I had spoken the sequence of digits to you, and then followed it with the spoken instruction 'Recall', the 'echo' of the last digit would have disappeared. The system involved in echoic memory of this type seems to be particularly geared to speech, since a simple but meaningless spoken sound such as 'bah' will disrupt performance whereas a pure tone of similar loudness and duration will not. A sequence of spoken digits is better remembered than a sequence of digits presented visually because auditory sensory memory appears to be more durable than visual.

Below left:
Skilled use of a
stethoscope depends
on a good memory for
breath sounds and
heart rhythms.

Auditory sensory memory is not limited to speech sounds. Suppose you are dubious about some component in your car engine and you listen to it while driving. What you will be trying to perceive is a repeated sound embedded in the relatively random engine noise. In order to perceive the repetition you need to be able to store a long enough 'bite' of noise to be able to detect the one feature that seems to be recurring. This effect has been used to study auditory memory. The listener is presented with a tape which recycles a sample of randomly fluctuating noise and the size of the sample is then systematically varied. If the sample is half a second long, the listener is required to perceive features that recur every half second. To be able to do this, he or she needs an auditory memory system that stores at least half a second's worth of sound. If the sample lasts for

Below right:
Listening for the
recurrent sound of
trouble. Auditory
memory is needed
for detecting any
disruption of the
regular rhythm of a
well-tuned engine.

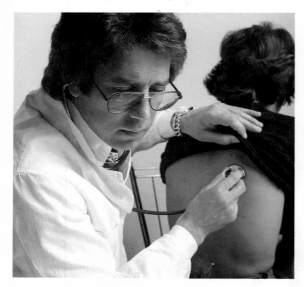

a full second, a more durable memory store would be needed to detect the rhythmic fluctuation. When faced with this task, subjects vary somewhat in their capabilities, but on average can detect repetitions separated by up to three seconds, indicating an auditory memory system of at least this duration.

Although we have touched only briefly on sensory memory, we shall not be returning to it. It is an important component of our overall memory apparatus, but it is probably best seen as part of the process of perception. To explore it further would demand far more detailed analysis of perception than is possible within the limits of the present book.

Short-term memory

To understand this sentence, you need to remember the beginning until you get to the end. Without some kind of memory for the words in it and the order in which they occur, it would be incomprehensible.

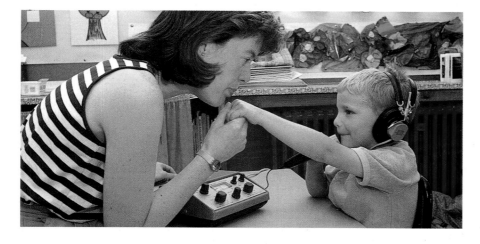

To learn to talk, you need to hear the sounds you are making. Feedback is an important component of learning to speak.

Suppose I ask you to multiply 23 by 7 in your head. Try looking away from the page and doing this. First of all, you need to remember the numbers involved. Then you will probably multiply 3 by 7, and remember that the answer is 21. Then you will remember the 1 and carry the 2. Then you will multiply the 2 by 7 and retrieve the 2 you carried, making 16. Then you will retrieve the original 1 and come up with the answer 161. All of this involves a good deal of temporary storage of numbers, all of which need to be retrieved accurately and at the appropriate time. Having completed the sum, there is no further need to retrieve information such as which number was carried, and after a couple of similar sums you will be unlikely to be able to remember this information.

In both language comprehension and arithmetic, therefore, there is a need for the temporary storage of information in order to perform various functions subsidiary to understanding or calculating. Once the task has been achieved, the subsidiary information is no longer required. Short-term or working memory is

Now I wonder why he did that? Evaluating alternative strategies in games like chess depends crucially on working memory.

the name given to this system, or, perhaps more appropriately, set of systems. Information which is essential for a brief period of time is very temporarily stored, then becomes quite irrelevant.

To what extent does short-term memory represent a system which is quite different from long-term memory? Here again there has been considerable controversy in recent years. One view is that short-term memory represents the same system as long-term memory, but is used under rather special conditions which lead to very little long-term retention. The alternative view, which I myself support, is that long- and short-term memory involve separate systems, although they are very closely integrated in operation. I myself would further argue that short-term memory represents not one but a complex set of interacting sub-systems which I shall refer to as *working memory.*

Long-term memory

Of the three types of memory — sensory memory, working memory and long-term memory — the one that corresponds most closely to the layperson's view of memory is long-term memory. This represents information that is stored for considerable periods of time. Indeed, as we shall see later, some theorists claim that information in memory never disappears, but simply becomes less and less accessible. Remembering your own name, how to speak, where you lived as a child, or where you were last year or indeed five minutes ago are all assumed to depend on long-term memory. Such memory is primarily concerned with storing information, unlike sensory memory and short-term memory where the storage is an incidental feature of other aspects of the system.

To an experimental psychologist the phrase 'long-term memory' refers to information which is stored sufficiently durably to be accessible over a period of anything more than a few seconds. The reason for this is that, on the whole, memory tested after one or two minutes seems to behave in much the same way as memory tested after one or two days, or years. The same does not apply, as we shall see in due course, to memory tested after one or two seconds, or even milliseconds. Is long-term memory a unitary system? This is still a controversial question. Distinctions of at least two types are commonly made, however.

Episodic and semantic long-term memory

A few years ago Canadian psychologist Endel Tulving made a useful distinction between two types of long-term memory: *episodic memory*, which involves remembering particular incidents, such as going to the dentist a week ago, and *semantic memory*, which essentially concerns knowledge about the world.

Knowing the meaning of a word or the chemical formula for salt or the capital of France would all be examples of semantic memory. There is no doubt that there are differences between specific personal memories of individual incidents and generalized knowledge of the world, which has often been acquired over a considerable period of time. Whether these represent separate memory systems or different aspects of a single system is still uncertain. However, the distinction is a convenient and useful one. In this book semantic memory has a chapter of its own.

A great deal of research on human memory has used verbal materials, since words are easy to present and people's responses are easy to record and score. In recent years researchers have increasingly asked whether memory for verbal materials is characteristic of all memory, and in particular whether memory for non-verbalizable sensory experiences relies on quite different memory systems. Undoubtedly we can remember the taste of cheese or the smell of burning rubber or the sound of the sea breaking on a rocky shore without using verbal descriptions of these experiences. Are there separate auditory and visual memory systems, or an all-embracing memory system which is capable of encoding all our experiences? Taking this latter view, much verbal learning is verbal only inasmuch as the material is presented verbally and subjects respond

A deaf child who learns sign language does not encode a conversation verbally or auditorily. Are there ways of encoding experience other than sight, sound, touch, taste, and so on?

verbally; what is stored is the experience conjured up by the verbal material. Fortunately the general rules which apply to the learning of verbal material also seem to apply, at least broadly, to remembering pictures or sounds, so the overall conclusions drawn in the chapters that follow are still likely to be valid whether we conclude that long-term memory is a unitary, dual or multiple system.

Implicit and explicit memory

It has been known for many years that densely amnesic patients such as Clive Wearing may still be capable of certain kinds of new long-term learning. The learning of motor skills such as typing is typically preserved, as is a whole range of phenomena known as *priming*. This term refers to the observation that when a word or object is seen or heard more than once, it will be seen or heard more readily on second and later occasions. Hence if you have recently read the word *rabbit*, then you will be better able to perceive it if I present it very briefly, and will be more likely to come up with the word if asked to produce something that will fit the pattern of letters R–B––T, than a subject who has seen a quite different word.

Learning measured in this way is called *implicit*. Because the subject is not asked about earlier presentations of material to be learned, their influence is reflected indirectly in the speed or nature of subsequent performance, typically in a non-memory task. Such learning is not affected by many of the factors which are important when learning is measured by recall or recognition. Processing a word in terms of its meaning, for example, enhances subsequent recall, but does not influence the magnitude of priming, whereas changing the physical presentation of the word, changing the typeface in which it is printed, for example, tends to reduce priming, but has little or no effect on recall.

Research in this area is currently extremely active. Some theorists argue that implicit and explicit learning reflect a single system operating under rather different constraints, while others argue for different learning processes. Typically the single system position is held by researchers who work principally with normal subjects, while those with a strong interest in neuropsychological deficits are more likely to advocate an approach based on two or more learning systems. My own current view is that both episodic and semantic memory are based on a single system that is damaged in amnesic patients, but that a number of implicit learning processes occur; what these have in common is the fact that they do not rely upon explicit episodic memory. However, this issue will be discussed in more detail in Chapter 4. The area is currently bedevilled by problems of terminology. While most people agree that there is an important distinction, they tend not to agree on how it is best conceptualized. Consequently they tend to use somewhat different terms to refer to the same phenomena.

Although there is disagreement about the theoretical interpretation of explicit and implicit learning, most people would agree that the preserved learning in amnesic patients is characterized by tasks in which the learning is measured indirectly. The subject does not need to remember having encountered the situation before in order to perform well on a skill task such as typing, for example, or to show a priming effect. In contrast, amnesic patients perform badly on tests that require them to recollect the learning experience — they would find it difficult to recall a newspaper story, for example, or decide whether a particular word had been presented earlier in a test session. For this reason some theorists prefer to use the terms *direct* and *indirect* (rather than *explicit* and *implicit*) to distinguish between the two types of learning and memory.

Another way of interpreting the two types of learning and memory is to call them *declarative* and *non-declarative*. Declarative memory refers to memory for facts or events, and non-declarative to the rest. I myself am sympathetic to this distinction, but must confess that I find the labels somewhat cumbersome.

In the chapters that follow I will describe short-term or working memory, and then go on to consider various aspects of long-term learning and memory. I shall then apply what we have learned to such practical issues as interpreting the testimony of witnesses, understanding amnesia, and studying memory in children and in the elderly.

Same location, different memories? No two people remember the same thing in the same way.

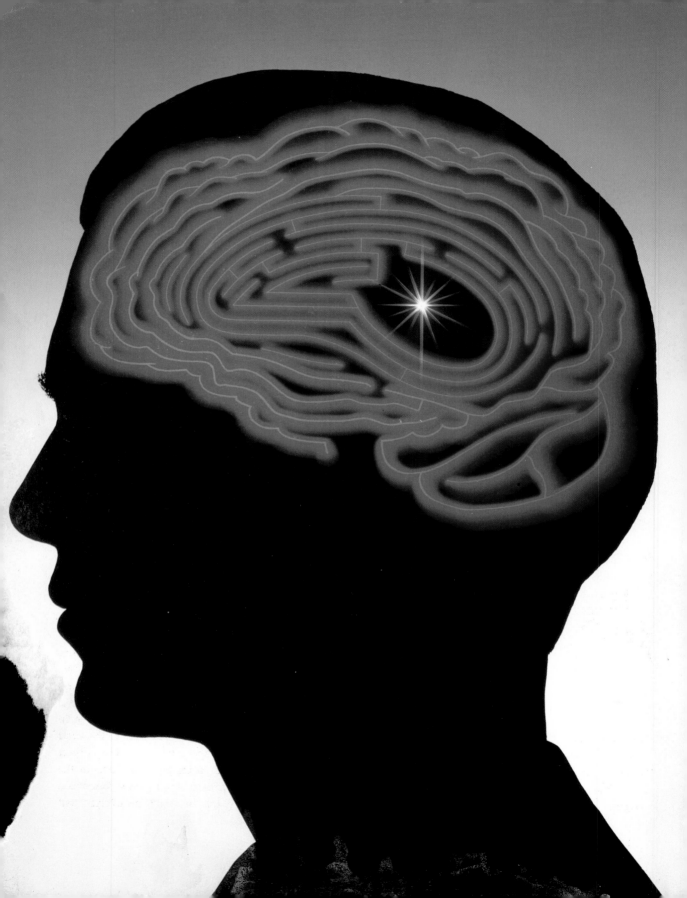

Chapter 2 Short-term memory

William James, the great nineteenth-century American psychologist whose views on attention and short-term memory are still influential.

How long is the present? A minute? A second? A millisecond? Or is it infinitesimally small? Suppose we hear the work 'bicycle' spoken. We do not have the sensation of needing to pull the initial syllable 'bi' out of memory when we come to the final syllable — the whole word appears to be present at the same time. William James referred to this sensation as 'the specious present', specious because it seems plausible, though is literally false, that the beginning and end of the word are present at the same time. Sir Frances Galton, the nineteenth-century British scientist, gave the following description of a similar phenomenon: 'There seems to be a presence-chamber in my mind where full consciousness holds court, and where two or three ideas are at the same time in audience, and an ante-chamber full of more or less allied ideas, which is situated just beyond the ken of full consciousness. Out of this ante-chamber the ideas most nearly allied to those in the presence-chamber appear to be summoned in a mechanically logical way, and to have their turn of audience.'

This concept of limited consciousness is closely related to but not identical with the concept of short-term memory, a system for storing information over brief intervals of time. The nature of consciousness is a fundamental and fascinating problem, but one which is beyond the scope of the present book. In considering short-term memory, however, we will be looking at one aspect of the problem, namely the characteristics of the system which allows the holding and manipulation of limited amounts of information. It is as if the system can grasp fleeting ideas which would otherwise slip into oblivion, hold them, relate them and manipulate them for its own purposes. The number of items or ideas that can be grasped is limited, but capacity can be supplemented in various ways.

Digit span

The audience chamber of the human mind where full consciousness reigns?

The question of the capacity of immediate memory was one which preoccupied a number of philosophers during the nineteenth century. Sir William Hamilton, for example, observed that if one flung a handful of marbles on the ground, the maximum number that could be perceived reasonably accurately would be about seven. The first systematic experimental work to be done on this problem was carried out in 1887 by a London schoolteacher, J. Jacobs, who was interested in measuring the mental capacity of his pupils. He devised a technique, the *digit span*, which has played an important role in psychology ever since. The subject is presented with a sequence of digits and required to repeat them back in the same order; the length of the sequence is steadily increased until a point is reached at which the subject always fails; the sequence length at which he is right half the time is defined as his digit span. Try it for yourself. Read out loud the digit sequences shown below at a steady rate. After each sequence, close your eyes and try to repeat the numbers in the correct order. Note in each case whether you get the sequence completely correct or not. If you do, move on to the next length of sequence. If you make a mistake, try the next sequence of the same length, and continue testing yourself until you reach a length at which you are always incorrect. Your span is the length at which performance reaches its limit, which for present purposes can be regarded as the longest sequence you recall correctly on at least one of the three permitted attempts.

```
9 7 5 4
3 8 2 5
6 5 1 4
9 4 3 1 8
6 8 2 5 9
3 8 1 4 7
9 1 3 8 2 5
6 4 8 3 7 1
5 9 6 3 8 2
7 9 5 8 4 2 3
5 3 1 6 8 4 2
7 9 1 8 5 4 6
8 6 9 5 1 3 7 2
5 1 7 3 9 8 2 6
5 1 3 9 8 2 4 7
7 1 9 3 8 4 2 6 1
1 6 3 8 7 4 9 5 2
6 2 5 9 4 3 8 2 6
9 1 5 2 4 3 8 1 6 2
7 1 5 4 8 5 6 1 9 3
1 5 2 8 4 6 7 3 1 8
```

Most people can manage six or seven digits, but there is quite a large range of capacity, with some people managing only four or five and others getting up to ten or more. Needless to say, tests would normally be carried out in much more controlled conditions than this!

If you speak the sequences aloud, you will probably do somewhat better than if you simply read them to yourself. The reason for this is that articulating and hearing the sounds of the numbers registers them in a brief auditory memory store (of which more later on).

Another way of improving your performance would be to group the digits rhythmically. This technique appears to help reduce the tendency to recall them in the wrong order. Studies comparing different modes of grouping seem to come up with the conclusion that grouping in threes is best and that even a tiny gap between successive groups is helpful, provided the listener can hear it. So if you are telling someone your telephone number and you want to ensure that they write it down correctly, group it in threes, or if it is not divisible by three, in threes and twos. Having done so, you would be wise to check it, since there is a surprisingly high error rate in reproducing telephone numbers, even when one is simply remembering a number for the brief period needed to copy it from one sheet of paper to another.

The role of rhythm in memory is one which we rather tend to neglect, possibly because it is associated with nineteenth-century ideas of memory drill which emphasized the parrot-like repetition of often useless information. Rhyme and rhythm are what make poetry particularly easy to commit to memory.

Rhythm certainly played an important role in the memory of the late Professor A. C. Aitken of Edinburgh University. Aitken was a very talented mathematician and had amazing memory abilities; he was, for example, a lightning calculator. One of Aitken's mnemonic feats was to recall, to the first thousand decimal places, the value of *pi* (the symbol of the ratio of the circumference of a circle to its diameter). Ian Hunter, a psychologist who studied his remarkable talents, reports that Aitken thought this 'a reprehensibly useless feat had it not been so easy.' Aitken discovered that by arranging the digits in rows of 50, with 10 groups of 5 digits in each row, and reading them over in a particular rhythm, they were very easy to memorize: '. . . the learning was rather like learning a Bach fugue.' Hunter tape-recorded Aitken's recall, describing it as follows: 'Sitting relaxed and still, he speaks the first 500 digits without error or hesitation. He then pauses, almost literally for breath. The total time taken is 150 seconds. The rhythm and tempo of speech is obvious; about five digits per second, separated by a pause of about half a second.'

When tested using the standard digit span procedure of one digit per second, Aitken's performance was unremarkable; he complained that the presentation rate was far too slow, 'like learning to ride a bicycle slowly'. When the digits were read at a rate of five per second he had no difficulty in repeating back 15 in the order of presentation, or indeed in reverse order. Recalling in reverse order is much more difficult than normal auditory recall. Try it for yourself, using a sequence length from the digit span list opposite.

Aitken's amazing memory capacity was not limited to remembering numbers. In 1937 he had been tested using a passage of prose and a list of 25 words. Some 27 years later Hunter asked him to recall this material. Not only did he recall all 25 words correctly and in the right order, but the passage of prose was recalled virtually word for word. Aitken also had a remarkable memory for events and conversations, and on committees could always be relied on to give an accurate and detailed account of what had occurred at previous meetings. He himself took little pleasure in being used as a walking minute-book and was distinctly unimpressed by his abilities as a lightning calculator. In fact he ceased to practice many of his calculative skills as soon as automatic calculators became available.

Even to write a telephone number on your hand is likely to require rehearsal of the number while you are writing.

The longest name in Britain belongs to a village on the island of Anglesey. A suitable case for chunking? A nineteenth-century clergyman is said to have invented the name with a view to boosting the tourist trade.

Chunking

A crucial element in Aitken's success was his ability to parcel several digits into a single 'chunk'. The capacity of immediate memory is determined by the number of chunks rather than by the number of digits, a point made more obviously if we move on to memory span for sequences of letters rather than sequences of digits. Try reading off and repeating back the following sequence of letters: *I A R F T S K B G N I*. Were you able to repeat it correctly? If you were, you have a remarkably good immediate memory. Now try the next sequence, which in fact comprises exactly the same letters: *F R I K B A S T I N G*. No prizes for getting that one correct. What is the difference between the two sequences? The first comprised 11 unrelated letters, and although it is possible to chunk a few of them together into a single sound, *ARF* for example, in general the number of chunks remaining would be likely to exceed the six or seven that our short-term memories can hold. The second sequence can very easily be chunked into three speech sounds, or possibly even two if you regard *B A S T I N G* as a single word. The task would have been even easier had the 11 letters made up an already existing word such as *intelligent*.

Chunking is something which the memorizer himself does with the material presented, but obviously some sequences lend themselves to this

This graph shows the effects of two factors, predictability and sequence length, on recall of pseudo words and real words. The more word-like sequences are, the easier they are to remember. (Baddeley and Conrad, 1960)

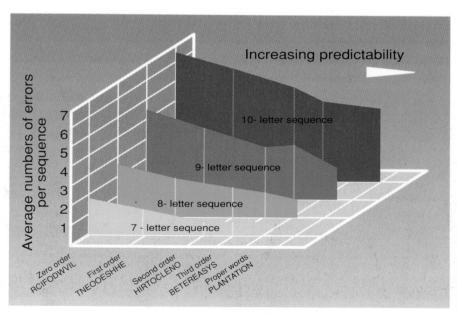

process much more readily than others. One factor that assists chunking is the redundancy, or predictability, of the material. Consider the structure of the English language: certain letters occur much more frequently than others. If I were playing a guessing game and trying to determine what the first letter in a sequence was, I would be much more sensible to guess *S* or *T* than *X* or *Z*. Similarly, certain combinations of letters occur particularly frequently; there is a general tendency for vowels and consonants to alternate, and for certain letters to follow others. If I told you that the first letter in a word was a *Q,* it would not take great foresight to guess that the letter following would be a *U*. Such relationships are not limited to adjoining letters. If I tell you that the first two letters of a word are *T* and *H*, you would be more likely to guess *E* than *U* as the following letter, and more likely to choose either of these than another consonant such as *S*.

These various probabilities can be calculated simply by feeding a sample of normal English into a computer and asking it to count the frequency with which individual letters occur on their own, and in association with preceding letters or pairs of letters. My colleagues, R. Conrad and W. E. Thompson, and I performed such an analysis several years ago using as our two samples leading articles from *The Times* newspaper, written in a rather formal kind of English, and scripts from a BBC soap opera, which used a much more colloquial English. The computer gave us information on the frequency of individual letters, pairs of letters, and triplets. Using the results, we were able to produce letter sequences that ranged from completely random through so-called first order approximations (where letters occurred with the frequency typical of English), second order approximations (where pairwise associations were mimicked), third order approximations (based on triplets of letters), and real words. Samples of the various types of material are shown below. Try testing yourself on some of the sequences by reading them aloud, then closing your eyes and trying to repeat them back. If you would like to plot your performance more systematically, simply count how many times you get the sequence right for each order of approximation, then compare your results with what our subjects achieved, as shown in the graph opposite.

Random sequences	First order (frequency of individual letters the same as in English)	Second order (pairs of letters occurring with same frequency as in formal English)	Third order (letter triplets occuring with same frequency as in normal English)	Real English words
RCIFODWVIL	*TNEOOESHHE*	*HIRTOCLENO*	*BETEREASYS*	*PLANTATION*
GKTODKPENF	*INOLGGOLVN*	*DOVEECOFOF*	*CRAGETTERS*	*FLASHLIGHT*
TZXKHAWCCF	*PDOASLOTPP*	*SESERAICCG*	*TOWERSIBLE*	*UNCOMMONLY*
NGORHQIYWB	*AEOCAOIAON*	*AREDAGORIZ*	*DEEMEREANY*	*ALIENATION*
BVNJSYZXUA	*IRCRENFCTN*	*CUNSIGOSUR*	*THERSERCHE*	*PICKPOCKET*

Why did we go to this trouble? We were interested in the design of codes in connection with the British Post Office's plans to introduce postal codes as an aid to automatic sorting of letters. Using the structure of English allowed us to create a series of codes, producing the most memorable sequences based on real words first, before moving on to slightly less memorable pseudo-words, and working down to sequences which bore no relationship to English whatsoever. In fact the codes that were eventually adopted were very different from those we produced (and much less easy to remember!), largely because of operational and engineering constraints.

Short-term forgetting

So far we have concentrated on one measure of memory, memory span, a measure used steadily over the last 60 or 70 years. Intensive interest in short-term memory did not develop until the late 1950s and it did so as the result of two studies, one by John Brown in England and one by the Petersons in the United States. These showed that even sequences within the memory span would show clear forgetting if the subject was prevented from thinking about the item or rehearsing it in any way. Peterson and Peterson presented their subjects with sequences of three unrelated consonants. Immediately the subject had read them he was shown a three-figure number and asked to start counting backwards from it in threes. After an interval ranging from between 3 and 128 seconds he was asked to recall the original three consonants before going on to the next three, which would again be followed by the backward counting task and then recall. Try it for yourself with the material at the top of the next page. As you can see, the numbers and letters are arranged in six columns. Beginning with the far left-hand column, cover up the figures with a sheet of paper and read out the three consonants *B, K, Q*. As soon as you have read them out, cover them up and do the simple sum below them. Cover up the whole column and move on to the next column, and so on. As soon as you finish each sum, write down the answer and then try to remember the letters above. Then move on to the next column of letters and numbers. When you have completed all the columns, read on.

The results obtained by Peterson and Peterson and their subjects are shown opposite. Also illustrated are the results from an experiment by Murdock using either one or three unrelated three-letter words. As you will see, the forgetting curve is the same whether one is trying to remember three letters or three words. Nevertheless, single three-letter words show very little forgetting, indicating that, as with memory span, the important fact is the number of chunks remembered rather than the number of letters.

How did you get on with the six columns of letters and sums? Clearly our attempted version of the experiment was very rough-and-ready. We did not, for example, systematically vary the length of time for which you had to remember each set of letters. Furthermore, some of the triplets of letters are easier to remember than others. However, I suspect that you probably got the first triplet

B	L	Q	F	P	D
K	Z	X	J	K	L
Q	M	C	V	H	X
7	8	5	9	6	8
+ 9	- 2	+ 8	- 4	+ 3	- 5
+ 3	+ 6	- 2	+ 5	- 4	+ 9
- 6	+ 3	+ 9	- 7	+ 9	- 4
+ 8	- 9	- 7	+ 3	+ 2	- 6
- 3	+ 7	- 3	+ 6	- 7	+ 7
- 5	- 5	+ 9	- 2	- 8	+ 2
+ 4	- 2	- 7	+ 8	+ 5	- 4
Total?	Total?	Total?	Total?	Total?	Total?
Recall	Recall	Recall	Recall	Recall	Recall

right, and possibly the second, but did rather worse on the later ones. This is the normal pattern of results and it has an important implication for the explanation of the Peterson effect. It was initially thought that the sort of curve yielded by the Murdock and Peterson experiments indicated that the memory trace left by the triplet sequences was becoming more and more faded and decayed as time elapsed, making it less and less likely that they could be accurately recalled. However, it was subsequently pointed out that on the first trial of such an

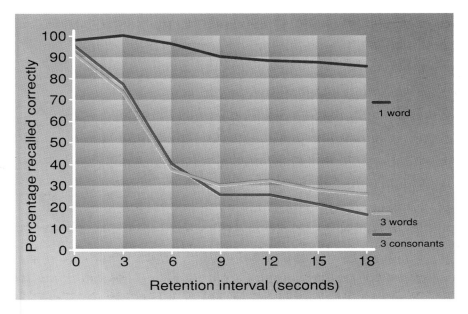

These were the forgetting curves found by Murdock and the Petersons when they prevented their subjects from rehearsing the items they were asked to recall after intervals ranging from 3 to 18 seconds. (Peterson and Peterson, 1958; Murdock, 1961)

experiment very little forgetting occurred; only the later triplet sequences showed the dramatic forgetting that is so characteristic of this procedure. The reason for this seems to be that the subjects have difficulty discriminating between the three letters they have just been shown and the various triplets that have previously been presented; the greater the interval, the greater the confusion. The Peterson task is not of course limited to use with letters; very frequently it is used with word threesomes, and if you are prepared to try another eight trials it should be possible to demonstrate another characteristic of the procedure. Move on to the lists below and carry out the task as before. The only difference is that this time you are being asked to remember triplets of words rather than triplets of letters. As before, concentrate entirely on the column you are working on and blank out the others with a piece of paper or card. Once again you should read out the three words, cover them up, and go on to the arithmetic task. Then recall and write down the three words in the order in which they were presented. Move straight on to the next column and so forth until you have completed all eight columns. Then go back and mark how many word triplets you got right.

bear	horse	zebra	dog	grape	banana	cherry	copper
cow	sheep	fox	camel	plum	orange	lemon	zinc
lion	tiger	cat	mouse	apple	strawberry	tangerine	lead
5	7	8	6	4	9	7	6
+ 9	- 4	- 7	+ 3	+ 9	- 5	- 4	+ 7
- 7	+ 9	+ 3	- 8	- 5	+ 7	+ 6	- 2
+ 4	- 3	+ 9	+ 6	+ 8	- 2	- 3	+ 9
- 8	+ 6	- 4	+ 9	- 2	+ 7	+ 5	- 3
- 3	- 5	+ 6	- 4	- 4	- 8	+ 2	- 5
+ 2	- 7	- 8	- 5	- 7	+ 6	- 9	+ 4
- 5	+ 8	+ 6	+ 6	+ 2	+ 5	+ 8	- 9
Total?	**Total?**	**Total?**	**Total?**	**Total?**	**Total?**	**Total?**	**Total?**
Recall	**Recall**	**Recall**	**Recall**	**Recall**	**Recall**	**Recall**	**Recall**

As you no doubt noticed, the words above were not selected at random but come from within particular categories. You should again have observed the tendency for the first triplet to be well recalled, and for recall of subsequent triplets to decline, with one exception; when you changed from the category comprising animals to that comprising fruits your performance should have improved dramatically, before falling away again.

Why does performance improve with a change of category? Because you have been given a way to avoid confusing the words presented earlier with the words you are currently trying to remember. This effect is termed *release from proactive inhibition*. However, having moved on to a new category, by the second trial there are already previous items from that category getting in the way of recall. The release from PI technique was developed by the American psychologist Delos Wickens, who has shown that the effect can be produced by changing any of a wide range of different dimensions, including switching from letters to numbers, from large to small items, or from dark to light backgrounds, although these effects tend not to be as dramatic as those obtained when a switch in meaning is used.

The phenomenon of release from PI is not limited to short-term memory, and may indeed have some practical value. In a study concerned with the memorability of TV news items, the investigators studied the accuracy with which news items were remembered when presented under two different conditions. In the first, all four items presented came from thematically similar topics. In the release from PI condition, however, the fourth item was switched so as to come from a completely different category.

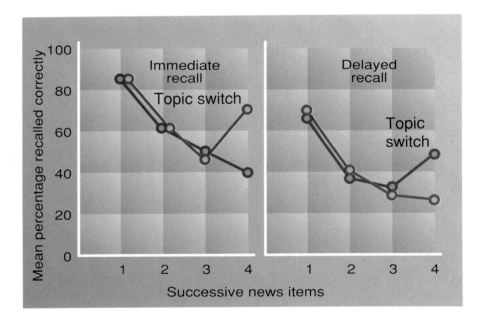

Recall of successive news items. When the topic was switched after three successive similar items, people remembered the new item better whether tested immediately (left panel) or after a delay. (Gunter, Barry and Clifford, 1981)

Free Recall

Another technique often used to study short-term memory is *free recall*, so named because the subject is presented with a string of items to remember and is free to recall them in any order; this is in contrast to *serial recall,* where the items must be recalled in the order in which they were presented. In free recall it is usual to present subjects with considerably more items than they are likely to remember. Once again, the best way of getting the flavor of such a task is to try it for yourself.

Look at the six lists below and work your way through the examples. Simply read through them at a comfortable pace, covering up each word with a piece of card as you go. When you get to the bottom of each list you will find either the instruction 'Recall', in which case you should write down the words in any order you like on a piece of paper, or a column of numbers to add up; in which case do the sum and then try to recall the words previously read through. Allow yourself about one minute to do the recalling — most of the words you are likely to remember will be recalled in this time. One or two additional words may pop up later; if they do, ignore them. I suggest that you work through all six lists before

List 1	List 2	List 3	List 4	List 5	List 6
barricade	armchair	icicle	proud	parchment	sepulcher
children	glow-worm	instructor	stirrup	gold	gnome
diet	outhouse	kidney	villain	baroness	stage
gourd	troll	lapel	zodiac	lever	patriarch
folio	handshake	crooner	deer	manservant	diploma
meter	hoarfrost	funnel	arbitrator	divan	minstrel
journey	elephant	carpet	beginner	emporium	mayonnaise
mohair	pumpkin	haystack	courtroom	wood	portcullis
phoenix	graveyard	hopper	hobby	gorge	dyke
crossbow	capsule	chancery	measles	windshield	effigy
alligator	file	simpleton	ogre	armada	tiger
doorbell	package	theater	nosegay	beverage	wage
muffler	playhouse	stencil	film	flowerpot	yacht
menu	ferry	urn	peg	lotion	maggot
nebula	dumpling	slug	flagon	archer	inspector
	overcoat		head-dress	pharmacy	deformity

List 1	List 2	List 3	List 4	List 5	List 6
Recall	**Recall**	**Recall**	3	9	6
			+ 7	- 5	- 3
			- 6	+ 6	+ 7
			+ 5	+ 3	- 2
			- 4	- 1	+ 9
			- 1	+ 4	+ 5
			+ 2	- 8	- 8
			+ 9	- 2	- 8
			- 8	+ 7	- 1
			Total?	**Total?**	**Total?**
			Recall	**Recall**	**Recall**

scoring for recall. Remember that you are allowed to recall the words *in any order you like*. Score your recall by comparing the listed words with those you have written down. Start by scoring Lists 1 to 3, adding up the number of times you got the first word right, the second, the third, and so on up to the sixth. Then score Lists 4 to 6 in the same way.

You probably found that on the first three lists you did only moderately well on the earlier and middle items, but rather better on the last one or two items. With the last three lists this tendency probably disappeared. Clearly under such uncontrolled conditions you are unlikely to get a very clear result. But the results that would have been obtained if a large number of people had been tested, each with a large number of lists, is shown on page 38. The curve relating presentation position to the likelihood that the word will be recalled is known as the *serial position curve*. Free recall without any intervening task gives rise to a very clear and characteristic curve, with the first one or two items moderately well recalled, a very flat middle portion to the curve, and excellent recall of the last one or two items. Such a curve is obtained across an amazingly wide range of conditions, whether the list is long or short, whether it contains words or nonsense material, whether it is presented rapidly or slowly, and indeed whether the subject is drunk or sober! The curve is not limited to Western culture either; students of an Islamic village school in Morocco whose education consisted of learning by rote sections of the Koran also showed this sort of curve when presented with unrelated words.

Rote learning of the Koran. The tendency to remember first and last items of information better than intervening items seems to be consistent across many cultures. Unfortunately, learning things parrot-fashion does not have a beneficial effect on the rest of one's memory.

As you probably noted from your own last three trials, and as the curve in the lower of the two graphs on page 38 shows, the picture changes dramatically when one is not allowed to recall immediately. Even a very brief interruption is enough to abolish the tendency of the last few items to be well recalled. This tendency is known as the *recency effect* because it reflects recall of the most recent items — the last few presented — and appears to behave very differently from performance on the rest of the curve, being unaffected by many other factors which influence performance. For example, familiar words are generally better recalled than rare words, but show no greater recency effect; presenting words slowly increases overall performance but leaves the recency effect unaffected; presenting words that refer to concrete objects rather than to abstract concepts increases perforance on the earlier part of the curve, but again leaves the recency effect intact. And yet the recency effect can be abolished very simply by interpolating a small amount of distraction, such as requiring the subject to add five single digits. Because of the apparent difference between recall of recent and early items it has been suggested that the former depends on short-term memory, while the latter reflects a longer-term aspect of memory.

The graph on the right illustrates the tendency for the last items in lists of items to be recalled fairly accurately. But this effect, the recency effect, disappears if recall is delayed, as shown in the graph below; after a 30-second delay recall of later items drops dramatically. (Postman and Phillips, 1965)

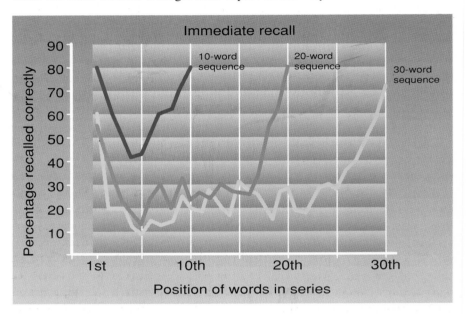

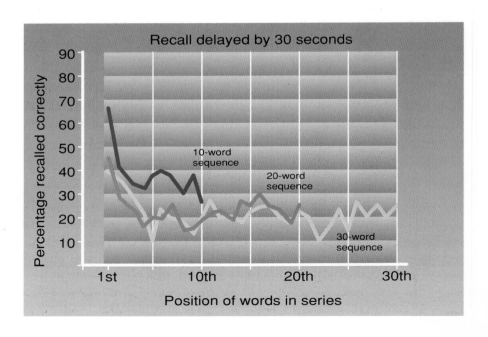

Are short-term and long-term memory separate systems?

A major controversy within experimental psychology during the 1960s was whether long- and short-term memory involved two separate systems or different aspects of one unitary system. Until the 1960s there was virtually no discussion of this point, partly because those people who were working on long-term memory did not work on short-term memory and vice versa. During this period long-term memory work was carried out largely in North America by a close-knit group who used mainly nonsense material and who were much more concerned with plotting the relationship between variables than with producing theories. The theories they did produce were based on the simple concept of association and interference between associations.

Work on short-term memory was particularly strong during the same period in Britain, where it has it roots in applied problems such as designing telephone numbers and codes. People working on short-term memory, both in Britain and North America, were very interested in explanatory models, often using concepts derived from digital computers which were developing rapidly at that time. However, work by Peterson and Peterson on short-term forgetting simply and elegantly focused the attention of both groups on a common problem. Was it necessary to assume that there were two separate kinds of memory, short-term and long-term, or could all the effects observed be explained in terms of the principles then assumed to govern long-term memory? This latter view was put forward by a highly respected advocate of the traditional North American approach to memory, Arthur Melton, in an influential paper which triggered off a whole series of attempts to argue for or against a separation of the two sytems.

The issue is still somewhat controversial, and I should therefore state that I myself believe that the data are far too complex to fit into a single unitary theory. There are indeed problems with the view that there are two systems, but here again I think that they stem from oversimplification; there are probably *more* than two memory systems in fact. Short-term memory is not a single unitary system; rather it is an amalgam or alliance of several temporary memory systems working together. The issue is too complex to be discussed in detail here, though it is perhaps worth describing some of the evidence that was used to argue for two memory systems rather than one, before going on to discuss the need for a more complex theory.

The first source of evidence has already been discussed; it concerns the fact that a number of memory tasks appear to have two components which behave in quite different ways. The clearest example is free recall where, as you may remember, the recency effect is very fragile, disappearing after a brief interval which has no effect on the retention of earlier items. On the other hand, performance on earlier items is sensitive to a wide range of factors that are known to influence long-term learning. These include: rate of presentation, with slow presentation leading to better performance; familiarity of the material, with familiar material being better remembered; distraction arising

from a request to do another task at the same time, thus impairing performance; and factors such as age, with elderly subjects remembering less than younger subjects. But none of these variables affects the recency component. One simple explanation of this is that they influence long-term memory but not short-term memory.

A second source of evidence comes from brain-damaged subjects, who occasionally have very specific memory problems. Certain amnesic patients, described in more detail in Chapter 11, have great difficulty learning new material. Their ability to remember free recall lists, such as those presented on page 36, is abysmal, and their everyday life performance is quite appallingly bad. They have great difficulty remembering where they are, what day of the week it is, or what they had for breakfast; you could spend all morning with such a patient who

Completing a jigsaw puzzle requires aspects of both long- and short-term memory. Unless you hold an image of the total pattern in your head, your efforts will be hit and miss.

would then fail to recognize you in the afternoon. Nonetheless, despite their dramatically impaired performance on the early part of free recall lists, such patients show normal recency. They also show good performance on memory span, and can in certain cases be quite normal on the Peterson task. In contrast, there are other kinds of amnesic patient who appear to have exactly the opposite set of symptoms. Their memory span may be limited to two or three items, their recency effect may be limited to one item and their Peterson performance may be extremely poor, particularly with auditory presentation. Despite this they may have apparently normal learning ability.

These two types of brain-damaged patient do of course have damage to different parts of the brain. Short-term memory problems are associated with damage to the left cerebral hemisphere in an area close to that involved in speech, and such patients may, but need not necessarily, have language problems. Amnesic patients who show defective long-term memory tend to have damage to the temporal lobes of the cortex and to deeper structures such as the hippocampus and the mammillary bodies. The fact that tasks associated with short-term memory are intact, and vice versa, speaks strongly for the view that different memory systems are involved.

A third source of evidence for separating long- and short-term memory comes from experiments which suggest that material in our short-term memory is processed largely in terms of speech sounds, while our long-term memory depends primarily on meaning. In the early 1960s experiments on memory for letter codes carried out by Conrad in connection with work for the British Post

Office threw up an interesting phenomenon. Conrad's subjects were presented with sequences of unrelated consonants and were required to write them down immediately afterwards as accurately as possible in their right order. He noted that the short-term memory errors made were not random, and more particularly that these errors tended to be similar in sound to the correct item, despite the fact that items were presented visually. Hence *B* was more likely to be remembered as *V* than as *R*. Conrad went on to show that sequences containing letters that sounded alike were much more likely to be erroneously remembered than sequences made up from letters that sounded different; hence a sequence such as *P D G C V B* (pee, dee, gee, see, vee, bee) was much more subject to error than a sequence such as *K X R Y L F*. He showed that similar effects could be produced using words that sounded alike, again indicating that they were remembered in terms of their sound rather than their visual appearance.

Acoustic cues

Conrad's data suggested that short-term memory relied on some form of acoustic, or at least speech-based, code. However, it is still possible to argue that *any* form of similarity has the potential to cause confusion, and that it simply happens to be the case that letters are more similar in sound than they are visually or in any other dimension. I decided to explore this possibility using words rather than letters and comparing the effect of similarity of sound with that of similarity of meaning.

The experiment I carried out was very simple. It involved presenting subjects with sequences of five words and asking them to write them down in the order presented — basically a memory span task. You may like to look at the word lists on the next page and try the test for yourself. Read off the first column of words in each group, look away, write them down in the correct sequence, and then test yourself on the second column and so forth. When you have finished, check how many words you got right in each column in each group.

As you may have noticed, all the words in Group A are similar in sound — *man, mad, mat, map, can, cat, cap, cad*; those in Group B are equally common words in English, but they have distinctive sounds — *pen, day, few, cow, pit, bar, hot, sup*; those in Group C are all adjectives with approximately similar meanings *high, great, big, long, tall, broad, large, wide*; and those in Group D are adjectives with distinctive meanings — *old, foul, late, strong, think, deep, hot, safe*. Was there a noticeable difference in your performance on the basis of these four categories? The bar graph on page 42 shows the percentage of sequences that my subjects recalled entirely correctly in the experiment. Two things are clear. First, I successfully repeated Conrad's finding; my subjects found the words that sounded alike very much harder to remember than that which did not. Secondly, I found that similarity of meaning had only a very slight influence on performance. It appeared that my subjects were relying much more on the sound of the words

Group A

mad	mat	can	map	cap
cap	can	cat	cat	map
cat	map	map	man	mat
map	mad	man	mad	man
cad	cat	cap	can	can
Recall	**Recall**	**Recall**	**Recall**	**Recall**

Group C

big	long	tall	broad	wide
wide	tall	broad	tall	large
high	wide	high	long	long
broad	large	large	big	great
tall	great	long	large	high
Recall	**Recall**	**Recall**	**Recall**	**Recall**

Group B

pen	few	sup	day	cow
cow	sup	day	sup	pit
bar	cow	bar	few	few
day	pit	pit	pen	hot
sup	hot	few	pit	bar
Recall	**Recall**	**Recall**	**Recall**	**Recall**

Group D

foul	late	thin	old	strong
strong	thin	hot	deep	old
hor	old	late	safe	late
old	foul	safe	foul	safe
deep	hot	strong	thin	thin
Recall	**Recall**	**Recall**	**Recall**	**Recall**

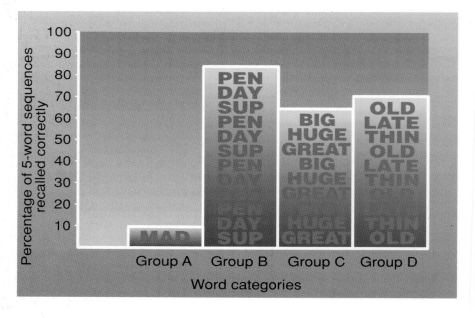

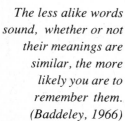

The less alike words sound, whether or not their meanings are similar, the more likely you are to remember them. (Baddeley, 1966)

than on their meaning. Thus it seems that Conrad was right in assuming that short-term memory is particularly closely associated with speech. But what of long-term memory?

In order to look at long-term learning I used the same experiment but extended the length of the word lists from five to ten, preventing subjects from relying on rote rehearsal by interrupting them after each presentation. To ensure that learning occurred I presented the lists four times and then tested recall after a 20-minute delay. Under these conditions the effects of similarity of sound disappeared; the words that gave subjects the most trouble were the adjectives with similar meanings. Or, to put it another way, this particular long-term memory task appeared to depend on the meaning of the words, not on their acoustic characteristics

Similar effects were observed in other experiments conducted at about the same time. Again it appeared to be the case that short-term memory was sensitive to the 'surface' or sound characteristics of the words, while long-term memory discarded such information, retaining only its meaning

Short-term memory store

By 1970 opinion favored the view that long- and short-term memory involved two quite separate systems. There were many divergent opinions on the exact nature of and relationship between the two, but most conformed more or less to the model of memory put forward in 1968 by two American psychologists; Richard Atkinson and Richard Shiffrin (see page 17).

Atkinson and Shiffrin considered memory to have three major constituents. The long-term memory system was concerned with storing information over extensive periods of time and was fed by a short-term memory that acted as a controller, feeding in new information and selecting particular processes for pulling information out of the long-term memory. The short-term system was itself fed by a series of *sensory registers* which were essentially micro-memories associated with perception. These registers acted as a system for selecting and collating sensory information, and could be viewed as an essential component of perception. The diagram on page 17 is not a literal representation of what happens in the brain, but it does help to make Atkinson and Shiffrin's theory more comprehensible. The same model could equally well be expressed mathematically, or in purely verbal terms.

At the heart of Atkinson and Shiffrin's model is the *short-term memory store*. It is important to note that they drew a distinction between short-term *memory*, which they used to refer to performance of a range of tasks in which small amounts of material need to be remembered for short periods of time, and the short-term *store*. This is a theoretical concept used to

A video mixer combining different information from different TV cameras. Similar mixing and selecting operations lie at the heart of short-term memory.

A morse code operator, like a typist, performs a task relying on information in both long- and short-termstorage.

explain results obtained in short-term memory experiments. Any experiment which tries to probe temporary working memory is likely to give results which are influenced not only by the performance of the short-term store but by other factors as well, in particular long-term memory. To take an extreme example, suppose I gave you the sequence *1 2 3 4 5 6 7 8 9 0* to remember in a memory span test; you would almost certainly remember it correctly, though I doubt if you have a memory span of ten items. If I were to ask you to repeat it five minutes later, you would still get it right, indicating that performance was in this case relying heavily on long-term storage. Many short-term memory tasks clearly do have a long-term component, and this inevitably makes theoretical interpretation difficult. The release from PI technique (see page 35), where subjects remember words from one category and are then switched to another, is a case in point. Although recall is typically requested after only a few seconds, this does not prevent the items being stored in long-term memory; indeed unpublished experiments of my own have shown that subjects, even when tested after a week, are able to recall many of the words presented in this type of experiment.

Levels of processing

Despite the fact that the Atkinson and Shiffrin model, or some variant of it, was extremely popular in the early 1970s, it was subsequently overshadowed by the *levels of processing* approach put forward by Fergus Craik and Robert Lockhart and discussed in more detail in Chapter 9.

A central characteristic of the Atkinson and Shiffrin view of memory was that the only way to learn new material and commit it to long-term memory was via the short-term store, which was capable of processing information in a range of different ways. The method most extensively studied by Atkinson and Shiffrin was that of *subvocal rehearsal*, whereby an item is repeated again and again. It was assumed that the longer an item is held in the short-term store, the more likely it is to go into long-term memory.

Such a view ran into problems. Certain brain-damaged patients have been shown to have very poor short-term memory, yet their long-term learning ability unimpaired. If the only route into long-term memory is via the limited capacity short-term store, then logically someone whose short-term store is almost non-existent should have enormous difficulties. However, such patients clearly do not have this handicap; they can learn normally and they appear to have remarkably few problems in coping with everyday life. This evidence clearly presents difficulties for the Atkinson and Shiffrin model.

However, a related problem, based on experimental evidence from normal subjects, has probably had more influence. The evidence came from a study by Craik and Watkins in which they were trying to assess to what extent keeping an item in short-term memory increases the probability of its passing into long-term memory. They required their subjects to hold a series of words in short-term memory for either long or short periods; after presenting many words, they asked their subjects, without prior warning, to recall as many of the previously presented and tested words as possible. Would holding a particular word for a long period increase the chances of its passing into long-term memory and being remembered subsequently, as Atkinson and Shiffrin's model suggested? There was no evidence that this was the case. Words held over a long period were no more likely to be recalled than those held only briefly.

From this Craik and Lockhart argued that the previous view of a short-term memory store relying on speech coding and feeding a long-term memory store was inappropriate. They proposed instead a view that assumed a short-term or primary memory system that could process material in a variety of ways, ranging from simply taking note of the visual characteristics of a printed word, through rehearsing it or paying attention to its sound, up to elaborate coding in terms of its meaning. They argued that all of these processes would lead to some long-term learning, but that the amount of learning depended on the type of processing, with 'deep' processing in terms of meaning leading to much better retention than 'shallow' processing. *Maintenance rehearsal* might keep material available, but would not enhance long-term learning.

The 'levels of processing' approach is essentially concerned with the role of coding in learning, the relationship between the manner in which material is processed and the probability that it will be subsequently remembered. As such, it is primarily a theory of long-term memory; it does assume a primary or short-term memory system that actually does the coding, but details of it are left unspecified. Indeed, so little emphasis is placed on the short-term component that the 'levels' approach has often mistakenly been assumed to represent a unitary approach to memory, and any success it has had in relating coding to long-term memory has sometimes been interpreted as evidence against the idea that long- and short-term memory involve separate systems. In fact the preoccupation with levels represented a reversion to the 1950s position of separate and parallel research on long- and short-term memory. The work stemming from levels tended to go more and more in the direction of studying the factors governing retrieval from long-term memory. Short-term memory studies became more closely associated with problems of attention, and with the role of short-term memory in other tasks such as reading and mental arithmetic. This led to the concept of a unitary short-term memory being replaced by that of a multi-component working memory.

3 Working memory

In this chapter I shall take the liberty of talking in somewhat greater detail than elsewhere about my own principal research interest. Underlying my approach is the assumption that a model or theory is useful if it helps one to come to grips with a problem. From this standpoint, a working memory approach to problems of short-term memory is not 'truer' than a simple dichotomy between long- and short-term memory, but its greater flexibility allows one to capture much more of the richness of the remarkable cognitive skills that we all display.

In the early 1970s a colleague, Graham Hitch, and I were about to start a three-year research project. We had been given funds by the Medical Research Council to carry out work on the relationship between long- and short-term memory. One lunchtime, over coffee, we fell to discussing some of our misgivings about the general field of short-term memory at the time. It was just passing through a peak of popularity, and the psychological journals were full of short-term memory experiments using a bewilderingly broad range of techniques, and coming up with a disconcertingly large set of explanatory models. One single book published in 1970, for example, had 13 different contributors, each presenting a different model of short-term memory. Surely not all of them could be right! Of course the models had much in common with each other. Nevertheless we felt uncomfortably like those medieval scholastic philosophers who spent their time discussing how many angels could perch on the point of a pin.

We decided to step back from the complexity and ask a single basic question. What is short-term memory for? The patient with a memory span of only two digits seems to cope with life effectively. Perhaps short-term memory had no function other than to keep experimental psychologists amused. If that were so, we decided, we would rather amuse ourselves in other ways.

There had already been a good deal of discussion as to the probable role of short-term memory, and there was fairly general agreement that its function was to serve as a *working memory*, a system that allowed several pieces of information to be held in mind at the same time and interrelated. This kind of system is clearly useful if you are trying to understand a spoken sentence, where it may not be possible to process the beginning of the sentence fully until you have reached the end. Take the following sentence: 'He strode across the court and protested vigorously that his opponent was infringing the rules by using (an illegally strung tennis racquet) (inadmissible evidence).' It is not possible to tell until the last phrase whether the court is a tennis court or a court of law.

Some form of temporary storage is also necessary for a wide range of tasks

Fingers being used as an aid to the temporary storage of information required to do sums. Information is stored just long enough for the sum to be completed, then forgotten.

Wim Klein, the 'Human Computer', a specialist in lightning mental arithmetic. The number he has written on the blackboard exactly tallies with the answer given by a computer. Mental arithmetic involves visuo-spatial and auditory processing of information in working memory.

such as mental arithmetic, reasoning and problem solving, and it is surely not accidental that virtually all attempts to simulate complex human behavior by computer have ended up requiring some type of working memory, a subcomponent of the overall system which holds and manipulates material that is being processed. If the short-term store does fulfil this role, then it is clearly a very important component of human behavior. Unfortunately, however, although many people had suggested this possibility, there was virtually no direct evidence. So Graham Hitch and I decided that we would attempt to collect some.

Capacity and limitations

One of the first problems in trying to decide whether short-term memory functioned as a working memory was the lack of agreement as to what the characteristics of short-term memory were. Taking all available models of short-term memory and testing them one after the other was likely to be a long job. Fortunately there were two features assumed by all the models, namely that short-term memory has a limited storage and processing capacity and that verbal memory span, the maximum length of telephone number you can repeat back, for example, relies heavily on short-term memory.

We reasoned that, if short-term memory does function as a working memory, subjects whose available capacity was used up by being required to remember strings of digits should have great difficulty in simultaneously performing other information processing tasks, such as reasoning or comprehending, even though these are not usually thought of as tasks involving memory. This approach assumes that the short-term memory system is like the control tower of a major airport, responsible for scheduling and coordinating all incoming and outgoing flights. Our experimental procedure was analogous to jamming the control room with additional high-priority demands which had to be met before the routine functioning of the airport could be continued. The outcome should be a dramatic disruption of performance.

The task that we chose to inflict on our subjects at the same time as they were remembering strings of digits was a verbal reasoning task, which is itself worth explaining briefly. During the 1960s both psychologists and linguists became very interested in grammar, and in the way in which syntax is processed. A number of experiments were run to show that active sentences such as 'The boy kicked the ball' were more rapidly processed than passive sentences such as 'The ball was kicked by the boy', or negative sentences such as 'The boy did not kick the ball'. At about that time I myself was interested in the effect on deepsea divers of nitrogen narcosis, the 'drunkenness' that develops if one breathes air at pressures exceeding that experienced at depths around 100 feet (30 meters).

To demonstrate the effect of nitrogen narcosis I needed a simple reasoning task that could be performed by my divers underwater; it had to be one which could be administered very quickly since bottom time was strictly limited, and I wanted it to be a task which required very little learning. I therefore borrowed the techniques being developed by the psycholinguists and produced a grammatical reasoning test. This involved presenting subjects with a series of sentences, each describing the order of presentation of two letters, A and B. Each sentence was followed by the pair *AB* or *BA*, and the subject's job was to decide whether the sentence correctly described the attached letter pair. The sentences used varied from simple active sentences such as 'A follows B — *AB*', to which the correct answer is obviously 'False', passive sentences such as 'B is followed by A — *BA*', to which the correct answer is obviously 'True', to more complex versions such as 'A is not preceded by B — *BA*', to which the answer would be 'False', and so on. Try it yourself, checking off your answers in the True/False column.

			True	False					True	False
1.	B is followed by A	—BA		✓	14.	B precedes A	—AB		
2.	A does not follow B	—BA		✓	15.	B is not preceded by A	—AB		
3.	A is not followed by B	—BA	✓		16.	B is preceded by A	—AB		
4.	A is not preceded by B	—BA		✓	17.	A is not preceded by B	—BA		
5.	B follows A	—AB	✓		18.	A does not precede B	—AB		
6.	B is not preceded by A	—BA	✓		19.	A follows B	—BA		
7.	B does not follow A	—AB		✓	20.	A is not followed by B	—BA		
8.	A follows B	—BA	✓		21.	B precedes A	—BA		
9.	B is preceded by A	—BA		✓	22.	A does not precede B	—BA		
10.	A does not precede B	—BA	✓		23.	B is followed by A	—AB		
11.	B is not followed by A	—AB	✓		24.	A does not precede B	—BA		
12.	A is followed by B	—BA		✓	25.	A is followed by B	—AB		
13.	A is not followed by B	—AB		✓	26.	A is not preceded by B	—BA		

The test proved very successful for the purpose and could be carried out after a small amount of practice by virtually all the subjects I tested. By counting how many sentences my divers could complete correctly in three minutes I was able to get a very rapid measure of their mental capability at depth. It also proved to be reasonably sensitive, picking up impairment even at 100 feet (30 meters), about the shallowest depth at which one can reliably detect impaired performance.

Now if short-term memory is indeed required for reasoning, one should have difficulty doing a sentence-checking test of the kind just described while remembering telephone numbers! We were anxious not to overload our subjects, so we began by giving them just one or two items to remember while doing the test. We found absolutely no effect, so progressed to giving them strings of six numbers to remember (you will recall that six numbers approaches the average digit span, and so ought to occupy a great deal of one's short-term memory system).

This is how we ran the experiment. Each subject was given a six-digit number such as 731928; he was then required to say it aloud, and to continue saying it. Meanwhile a sentence such as 'A precedes B — *BA*' was shown to him and he was required to press a key marked 'True' or one marked 'False', as appropriate, while continuing to rehearse the telephone number. Our subjects were initially rather horrified at being asked to do these two things at the same time, but somewhat to their surprise they discovered that they made very few errors on either the digit span or sentence-checking task. With six-digit numbers, however, there was a consistent tendency for reasoning to be slowed, though the magnitude of the disruption was much less than we had expected. Was this slowing-down evidence that short-term memory acts as a working memory system?

All things considered, our results seemed to be telling us that the short-term store is involved in the system used for reasoning, comprehending and learning, but that this involvement is by no means total; the two systems appeared to have some overlapping components but were by no means entirely

A simple representation of the model of working memory proposed by Baddeley and Hitch. An attentional control system, the central executive, is supported by two subsystems, one visual and one verbal.

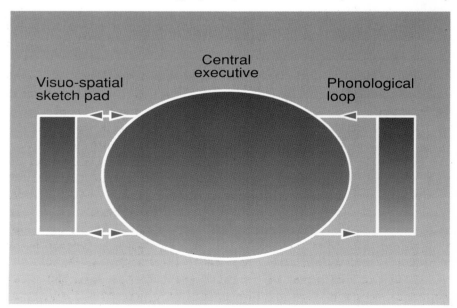

dependent on the same limited capacity system. As a result, we began to reformulate our concept of short-term memory, and to attempt to sort out some of the subcomponents.

Starting from the premise that working memory was likely to be a complex and flexible system, we decided that our best strategy was probably to isolate certain subcomponents and attempt to understand them. We therefore began by assuming the existence of a core system, a system responsible for controlling the overall system, and termed this the *central executive*. We postulated that the central executive was assisted by a number of 'slave' systems which would allow it to offload some of its short-term storage functions, thereby freeing a portion of its own capacity for performing more demanding information processing tasks. An analogy can be drawn with a business executive who, if he is to avoid becoming overloaded, must delegate the more routine aspects of his job to subordinates, leaving himself free to give full attention to novel problems and dilemmas.

The phonological loop system

You may recall that one characteristic frequently assigned to short-term memory is its reliance on speech coding — most models of short-term memory involve some process of rehearsal, usually via subvocal speech, to maintain the memory trace. Separating this aspect of memory from the rest, we postulated a slave system which we called the *articulatory* or *phonological loop*. The assumption that such a slave system existed was supported by three clusters of evidence. The first of these was the *acoustic* or *phonological similarity effect*, shown by the tendency for subjects' errors to be phonologically similar to the correct item (*F* for *S* and *B* for *G*) and for sequences of items that have similar speech sounds to be particularly hard to remember in the appropriate order. For example, *D B C T P G* is harder to remember than *K W Y L R Q*; *mad can cap man map* is harder than *pen day cow bar rig*.

A second source of evidence came from the observation that the immediate recall of visually presented digits could be disrupted when one is asked to ignore irrelevant spoken material. Recall is disrupted just as much whether the irrelevant material is in English or Arabic, suggesting that the recall process is operating at the level of sound rather than meaning. The effect is not simply one of distraction, however, since meaningless noise does not disrupt memory, even when presented very loudly. We interpreted the irrelevant speech effect by assuming that the irrelevant spoken material gains access to the short-term speech-based store, even when the subject tries to ignore it; it then disrupts performance by corrupting the memory trace. We assumed that noise does not disrupt memory because it is kept out of the short-term memory store by some sort of filter that is capable of distinguishing between noise and speech. We found that singing was just as disruptive as speech, but that instrumental music had a smaller effect, a result that has implications for the nature of the proposed sound filtering process.

A third source of information about the articulatory loop came from other experiments we were carrying out on the effect of word length on memory span. We found a very clear link between word length and increased memory span. You can demonstrate this for yourself by using the columns of words below. Read down each column silently, then look away and write down the words, or the first two or three letters of each word. Each correct word scores 1.

some	twice	yield	bond	hate
harm	harm	worst	harm	bond
bond	worst	harm	worst	some
yield	wit	twice	yield	twice
hate	come	hate	twice	yield
Recall	**Recall**	**Recall**	**Recall**	**Recall**
association	considerable	university	considerable	immediately
considerable	representative	representative	opportunity	considerable
representative	individual	association	organization	individual
individual	association	individual	university	association
immediately	opportunity	immediately	representative	opportunity
Recall	**Recall**	**Recall**	**Recall**	**Recall**

Your score on the shorter words was almost certainly better than on the longer words. We also had our subjects remember sequences like *Malta, Chad, Kenya, Burma, Chile* as compared with *Czechoslovakia, Switzerland, Ethiopia, Australia, Afghanistan* to reassure ourselves that this effect had nothing to do with English monosyllabic words being of generally Anglo-Saxon origin and polysyllablic ones of Latin origin. It didn't.

We assumed that the reason why long words were harder to remember was because our subjects said the words to themselves under their breath. The longer the word, the longer it takes to say, and the greater the time taken to rehearse the sequence of syllables, the more time there is for the memory trace of earlier words to fade away.

If we were right, then it should prove possible to get rid of the word-length effect by preventing our subjects from rehearsing. We did this by having them say an irrelevant word such as 'the' repeatedly out loud. As predicted, this reduced the level of performance, since it stopped the subjects gaining the advantage of rehearsal, and also removed the influence of word length. Since subjects were unable to rehearse subvocally, the length of the words ceased to be important.

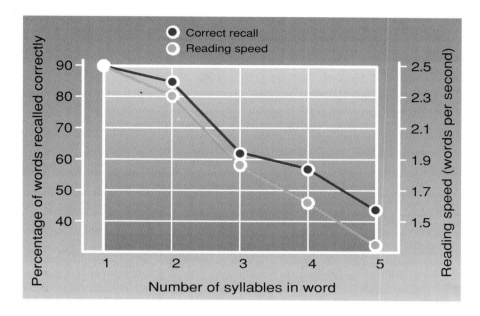

This graph shows the relationship between word length and recall, and between word length and reading speed. Such results suggest that longer words are more difficult to recall because they take longer to articulate during rehearsal. (Baddeley, Thomson and Buchanan, 1975)

Preventing rehearsal by requiring the subject to generate repetitive speech is termed *articulatory suppression*, and it has a further effect on performance. When they are suppressing articulation, subjects appear to be unable to transfer visually presented material to the phonological short-term store. Because of that, suppression also gets rid of the acoustic similarity effect, provided material is presented visually. It also gets rid of the irrelevant speech effect. If subjects cannot subvocalize the digits they are seeing, the digits do not get translated into a phonological code. They are therefore not registered in the store, and hence are not disrupted when irrelevant spoken material enters the store.

The concept of the articulatory loop quite neatly tied together this cluster of findings. We assumed that a process of subvocal rehearsal is used, probably to refresh a fading memory trace before it decays into inaccessibility. The process seems to involve subvocal speech and can be hindered if the subject's speech system is kept busy uttering irrelevancies. Is it simply that long words take longer to articulate than short ones? Or does the effect stem from the greater complexity of long words, comprising more speech sounds, causing overloading of some part of the speech system? We were in fact able to investigate this relatively simply by comparing memory span performance on two sets of words, both of which had the same number of syllables, letters and phonemes, but differed in the time they took to utter.

We required our subjects to remember either sequences of words with long vowel sounds, such as *harpoon* and *Friday*, or sequences of words containing the same number of syllables, but which are spoken relatively rapidly, such as *bishop* and *wicket*. We found a clear tendency for slowly spoken words to be remembered less well, implying that the articulatory loop's limitation is purely one of time. Consistent with this, we found that there was a clear relationship between the

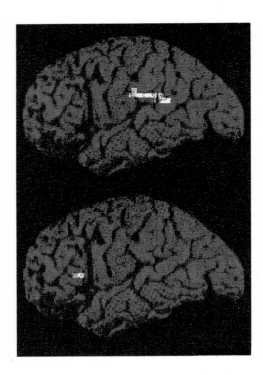

A PET scan showing areas of the brain involved in the phonological loop component of working memory. The yellow area in the upper figure represents the region of the brain principally concerned with the short-term storage of sound, while the lower figure highlights the area principally concerned with active subvocal rehearsal. (Based on Paulesu, Frith and Frackoviak, 1993)

speed with which an individual could read out sequences of words and his memory span; fast talkers were good rememberers, on this task at least.

The relationship between the time it took to speak words of particular lengths and memory span for them was very orderly, as the graph on page 53 shows. On the basis of this, memory span can be redefined: it is the amount of time that is constant, not the number of items. Our subjects could only remember as much as they could say in just 1.5 seconds.

One spin-off from our work on the articulatory loop was provided by a colleague, Nick Ellis, working at the University of Bangor in Wales. Bangor is in a strongly Welsh-speaking area, and so when an educational psychologist wants to test a child whose first language is Welsh the standard psychometric tests are given in Welsh. Nick Ellis noted that the norms which indicated the expected level for an average child of a given age showed a curious discrepancy; in the case of digit span, Welsh-speaking children appeared to lag consistently behind the norms based on English-speaking American children. Was there some mysterious genetic deficiency in the Welsh, compensated for by a super-abundance of genes related to choral singing and passing rugby balls? Perish the thought. Actually, numbers in Welsh all tend to contain relatively long speech sounds, and so are likely to be spoken more slowly even though they have just the same number of syllables as English numbers. Ellis and a colleague, R. A. Hennelly, decided to explore this factor to try and account for the lower spans of Welsh-speakers. They did so by taking a number of students who were bilingual in English and Welsh, but who spoke Welsh for preference.

First of all they showed that their students had a greater digit span in their non-preferred language, English, thus supporting their view that the difference was based on the language, not on the individual. They then showed that the time required to read out Welsh numbers was indeed longer than that taken to read out a similar number of English numbers, and that when digit span was adjusted on account of this, the difference between English and Welsh disappeared. In other words, the span was determined not by the number of items but by the amount of speaking time a sequence took. In a further experiment they showed, as one would expect, that when their subjects were prevented from using the articulatory loop by being asked to repeat irrelevant speech sounds, the difference between their English and Welsh digit spans vanished.

Suppose then that we accept as a useful working hypothesis the concept of an articulatory loop. What purpose does it serve? It seems somewhat unlikely that evolution has specifically equipped us to remember telephone numbers. We have, however, begun to explore a range of tasks which might utilize the articulatory loop. These tend of course to be cognitive tasks with a speech component.

Counting is an obvious example. Try counting the number of letters in the next line, while at the same time repeatedly and rapidly saying the word *the*. Time yourself, and then repeat the procedure without articulatory suppression. I think you will find that subvocalization plays an important part in normal counting, at least in our culture.

Nevertheless people are quite ingenious at finding ways around the problem of not being allowed to subvocalize. Indeed there are many cultures which do not use subvocal counting, relying on something analogous to counting on the fingers, but often using many more parts of the body — hence allowing them to count well above 10. Arithmetic in general probably uses the articulatory loop. Graham Hitch has begun to analyze the processes underlying simple arithmetic from a working memory viewpoint, and Ellis and Hennelly have shown that their bilingual subjects are particularly prone to error when doing arithmetic in Welsh.

A task in which subvocalization might be assumed to play an important role is that of reading. People commonly 'hear' what they are reading spoken in some form of inner voice, and it is tempting to attribute this to the articulatory loop. However, although 'the mind's ear' may possibly be important in learning to read, it seems to play a much less crucial role in the fluent adult reader. If you remain to be convinced, try reading the next couple of sentences while repeating the word *the* under your breath. It may be a little uncomfortable, but you should have no great difficulty understanding what has been written. We have conducted a number of experiments along these lines, and find that people appear to read just as rapidly and have no difficulty in understanding the gist of what is written while suppressing subvocalization. They are less good at picking up deliberate errors in prose passages, however. If, for example, I had reversed the order of two of the words in a sentence, you would have been much less likely to notice it while suppressing subvocalization.

So the articulatory loop appears to be a checking mechanism that is particularly good at preserving the order of information. You probably use it when reading difficult prose — a legal document, for example — where accurate understanding is essential, but I suspect that you do not subvocalize very much when reading a novel. You might well argue that, although you do not subvocalize, you still think you hear a voice when you read; I suspect that this 'voice' is based on another system, an *auditory imagery system*, related to but different from the articulatory loop.

Auditory imagery

We clearly do have some form of auditory imagery which allows us to imagine the voice of a great singer, the sound of waves crashing on the beach, or a symphony orchestra tuning up. These are all sounds which we ourselves cannot possibly reproduce. It is therefore unlikely that our imagery is based on subvocalization. Experiments have shown that if people are shown a series of words, they are capable of imagining themselves saying them in either a male or female voice. If they have imagined a given word in a female voice, they are more likely to recognize it later if it is spoken by a female rather than a male, and vice versa. Curiously, but conveniently, one's own voice appears to be hermaphrodite! One recognizes words that have been rehearsed in one's own voice equally well regardless of whether they are presented by a male or female voice.

Returning to the question of reading, one might imagine that judging the spoken sound of written words would require some form of subvocalization. We tested this by having subjects judge whether pairs of words were similar in sound or not, choosing words which were sometimes spelt irregularly; hence *dough* and *doe* should be given a 'Same' response, *dough* and *rough* a 'Not same' response. Our subjects made these judgements either unimpeded or while suppressing articulation by repeatedly counting from one to six.

How good is your imagination for sounds? Can you hear the sounds implied by each of these pictures? In what sense do you 'hear' them? To what extent are you trying to convert them into subvocal speech sounds? Do you think you have a non-verbal auditory imagery system?

Another way of making the same point would be to ask you to read a series of 'nonwords' which, when pronounced, sound the same as real words, *cote* for *coat* and *eeggl* for *eagle*, for example. Try reading Sentence 1 below, and when you have completed that, begin suppressing articulation and attempt to read Sentence 2.

1. *Iff yue sowned owt thiss sentans tew yoreselph, yoo wil komprehenned it.*

Now begin repeating the word 'the' under your breath and read Sentence 2.

2. *Moast peepul seem tue bee aybul tue heer thuh wirds eevan wen thay arr surpresing artikulashun.*

I suspect that you had little difficulty in understanding either sentence, although the laborious nature of the process indicates, I think, that we probably do not normally read by sounding out the words in a text and listening to the sounds, although we may well have gone through a process of sounding and listening when we were learning to read. The role of the sound or phonological component in fluent adult reading is still a controversial one, but it is by now, I think, fairly generally accepted that it is not necessary to be able to produce the sound of a word in order to understand it.

Of particular interest in this connection is a rare group of patients whose reading performance has been disturbed by brain damage, often following a stroke. A subgroup of such dyslexic patients, known as 'deep dyslexics', have great difficulty in reading words aloud and are quite incapable of reading out pronounceable 'nonwords' such as *fleep* or *spart*. They experience further problems in reading abstract words such as *hope* or *justice*, but find imageable words such as *castle* and *trombone* much easier. One such patient, for example, could read the concrete noun *inn* but not the much more common preposition *in*, and the word *bee* but not *be*. Errors like this are also interesting in that they suggest it is possible to understand a word approximately but not be able to access its spoken sound. For example, *pray* might be read aloud as *chapel*, or *sepulcher* as *tomb*. This problem does not stem from an inability to pronounce the words, since the subject can repeat them with no difficulty; it is simply that the written version of a word appears to access certain aspects of its meaning but not its spoken form.

The phonological loop as a language-acquisition device

Although we had shown that the phonological loop played some role in counting and proofreading, the effects of blocking the phonological loop were far from dramatic, causing a colleague to speculate that the phonological loop was little more than 'a pimple on the face of cognition'. (He has subsequently corrected me on this point; the anatomical location he suggested was apparently rather less elevated than the face!) Consistent with this view was the observation that patients who had acquired a specific deficit in phonological loop performance following brain damage appeared to have very few problems in coping with everyday life. Did the loop have any role other than keeping cognitive psychologists busy?

We began to explore this question by testing a young Italian lady, whom we will call PV, who had been left with a very pure deficit in auditory short-term memory following a stroke. In a series of experiments carried out jointly with Italian colleagues Giuseppe Vallar and Costanza Papagno, we first explored PV's capacity for understanding spoken and written prose. She did prove to have some problems, particularly with certain types of complex long sentences, but for practical purposes the effects were not large, perhaps suggesting that the phonological loop might provide a back-up process rather than playing a central role in language comprehension.

We then decided to explore PV's capacity for new phonological learning, attempting to teach her Russian vocabulary. We knew that her learning abilities in general were excellent, but most standard tests of long-term memory are probably based on meaning or on visual memory; her phonological long-term learning had never been tested. We therefore carried out two experiments, one in which she learned to associate pairs of words in her native Italian (e.g. *cavallo — libro*, i.e. horse — book). We expected her to learn these in terms of their meaning, and to perform normally, which she did when compared with a group of control subjects of equivalent age and educational background. The second experiment required her to learn to associate an unfamiliar Russian word with its Italian equivalent (e.g. *rosa* [rose] — *svieti*). As the lower of the two graphs below shows, her performance on this task was appalling; indeed she failed to learn a single Russian word. These results support the view that the phonological loop might indeed be specialized for language learning.

Patient PV had a very pure deficit in short-term auditory memory. As the upper graph shows, when meaningful words were involved, her capacity for learning was normal. The lower graph, however, shows that she was very bad at learning foreign words, indicating that short-term auditory memory problems were impairing long-term auditory learning. (Baddeley, Papagno and Vallar, 1988)

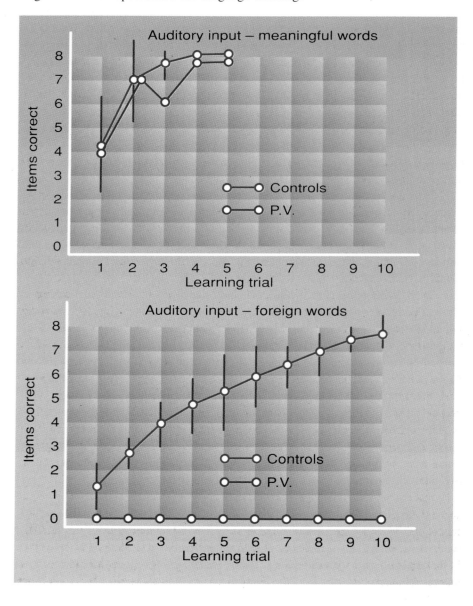

Individuals like PV, with a very pure deficit of phonological short-term memory, are extremely rare. The deficit results from damage to the left hemisphere of the brain, which is specialized for language. However, most patients with defective short-term memory also have more extensive language processing problems, which makes it difficult to interpret their memory results. We therefore attempted to simulate PV's deficit using normal subjects. We did not of course try to remove parts of their brains, but instead tried to interfere with the operation of the phonological loop by requiring them to suppress articulation. When we did so, we found that it impaired their capacity for learning foreign vocabulary, but had no such effect on their capacity to associate pairs of words in their native language. My colleagues carried out further experiments which also pointed to the importance of the phonological loop in vocabulary learning; they capitalized on the phonological similarity effect, showing that the rate of acquiring Russian vocabulary was impaired when the Russian words were similar in sound, while similarity had no effect on learning pairs of familiar words. They went on to show that learning was slower for long than for short words, while word length did not influence paired-associate learning in the subjects' native tongue. It appears to be the case, therefore, that normal subjects also rely on the phonological loop for acquiring foreign language vocabulary, while relying on semantic coding to associate pairs of familiar words.

These results suggest that phonological loop capacity may be an important determinant of foreign language acquisition rate, a conclusion supported by a recent study of language learning by Ellis and Beaton that will be discussed in more detail in Chapter 14. They found that although an imagery mnemonic was helpful in learning the meaning of foreign nouns, learning to produce the foreign words was better following rote rehearsal.

A link between the phonological loop and foreign language learning is also supported by two recent single case studies. An American graduate student whom I tested, who proved to have a remarkably short digit span, also had difficulty learning foreign language vocabulary; indeed he had found it impossible to learn foreign languages, although this was very important to him for university admission. Rather more dramatically, my Italian colleagues have recently reported the case of a young lady suffering from Down's syndrome, who is clearly below average in general intelligence, but nevertheless is able to speak three languages fluently; she proved to have an excellent digit span, and to be just as good as controls at learning new foreign language vocabulary, although substantially poorer at learning to associate words in her native language.

So far we have shown that the phonological loop appears to be involved in second language learning, but what about the acquisition of one's native language? A colleague, Susan Gathercole, and I have explored this, initially working with a group of children identified as having a specific language deficit, in that their vocabulary and reading skills were at least two years behind their age norms although their non-verbal intelligence was above average. We found that our young subjects had a particularly marked deficit in a task involving hearing and repeating back nonwords such as *bannow, skiticult* and *contraponist*. Not only did they have the vocabulary of children two years younger, but the repetition abilities of children four years younger. Was it poor repetition ability that was responsible for their delayed language development? We checked that this was not readily attributable to problems of hearing or speech production, and discovered, using familiar material such as proper words, that they did indeed have severely reduced verbal memory span. The most likely interpretation of their below average performance therefore seemed to be a deficit in the performance of the phonological loop component of working memory.

Our next question was concerned with whether the phonological loop, insofar as it is measured by nonword repetition, limits the language development of children within the normal population. We tested about 100 children who were starting school, aged between four and five years, correlating their performance on our nonword repetition test with their vocabulary score. We found that nonword repetition correlated highly with vocabulary, and was indeed a better predictor of vocabulary than was performance on a general intelligence test. Of course correlation does not necessarily imply causation. It is, for example, as plausible to assume that a good vocabulary helps in nonword repetition tests, as it is to assume that good nonword repetition performance indicates a good memory system, which in turn leads to good vocabulary. There is, however, at least one way of teasing apart the direction of causation, and that is to test subjects again after a lapse of time, and look at the relationship between the various measures on the two occasions. If good memory is causally linked to good vocabulary, then it ought to be possible to demonstrate that nonword repetition performance at age four predicts

Building a Tower of Babel? If non-verbal abilities outstrip the ability to read and spell, a short verbal memory span may be the culprit.

vocabulary at age five rather better than vocabulary at age four predicts nonword repetition at age five. This is indeed what we found. Nonword repetition performance at age four predicted vocabulary at age five significantly better than vocabulary predicted later nonword repetition. Beyond age five the pattern begins to change. For older children and adults the causal direction changes, with existing vocabulary probably providing a useful tool for performing nonword repetition.

Another way of tackling the question is to try to teach children new vocabulary. We did this using toy monsters and teaching the children either familiar names for each monster (e.g. Michael) or unfamiliar (e.g. Pikle). We found that children who were high on a test of nonword repetition were better name learners than equally intelligent low repetition children, particularly at learning the unfamiliar names. A similar conclusion was reached by Elizabeth Service, independently carrying out a study on Finnish children learning English. Before the children began the course, she gave them a range of tests, which she then related to their performance on English language skills two years later. The best predictor was a nonword repetition test that involved hearing and repeating back pseudo English nonwords.

In conclusion, then, we now appear to be in a position to argue that, far from being 'a pimple on the face of cognition', the phonological loop is the system that evolution has developed for the crucial task of language acquisition. Adults who have a disruption to this system do not have too many problems, provided they are not required to learn new languages. However, children with a deficit in the phonological loop are likely to have substantially more problems. The evidence suggests that an intelligent child is likely to catch up on vocabulary, since many factors other than phonological coding are important, but that he or she may well encounter problems in reading and spelling.

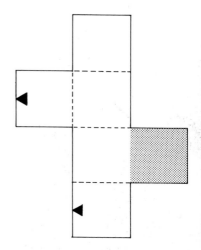

The visuo-spatial sketch pad

A great deal of interest has been focused on the topic of visual imagery in recent years, partly because it plays such an important role in learning verbal material. Visual imagery mnemonics are an extremely effective way of remembering lists of words, and words which are imageable are more easily memorized than those that aren't. In particular, there has been a great deal of controversy as to whether images are in some sense stored directly in the brain or created from some more abstract representation. Supporters of the former view have tended to look for similarities between the process of reading information from a mental image and the process of perceiving, and they have met with a good deal of success. Strongly associated with this approach is Roger Shepard of Stanford University in California. Shepard has carried out a range of experiments which explore the similarity between imaging and perceiving.

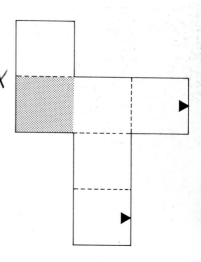

One of his early experiments is shown on the right. Both the shapes depicted could, if they were made out of paper, be folded to create a solid, with the shaded area being the base. Your task is to imagine folding the shapes and to decide whether the arrows will meet head on. Shepard found that the time it took his subjects to come to a solution was systematically related to the number of folds that would have been required had they actually been doing the folding. It was as if they were folding the cube in their heads.

A similar effect was demonstrated even more elegantly using the clusters of two-dimensional cubes shown on page 63. Subjects were shown pairs of clusters and asked to decide whether they were the same but seen from a different angle, or were built up quite differently. The angular difference between the orientation of the two figures was varied systematically.

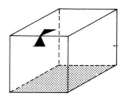

See how good you are at mental rotation! Figures A and B below show two clusters of cubes seen from different angles. If you mentally rotate Figure B you will see that it is exactly the same as Figure A. Figures C and D, however, show two different clusters of cubes. No matter how you rotate them, they will never match each other.

On the cube cluster rotation test opposite Shepard's subjects showed a linear relationship between the time it took them to make the comparison between each pair of clusters and the angular difference between them. It was as

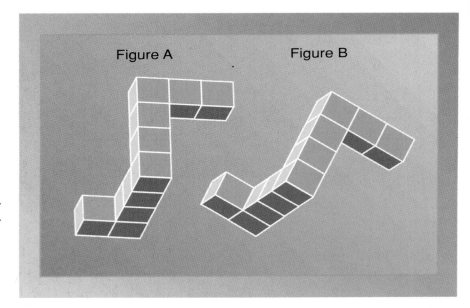

Below:
Another 'mental manipulation' exercise. Can either of these flat pieces of paper be folded into a pyramid? The top one can, but the bottom one can't.

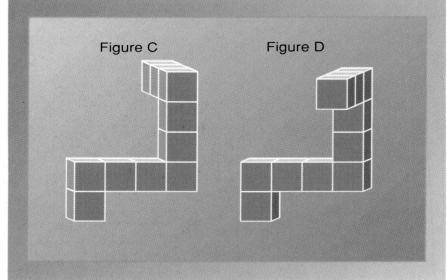

if they were rotating one cluster in their hand at a constant rate until it was in line with the second, then making their judgement.

Stephen Kosslyn of Harvard University produced a related set of demonstrations. In one experiment he had his subjects memorize a series of pictures, such as a simple drawing of a boat, for example. He then asked them to scan their image of the boat in order to report on a particular detail. Kosslyn showed that a subject who had just responded to a question about the stern of the boat took longer to respond to a question about the bow than one who had just

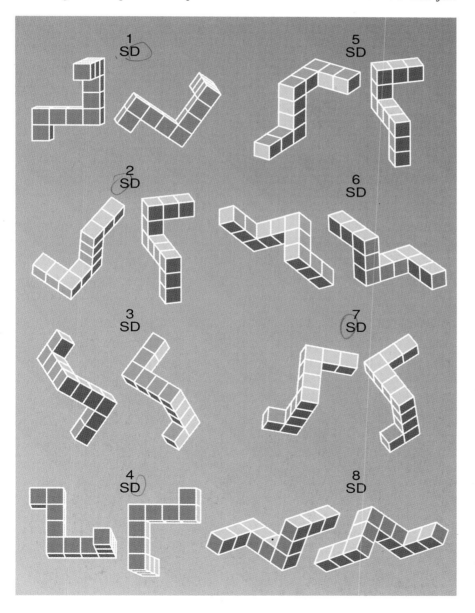

Mentally rotate these pairs of cube clusters, circling S if you decide they are the same and D if you decide they are different. The correct answers are (S) *for 2, 3, 6, 7 and 8, and* (D) *for 1, 4 and 5.*

responded to a question about the portholes. It was as if the subject were taking time to scan across the boat, and the greater the distance that had to be scanned the longer it took to respond.

One characteristic of our visual images is that we appear to be able to manipulate their apparent sizes. We can for example consider a cat as a whole or 'zoom in' on its whiskers or the tip of its tail. When imaging two different sized animals together, say an elephant and a rabbit, Kosslyn showed that it took longer to answer a question about the rabbit's ears, a relatively small detail in relation to the elephant, than it took if the subject were imaging a rabbit next to a fly, for example, the rabbit's ears being large in relation to the size of the fly. However, since our imagery system is conveniently flexible, it is also possible to reverse the effect by imaging a giant fly towering over a rabbit, or a tiny elephant no bigger than a rabbit's foot. All these effects show that, in some respects at least, visual images do behave like visual percepts. It is important, however, not to regard them simply as pictures stored in the head. Consider the cat just mentioned; if our mental image of a cat had to contain all the information necessary to specify every whisker and piece of fur, this would be enormously costly in terms of information storage. There is considerable evidence to suggest that we simply do not have this degree of information about items that we image.

What has visual imagery to do with working memory? Our own approach is to suggest that spatial information is probably stored in some abstract code in long-term memory, but that one method of displaying and manipulating such information is via a spatial slave system. Such a system uses some of the same equipment as is used in perception, and depends for its functioning on the central executive component of the working memory system. What is our evidence for such a view?

As with our other research on working memory, we have relied heavily on the technique of selectively interfering with some aspect of processing. In the case of our work on imagery, we were heavily influenced by some ingenious work by a Canadian psychologist, Lee Brooks. In one of the tasks devised by Brooks subjects were shown a block capital letter such as the F shown here. They were asked to hold it in their mind's eye and, starting at the bottom left, to classify each corner as a 'Yes' if it involved the bottom or top line of the letter and as a 'No' if it did not. In this case the correct sequence of responses would be 'Yes, Yes, Yes, No, No, No, No, No, No, Yes.' Subjects performed this task and responded either verbally or by pointing to the word 'Yes' or 'No' located at different points down the page. Brooks' subjects found much more difficulty in responding by pointing than by speaking, as if the act of pointing interfered with the process of imagery. Brooks contrasted this task with a second in which subjects were given a sentence such as 'A bird in the

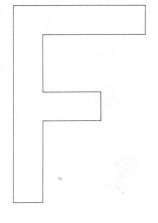

One of the original Tenniel illustrations to Lewis Carroll's Alice in Wonderland, *a story that makes full use of the exciting possibilities of visual imagery. One moment Alice is huge, and the next she is tiny enough to peep over the edge of a mushroom and talk to a caterpillar.*

hand is not in the bush' to remember and required to classify each word in the sentence as a noun or as a non-noun; in this case the correct sequence of responses is 'No, Yes, No, No, Yes, No, No, No, No, Yes'. With this task, performance was much better when the responses were made by pointing rather than by speaking. The reason is obvious. In a visual imagery test a visuo-spatial task such as pointing appears to use some of the capacity of the imaging equipment, leaving less capacity available for mental imagery; but the same sort of task does not interfere with heavily verbal tasks such as classifying nouns, remembering sentences, or making judgements based on knowledge of syntax.

Our first experiment was somewhat similar to that of Brooks, but it was derived, at least in part, from a rather disconcerting personal experience. While spending a year in the United States I became very interested in American football, and on one occasion decided to listen to a game while driving along a Californian freeway. In order to understand the progress of the game it was necessary to form a fairly clear and detailed image of the proceedings, and I observed that as I did so my car began to drift out of lane and back again. I rapidly switched to music, but remembered the experience and decided to explore it in the laboratory. In order to do so I used a task somewhat similar to the one just described. I had my subjects perform it either on its own or at the same time as they were doing a simple tracking task which had some of the characteristics of steering a car. The task involved a spot of light that moved along a circular path; subjects had to try to keep a pointer in contact with the spot of light, their success being measured by how much of the time they were on target. We began by checking that this task would disrupt imagery in the same way as the pointing task used by Brooks. In one experiment we gave our subjects one of several blocked letters and asked them to perform the Brooks task, saying 'Yes' for a top or bottom corner and 'No' for others while keeping the pointer in contact with the moving spot of light. We found that our subjects had great difficulty tracking the light spot while visualizing letters. A second experiment confirmed that an immediate memory task relying on imagery was disrupted by tracking, while one based on verbal coding was not.

Is imagery visual or spatial?

Further investigation of the Brooks task suggested that it was disrupted by non-visual spatial activity; for example, requiring a blindfolded subject to point to a moving sound source disrupted spatial memory. On the other hand performance on the Brooks task was not strongly disrupted by a non-spatial visual task that involved judging the brightness of a large pool of light. This tempted us to argue that the system is fundamentally spatial rather than visual. It now seems more likely that our conclusion stemmed from using a particularly spatial task, since other experiments using memory for pattern and shape have reported that non-spatial visual activity may be disruptive.

The strongest evidence in this area has come from the study of neuropsychological cases. During World War I the neurologist Gordon Holmes reported the case of a brain-damaged soldier who was able to identify objects, but not locate them spatially. One such patient was able to identify a pocketknife, but reached in the wrong direction to grasp it, while another had great difficulty locating a soup bowl with a spoon, but once this had been achieved was capable of using the spoon entirely appropriately. Conversely, there are patients whose spatial skills are normal, but who appear to have lost the capacity to form color images; for example, they are unable to answer questions such as 'What color is a banana?' or to color a drawing of a banana realistically with crayons.

More recent work has taken advantage of the techniques developed to study visual imagery. Martha Farah, for example, describes a patient who is unable to perform tasks that depend on the visual characteristics of objects, such as judging the relative size of a dog and a cow, reporting on the shape of a spaniel's ears, or judging the color of a lettuce. The patient can nonetheless perform spatial manipulation tasks such as Shepherd's cube rotation task (see page 63) or Kosslyn's mental scanning tasks (see page 64), and is able to demonstrate geographical knowledge by marking the locations of cities on maps. Other patients show the opposite pattern, arguing for a clear separation between visual and spatial aspects of imagery.

Psychophysiological studies measuring either the electrical activity of the brain or the blood flow in different cortical regions suggest that the more visual aspects of pattern and color imagery depend upon the occipital lobes — located at the back of the brain — while the more spatial aspects appear to reflect activity in the parietal region around the center of the brain. Work done by Patricia Goldman-Pakic, involving electrical recording from cells in monkeys who are awake and performing memory tasks, suggests that the frontal lobes may also be involved, possibly performing an executive or imagery controlling function.

Imagery and long-term learning

Thus far we have been concerned almost entirely with the process of representing and manipulating images. However, imagery may play a prominent role in long-term memory too. This prominence can be inferred from two pieces of evidence: first, there is a strong relationship between the imageability of a word and the ease with which it can be memorized; and second, imaging plays an important part in mnemonic strategies. Is there a relationship between our proposed visuo-spatial sketch pad system and imagery in long-term memory?

If the sketch pad system is used for displaying imageable words and for manipulating images in mnemonic schemes, performing a light tracking task during learning ought to disrupt both these processes. If, on the other hand, our sketch pad system is quite unrelated to imagery in long-term memory, a visual tracking task would disrupt non-imageable material just as much as imageable, and would interfere with simple rote learning just as much as with learning based on an imagery mnemonic.

In our first experiment we tried to abolish the effect of imageability by testing peoples' memory for pairs of abstract and concrete words. The abstract pairs we used were noun-adjectives such as *mood-cheerful, idea-original* and *gratitude-infinite*; the concrete pairs were noun-adjective combinations such as *strawberry-ripe*, *bullet-gray*, *table-square* and so on — highly imageable. With half the pairs of words on our abstract and concrete lists subjects were free to devote their attention entirely to learning; with the other half they were required to perform a tracking task which again involved keeping a pointer in contact with a moving spot of light. Our results were very straight-forward: we obtained the usual massive effect of imageability (the concrete pairs being remembered better than the abstract), and the tracking task im-paired performance slightly, but the impairment was just as great for the abstract pairs as it was for the imageable ones. Whatever the mechanism whereby imageability has an effect, it does not appear to depend very crucially on the visuo-spatial sketch pad.

What about the process of using imagery mnemonics? Do these make demands on the visuo-spatial sketch pad, or are all the long-term memory effects of imagery quite separate from the working memory system we have been describing? In order to test this we selected a mnemonic with a strong spatial component; we taught our subjects a series of locations and instructed them to imagine each of a series of objects in one of these locations. The experiment was run using University of Stirling students and we taught a route through the university campus which involved ten landmarks. Subjects were taught the sequence and then encouraged to use it in remembering lists of ten words. Suppose the first landmark was the university entrance and the second the entrance to the student bar, while the first two objects were, let us say, a pig and a lilac. They were instructed to imagine a pig at the entrance to the university and a lilac tree blocking the entrance to the student bar, etc.

Once again we relied on our light tracking task as our interference method. The results were again straightforward; under normal conditions subjects per-formed consistently better when they were using the mnemonic, but the advan-tage disappeared completely when they were required to perform the spatial tracking task as well. It seems then that the kind of manipulation and location of images used when applying a mnemonic *does* depend on the sketch pad. We noted incidentally that our subjects were able to use the sketch pad perfectly effectively whether the words they were using were imageable and concrete (*pig*) or abstract (*virtue, justice*). In the case of abstract words, they presumably created some serviceable form of representation.

The concreteness of a word, however, appears to have a quite different relationship to long-term memory. First, it does not seem to be mediated by the visuo-spatial sketch pad system, and second it is not affected by whether a person is instructed to conjure up images. The concrete/abstract difference probably has something to do with the way word characteristics are stored in semantic memory, with concrete words being more richly encoded than abstract ones. At the moment we know too little about how meaning is stored in semantic memory to do more than speculate.

The central executive

New uses for old objects. Creative problem solving is likely to depend on the central executive component of working memory.

The central executive component of working memory (see diagram on page 50) is assumed to be a limited-capacity attentional system that controls the phonological loop and sketch pad, and relates them to long-term memory. The executive is almost certainly considerably more complex than either of the two slave systems, which makes it considerably harder to investigate. One approach to working memory which has run in parallel with our own model has tended to define working memory in terms of the need to combine memory and processing. Tasks that perform this function are designed and used to measure the working memory capacity of a range of subjects. Differences in capacity can then be related to differences in performing complex tasks such as comprehension or problem solving.

This approach has had considerable success in exploring the processes of language comprehension. For example, in one study Meredith Daneman and Pat Carpenter in Pittsburgh devised a task which they termed 'working memory span'. This involved presenting the subject with a series of sentences. The subject was required to read each one and then, after the final sentence, recall the last word in each sentence. Try it yourself using the sentences below, covering each one as soon as you have read it.

The greengrocer sold many apples and oranges.

The sailor had been round the world several times.

The house had large windows and a massive mahogany door.

The bookseller crossed the room, scowled and threw the manuscript on the chair.

Now recall the final word in each sentence. Were you correct? Four sentences is quite a good span for the average subject, and indeed some people have difficulty managing more than two. When this test was given to a range of university students, whose reading comprehension had been measured, there proved to be a good relationship between working memory span and reading comprehension. Other more detailed studies have shown that subjects with high working memory spans are better able to cope with passages such as the following: 'There was a strange noise emanating from the dark house. Bob had to venture in to find out what was there. He was terrified: rumor had it that the house was haunted. He would feel more secure with a stick to defend himself and so he went and looked among his baseball equipment. He found a bat that was very large and brown and was flying back and forth in the gloomy room. Now he didn't need to be afraid any longer.' Most people reading this passage tend initially to assume that the large brown bat is a baseball bat rather than a flying creature. However, subjects with a high working memory span are able to correct their misapprehension on about 75 per cent of occasions, while low span subjects are correct only about 25 per cent of the time.

Jane Oakhill, an English psychologist who taught reading before she took up research in psychology, was interested in children who appeared to be able to read words aloud with considerable accuracy but nevertheless had difficulty in understanding the content of what they read. Such children are sometimes described as 'barking at print' rather than genuinely reading. She found that such children tend to have a low working memory span, and that their comprehension skills are poor, even when they are listening rather than reading. In one study the children were read a story containing what appeared to be an inconsistent response by an adult to a child, but where the inconsistency was explained later in the text. For example, a child might be praised for refusing to share a piece of cake with his sister, who later in the passage was revealed to be on a diet. After hearing the passage the children were questioned about the appropriateness of the adult's action. Low working memory span children were likely to miss the link between the two pieces of information in the passage, and criticize the parent. Oakhill interpreted her results in terms of a central executive deficit rather than a specific language problem.

Patrick Kyllonen who works for the U.S. Air Force has been exploring the possibility that measures of working memory capacity might provide an alternative to traditional measures of intelligence based on reasoning. The U.S. Air Force is concerned with this issue since it needs to recruit people from many different backgrounds, not all of whom will have been equally well educated, a factor that can have a major effect on many standard intelligence test measures. Using a range of working memory tasks, defined in terms of the need for simultaneous memory and processing, Kyllonen found that working memory performance correlated very highly with reasoning skill. The main difference between the two was that working memory measures were slightly more dependent upon speed of processing, while reasoning tasks depended more on prior knowledge.

In a later experiment subjects were given working memory and reasoning measures, and then required to take a two-week training course in computer programing. Although reasoning and working memory measures were highly correlated, working memory was a better predictor of programing success than standard academic measures. A similar result was obtained in another study in which subjects had to learn about logic gates. Consequently, although our knowledge of the central executive is still very limited, the concept of working memory is already proving valuable.

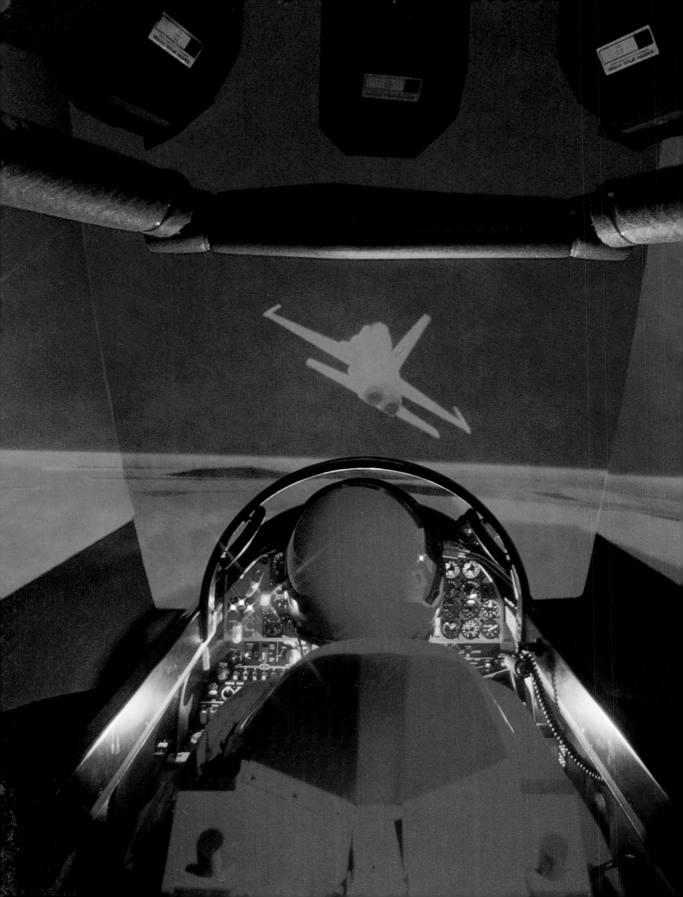

4 Learning

The scientific study of memory began in the early 1880s when a German philosopher, Hermann Ebbinghaus, came up with the revolutionary idea that memory could be studied experimentally. In doing so he broke away from a 2000-year-old tradition that firmly assigned the study of memory to the philosopher rather than to the scientist. He argued that philosophers had come up with a wide range of possible interpretations of memory but had produced no way of deciding which among these theories offered the best explanation of memory. He aimed to collect objective experimental evidence of the way in which memory worked in the hope that this would allow him to choose between the various theories.

Ebbinghaus decided that the only way to tackle the complex subject of human memory was to simplify the problem. He tested only one person, himself, and since he wished to study the learning of new information and to minimize any effects of previous knowledge, he invented some entirely new material to be learned. This material consisted of nonsense syllables, word-like 'consonant-vowel-consonant' sequences, such as *WUX, CAZ, BIJ* and *ZOL*, which could be pronounced but had no meaning. He taught himself sequences of such words by reciting them aloud at a rapid rate, and carefully scored the number of recitations required to learn each list, or to relearn it after a delay had caused him to forget it. During his learning he carefully avoided using any associations with real words, and he always tested himself at the same time of day under carefully controlled conditions, discontinuing the tests whenever 'too great changes in the outer or inner life occurred'. Despite or perhaps because of using this rather unpromising material, he was able to demonstrate to the world that memory can be scientifically investigated, and in the short period of two years was able to show some of the fundamental characteristics of human memory.

If you want to assess any system for storing information, three basic questions must be answered: how rapidly can information be fed into the system, how much information can be stored, and how rapidly is information lost? In the case of human memory, the storage capacity is clearly enormous, so Ebbinghaus concentrated on assessing the rate of input and, as we shall see in Chapter 6, of forgetting.

A pilot in a flight simulator. 'Refresher' training is part of a military and commercial pilot's life.

Rate of learning

Consider the rate at which information can be registered in memory. If you spend twice as much time learning, do you remember twice as much information? Or is there perhaps a law of diminishing returns, with each additional learning episode putting a little less information into storage? Or perhaps the relationship is the other way round; the more information you have acquired, the easier and quicker it is to add new information, rather like a rolling snowball picking up more snow with each successive revolution. Ebbinghaus investigated this problem very simply by creating a number of lists each containing 16 nonsense syllables. On a given day he would select a fresh list (one he had not learned before) and recite it at a rate of 2.5 syllables per second for 8, 16, 24, 32, 42, 53 or 64 repetitions. Twenty-four hours later he would find out how much of the list he had remembered by seeing how many additional trials he needed to relearn the list by heart. To get some idea of what his experiment was like, try reading the following list of nonsense syllables as rapidly as you can for four successive trials: *JIH, BAZ, FUB, YOX, SUJ, XIR, DAX, LEQ, VUM, PID, KEL, WAB, TUV, ZOF, GEK, HIW.*

The results of this very tedious exercise are shown in the graph below. The relationship between the number of learning trials on Day 1 and the amount retained on Day 2 is a straight line, signifying that the process of learning shows neither diminishing returns nor the snowball effect, but obeys the simple rule that the amount learned depends on time spent learning — if you double the learning time, you double the amount of information stored. In short, as far as learning is concerned, you get what you pay for. This relationship has been explored extensively in the 100 years since it was discovered by Ebbinghaus and is known as the *total time hypothesis.* This is the basic relationship that underlies the whole of human learning.

Hermann Ebbinghaus (1850–1909) was the first person to study memory experimentally. He invented nonsense syllables in order to circumvent the effects of meaning on recall.

As Ebbinghaus discovered, the relationship between the amount learned and the time devoted to learning is fairly simple. Here, in graph form, are the results of one of his early experiments. The greater the number of repetitions initially, the less time relearning takes.

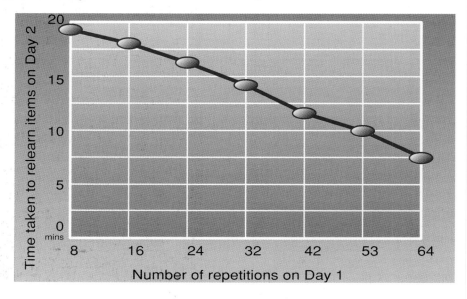

The generalization that 'you get what you pay for' is a reasonable rule of thumb, but within this broad framework there are good buys and bad ones, bargains and items which are not worth the asking price. Despite the general relationship between practice and the amount retained, there are ways in which one can get better value for time spent. The rest of this chapter will be concerned with ways of beating the total time hypothesis.

Distributed practice

If you examine the Ebbinghaus learning graph closely, bearing in mind the amount of time spent in practice on Day 1, you will notice that total time for learning is not in fact constant, since time spent on Day 1 gives a disproportionate saving on relearning the next day. For example, 64 trials on Day 1 take about 7.5 minutes; a similar time is needed to learn the list completely on Day 2, making a total of 15 minutes. However, if only 8 trials are given on Day 1 (about 1 minute), then it takes nearly 20 minutes to learn the list on Day 2. Dividing practice fairly evenly over the two days, therefore, leads to more efficient learning than cramming most of the practice into the second day. This is an instance of a very widespread phenomenon, known as the *distribution of practice effect*. What it means is that it is better to distribute your learning trials across a period of time than to mass them together in a single block of learning. As far as learning is concerned, 'little and often' is an excellent precept.

A good example of this arose a few years ago when my colleagues and I were asked to advise the British Post Office on a program that aimed to teach a very large number of postmen to type. Postal coding was being introduced, and it required the postmen doing the sorting to type out the codes on a keyboard resembling that of a typewriter. The Post Office had the option of either taking postmen off their regular jobs and giving them intensive keyboard training, or of combining the training with their regular jobs by giving them a little practice each day. There were four feasible schedules: an intensive schedule of two two-hour sessions per day, intermediate schedules involving either one two-hour or two one-hour sessions per day, or a more gradual approach involving one one-hour session of typing per day. We therefore assigned each postman at random to one of the four groups and began the training. The graph overleaf shows the rate at which the four groups acquired typing skill.

Constructive use of commuting time? Fifteen minutes' learning every morning and evening will probably yield better results than a solid day of studying.

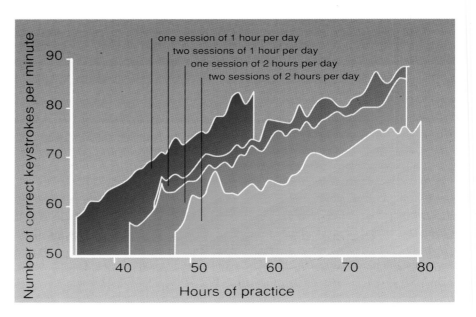

one session of 1 hour per day
two sessions of 1 hour per day
one session of 2 hours per day
two sessions of 2 hours per day

Four different training regimes produced varying rates of acquisition of typing skill. The point at which each curve starts reflects the time it took to learn the location of the individual keys. (Baddeley and Longman, 1978)

So the time it took to learn the keyboard and the subsequent rate of improvement were both strongly affected by the particular training schedule used. The postmen who worked for only one hour a day learned the keyboard on fewer hours of training and improved their performance more rapidly than those who trained for two hours a day, and they in turn learnt more rapidly than those who trained for four hours per day. Indeed the one-hour-per-day group learnt as much in 55 hours as the four-hours-per-day group learnt in 80. They also appeared to continue to improve at a faster rate, and when tested after several months without further practice they proved to have retained their skill better than the four-hours-per-day group. This result did not stem from fatigue or discontent on the part of the four-hours-per-day group. Indeed, when questioned afterwards, the one-hour-per-day postmen were the least contented with their training schedule since, when measured in terms of the number of days required to acquire typing skill, they appeared to be progressing less rapidly than their four-hours-per-day colleagues. In drawing practical conclusions of course this should be borne in mind; four hours per day may be a relatively inefficient way of learning to type when measured on an hourly basis, but it did mean that that group reached in four weeks the standard it took the one-hour-a-day group 11 weeks to achieve. Distributed practice is more efficient, but it may not always be practical or convenient.

The effect we have just described essentially says that a little every day is the optimal way of learning. What about the distribution of practice over shorter intervals? In recent years there has been a good deal of interest in what might be called *micro-distribution practice*. Suppose you are trying to learn French vocabulary and have the following list of words to master: *stable = l'écurie, horse = le cheval, grass = l'herbe, church = l'église.*

If you are presented with a single item on two occasions, do you remember it better if it is presented twice in rapid succession, or is recall better if the two presentations are spaced? Fortunately the answer is clear; spaced presentation enhances memory. On that basis one should go through the whole vocabulary list before representing and testing the first item, since that will maximize the space between two successive presentations. Unfortunately, however, life is not so simple, since it is also the case that if you succeed in remembering an item for yourself, this strengthens the memory more effectively than having it provided for you. The implications of this are exactly the opposite to the distribution of practice effect. The sooner an item is tested, the greater the probability that it will be correctly recalled, and hence the greater the probability that recall will be strengthened. The solution to this dilemma is to use a flexible strategy in which a new item is initially tested after a short delay. Then, as the item becomes better learnt, the practice interval is gradually extended, the aim being to test each item at the longest interval at which it can reliably be recalled. Hence a learning sequence for the list of French words just given might be as follows:

Teacher	Learner
stable—l'écurie	
stable?	*l'écurie*
horse—le cheval	
horse?	*le cheval*
stable	*l'écurie*
horse?	*le cheval*
grass—l'herbe	
grass?	*l'herbe*
stable?	*l'écurie*
horse?	*le cheval*
grass?	*l'herbe*
church—l'église	
church?	*l'église*
grass?	*l'herbe*
church?	*l'église*
stable?	*l'écurie*
grass?	*l'herbe*
horse?	*le cheval*

If the learner fails an item in the vocabulary list, it should be presented after a shorter delay; whenever the learner is correct, the delay should be increased. Having used this technique, invented by Tom Landauer and Robert Bjork, to teach my son French vocabulary, I can vouch that it does work. It also has the advantage of ensuring that the rate of failure during learning is low, so the learner does not become too discouraged. Indeed the invention of this ingenious new technique prompted Ulrich Neisser, normally rather skeptical about the achievements of modern memory research, to produce the following limerick:

You can get a good deal from rehearsal
If it just has the proper dispersal.
You would just be an ass to do it en masse:
Your remembering would turn out much worsal.

Motivation to learn

An important factor which has not been mentioned so far is motivation. This may seem strange in the light of most studies of animal learning, where motivation is regarded as of paramount importance. This is probably because rewarding or punishing the animal is the only way the experimenter can be sure that the animal will attend to the experimental conditions and exhibit what it has learnt. Fortunately experimental human subjects are in general rather more cooperative. Most subjects in memory experiments want to do well, to please the experimenter or to convince themselves that they have good memories, or perhaps because it is simply more interesting to attempt to do well than to display a complete lack of interest. Provided subjects give their full attention to a task, level of motivation is not an important factor.

A Swedish colleague, Lars Gören Nilsson, found his students very reluctant to accept this view, so set up the following experiment to prove his point. He had groups of students learn lists of words under various conditions. In one condition no pressure was put on any student to do well; they were simply told that they were taking part in an experiment on memory. In a second condition the students were not given motivating instructions during learning, but at the time of recall were told that a substantial cash prize would be given to the person who recalled the greatest number of words. A third group was told about the cash prize *before* they began learning. The learning performance of the three groups did not differ. A subsequent experiment included social competition as a means of increasing motivation and produced exactly the same result: no effect of motivation level on learning.

Does this mean that motivation is quite irrelevant to learning? As any schoolteacher will tell you, this is certainly not the case. The effect of motivation is indirect, however; it will determine the amount of time spent attending to the material to be learned, and this in turn will affect the amount of learning. Hence, if I were to ask you to learn a list of words comprising ten animal names and ten flower names, and I were to offer you a coin for each animal name recalled and a banknote for each flower, there is little doubt that you would remember more flowers than animals. The reason would be that you would simply spend more time on the flowers, producing a result that would be equivalent to my presenting the flowers for a longer time. In a classroom situation motivation is likely to affect learning because it affects the amount of attention children give to the material they are being taught. If they are interested, they will pay attention; if they are bored, they are likely to think about other things.

A good example of the importance of level of interest in the learner is provided by a series of experiments in which British students were asked to remember the results of professional football games. Each student was first given a test of knowledge of English league football, and then asked to remember a list of unrelated words, so as to provide a general measure of verbal memory performance. They were then asked to remember the results of a number of games, half of which were genuine and half of which were plausible but invented, a fact that was made clear to the them. Results showed that the more knowledgeable the subject, the better the recall of genuine results; on the other hand, success in recalling invented results was related to performance on remembering the lists of unrelated words rather than to football knowledge.

As a child learns to build structures of increasing complexity and meaning, one of his primary motivations is parental approval. At school, teacher approval is often a big incentive

A later experiment asked subjects about the teams they supported, and also about the relative importance for the outcome of the league championship of a range of actual games. Subjects subsequently attempted to recall genuine results. The important factor here proved to be the subjects' support for and interest in a particular team rather than the perceived importance of a game within the league. This suggests that commitment and enthusiasm were the principal determinant of memory performance, rather than knowledge of football and of the relative strengths of the various teams.

Learning and arousal

We are clearly not always equally alert. Our mood and general level of physiological arousal will tend to range from deep sleep through drowsiness to a normal waking state; occasionally we experience a state of high agitation or excitement, and, under extreme conditions, terror and panic. High arousal tends to be accompanied by changes in the electrical activity of the brain as recorded by electroencephalogram (EEG), and by an increase in heart rate, palm sweating and electrical conductivity of the skin. Arousal can also be altered by manipulating the environment or through drugs. Hence loud noises will tend to increase arousal, whereas deprivation of sleep will tend to cause it to decrease. Amphetamine or the caffeine in a cup of coffee will tend to lead to higher arousal, while a tranquillizer will tend to reduce it. Other drugs such as alcohol have more complex effects, initially increasing but then decreasing arousal.

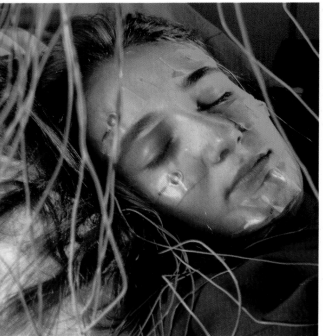

A volunteer wired up to an electro-encephalograph (and to apparatus that monitors muscle tension, heart rate and skin conductivity). For most of the night, level of arousal is too low for auditory stimuli to be registered, let alone processed and retained.

To what extent does arousal influence memory? Clearly, in an extreme case, it has a massive effect — a subject who is asleep has a very limited performance repertoire. It has in fact been suggested that we are able to learn when we are asleep, and there have been a number of attempts to market sleep teaching systems. These offer the unwary purchaser the attractive prospect of being able to learn easily and painlessly by playing a tape recording of the material to be mastered while he or she is asleep. Unfortunately objective measures of the effectiveness of sleep-teaching suggest that nothing is learned save the few scraps of information that are registered during the occasional periods during the night when we approach wakefulness, in between long periods of deeper sleep. If you wish to learn, it is advisable to be conscious at the time!

A very wide range of levels of arousal occurs in the fully conscious individual, and there is no doubt that performance is sensitive to arousal level. In general, performance improves as arousal increases up to some peak, beyond which it deteriorates, a relationship known as the Yerkes-Dodson law after the two people who first pointed it out. Neither somnolence nor blind panic are likely to be particularly efficient states of mind for the performance of any task. Different tasks are optimally performed at different levels of arousal. For example, the level at which you are likely to run fastest or hit hardest will be higher than that which is best for threading a needle or solving a complex intellectual puzzle.

What is the optimal arousal level for memory? Like much else in human memory, this proves to be a complex question. It depends crucially on when the learned material is subsequently recalled. If recall is immediate, then performance is best when level of arousal is relatively low; higher levels of arousal lead to poor initial performance, but in the long run they produce better learning.

This was shown most clearly in a series of experiments conducted by Kleinsmith and Kaplan in 1963 in which subjects were presented with the task of learning to associate numbers with words. The words were selected as being either relatively neutral *(swim, dance)* or as having emotional overtones *(rape, vomit)*. Three groups of subjects were tested, the first recalling after a delay of two minutes, the second after a 20-minute delay, and the third after a delay of one week. The low-arousal words were initially well recalled but showed marked forgetting. Recall of the high-arousal words actually improved with time. Kleinsmith and Kaplan argue that high levels of arousal help the memory trace to consolidate, but that during the early stages of consolidation they make retrieval difficult. The high-arousal items therefore have a short-term penalty by being difficult to retrieve, but in the long term they benefit from good consolidation. While I must confess I do not find this interpretation particularly compelling, there is no doubt that something approaching this phenomenon does exist, although it rarely presents itself as clearly as in the study quoted above.

Arousal level fluctuates systematically throughout the day, being relatively low shortly after waking up and gradually increasing throughout the day up to the evening, when it begins to drop again. It has been known since the time of Ebbinghaus that learning ability varies with time of day. However it has been shown by Folkard and his collaborators at the University of Sussex that the optimal time for learning depends crucially on whether you test recall immediately or after a delay. Folkard presented schoolchildren with a story either in the morning or in the afternoon. They were then tested either immediately or several days later. Folkard found that on immediate testing the children who had learned in the morning did better, but when tested after a delay there was a consistent advantage in having learned in the afternoon. He points out that the traditional school timetable tends to schedule most of the more demanding subjects in the morning, a state of affairs which might be justified if pupils are tested straight away, but which is not likely to lead to the best long-term learning.

Memory and anesthesia

One situation in which arousal level is explicitly manipulated occurs when a surgical patient is anesthetized. While this is obviously not an optimal state for learning and remembering, there is, worryingly, evidence of at least some capacity to experience, learn, and possibly remember in apparently anesthetized patients. On a small number of occasions patients have reported being aware of some aspect of an operation, and this has led to a number of attempts to investigate memory for material presented under anesthetic.

One early study, which I trust predates the current requirement of all research to be passed by ethical committees, involved a conversation within earshot of the patient in which the experimenter falsely suggested that an anesthetic crisis was occurring! The patients were reported as showing disturbances in subsequent behavior that implied that this information had been registered in some way. Later studies have tended to use positive conversation and reassurance, with results that are generally positive, although such effects are not always found.

Another approach, not dissimilar to post-hypnotic suggestion, involved telling the anesthetized individual that if he has understood the message, on recovery he should indicate this fact by making a sign or response. One study

The fact that a few patients remember hearing remarks made by surgeons and nurses during operations begs the question 'How unconscious are patients during operations?'

suggested that patients should pull their left ear. A greater incidence of ear-pulling was indeed observed. There has been some limited success in replicating this, although cultural differences appear to determine the sort of response that subjects will accept as natural — British subjects appear to prefer chin-stroking to ear-pulling, for example!

The growth in interest in implicit memory described earlier has had an influence on this area. The argument is that it may well be the case that information received during anesthesia will influence patients' subsequent be-havior, even though they are not able to remember experiencing the information during the operation, as is typically the case. One study, for example, presented patients with words from a particular semantic category, and later asked them to produce as many words from that category as possible. Suppose the category is *animals*; one patient might hear the words *dog, rabbit* and *hedgehog*, while a second patient might hear *cat, hare* and *fox*. There proved to be a greater tendency for patients to generate the words that had been presented during the operation, indicating that some form of learning had occurred. Typically patients cannot recall hearing any words under anesthetic, suggesting that the learning is implicit rather than explicit.

What limits learning under anesthesia? One possibility is that the subject simply does not experience the stimulus; this is of course one of the purposes of an anesthetic. Another possibility, however, is that the experience is very rapidly forgotten, possibly because of the lower level of arousal. A recent and as yet unpublished study carried out jointly with anesthesiologist colleagues throws some light on this. They were interested in developing measures of level of consciousness, with a view to ensuring that patients are indeed unconscious during surgical operations. As part of the validation of an electrophysiological measure, we carried out learning and memory experiments, with the anesthetists themselves as subjects. We used two principle measures, one to test hearing and understanding of spoken words, and the other to test retention. The subject had to decide whether each of a series of spoken words belonged to a particular category; it it did, he or she was required to raise the right hand (the particular anesthetic used did not include a muscle relaxant). Then the subject was presented with a string of words, some of which were new, while others were repetitions. Whenever an old word appeared, the subject was instructed to signal recognition by raising an arm. The gap between successive repetitions ranged from immediate to 16 interpolated words. The level of anesthetic was varied from zero up to a level at which subjects ceased to respond to the categorized word list, at which point an electric shock was delivered (ethical approval was granted for anesthetists to inflict this on each other, but not on the general public). This simulated the possible effect of a painful incision. The overall number of words categorized correctly dropped as anesthetic concentration rose, with no response being made at the highest concentration. Under normal conditions, subjects were well able to detect repetitions, even after 16 interpolated items, but as the anesthetic dose increased, forgetting became more rapid. The electric shock slightly revived performance, possibly because it increased level of arousal.

While it would obviously be unwise to generalize our results to other anesthetics, it seems that some ability to commit material to memory is retained under conditions of mild sedation, but as the dose increases forgetting becomes more rapid until a point is reached at which there is no evidence of material being perceived at all. Whether implicit learning can be observed under these conditions remains to be seen.

Repetition and learning

Some theories of learning have suggested that all that is required is repetition of the material to be learnt. Such a view would probably have appealed to Victorian educators with their emphasis on learning by heart. However a number of experiments have recently suggested that rote repetition, with no attempt by the learner to organize the material, may not lead to learning. A colleague, Debra Bekerian, and I were able to explore this question in connection with a saturation advertising campaign.

A number of years ago a new international agreement among European radio stations made it necessary for the BBC to reassign some of the British wavelengths. In order to acquaint the public with this fact, and to familiarize them with the changes, the BBC embarked on a saturation advertising campaign. Over a period of two months radio programs were regularly interrupted by detailed information about the new wavelengths, supplemented by slogans and complex jingles.

Debra Bekerian and I decided to test the effectiveness of the campaign by questioning about 50 members of our panel of subjects — these are people who volunteer to come along to the Applied Psychology Unit in Cambridge to take part in experiments on functions such as memory, perception and hearing. In this instance most of our volunteers were Cambridge housewives. We asked them how much time they spent listening to each radio channel and, on the basis of this and information provided by the BBC about the frequency of announcements, we estimated that most of them had heard the announcements about the new wave-lengths well over a thousand times. We asked them to recall the new wavelengths both by writing down the numerical frequencies and by marking a visual display resembling a radio dial.

How much had our subjects learnt? The BBC had been successful in conveying the fact that the change was about to occur, since virtually every subject was aware of it. There was also considerable knowledge about the exact date of the change, with 84 per cent of our subjects reporting it correctly. However, memory for details of the new wavelengths was appalling. Only 25 per cent, on average, even attempted to give the numerical frequencies, and while more people were prepared to attempt to represent them by marking the dial display, most of these attempts were little better than one would have expected on the basis of pure guessing.

Why was performance so poor? Surely a thousand trials ought to have been enough to teach anyone the necessary numerical information? First of all, mere repetition of information does not ensure that it is well remembered; the way in which information is processed by the learner is crucial. Second, when it was first presented the advertising was describing an event that was two months away, far enough ahead to be temporarily ignored. Towards the end of the two months the message had become so repetitious and tedious that it was automatically ignored — there is very good evidence to suggest that auditory messages which we try to ignore leave very little impression on our memory. Finally, the advertising assumed that listeners were tuning their radios on the basis of the numerical frequency of the wavelength of the station required. Although most of our subjects were unable to give details of the new frequencies, their knowledge of the old frequencies was little better. Presumably they relied on visual cues on the dial to tune in to their favorite programs.

Fortunately, in addition to the radio advertising campaign, the BBC also circulated every household by mail with information about the new wavelengths together with adhesive stickers. When we conducted a follow-up survey shortly after the changeover, we found that it was these stickers that had saved the day for most people. Seventy per cent of our follow-up group had indeed had difficulty learning the new wavelengths, but for the most part they coped successfully by waiting until the changeover had taken place, then hunted for the new wavelengths and marked them with the stickers which the BBC had so sensibly provided.

What conclusions can we draw from this? One is that saturation advertising is not particularly suitable for conveying complex information. If one simply wants people to remember 'Botto washes whitest', telling them so a thousand times will cause the message to be retained, though not necessarily believed. In the case of complex information which does not map onto one's existing way of thinking, however, the total effect appears to be minimal learning and maximum frustration.

There is surprisingly little published work on applying psychology to advertising. About the only work that I have come across attempts to apply the principles of conditioning initially discovered by Pavlov, who found that frequent association between a bell and feeding led to dogs salivating when they heard the bell. The advertising study, however, was not concerned with encouraging salivation, but with evaluative conditioning, the process whereby presenting a neutral item together with something pleasant causes it to acquire a pleasantness by association. Subjects were presented with a slide picture of a 'new' brand of toothpaste in a green and yellow tube, labelled 'Brand L Toothpaste'. The toothpaste was presented with three other fictitious commodities, 'Brand R Cola', 'Brand M Laundry Detergent', and 'Brand J Soap', which were paired with neutral pictures, while the toothpaste was always followed by one of four particularly pleasant slides, sunset over an island, for example, or sky and clouds seen through the mast of a boat. Different groups experienced the items from one to twenty times, and then were asked about which product they would probably buy. As the graph overleaf shows, the toothpaste was rated as more likely to be bought than the other three items, with likelihood of purchase increasing as the number of exposures increased.

A session in a language laboratory. Repeating foreign words and phrases helps with pronunciation, while processing in terms of imagery and associations helps in remembering the meaning of foreign words.

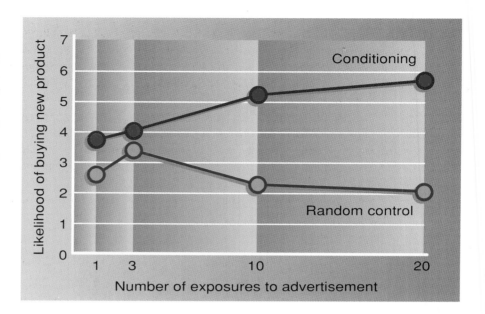

Conditioning and advertising. When an unfamiliar brand of toothpaste was repeatedly associated with pleasant scenes, subjects rated themselves as more likely to buy it. When the pleasant scenes were presented but not associated with the toothpaste, there was no urge to buy. (Stuart et al., 1987)

The investigators went on to test two more detailed predictions from the conditioning laboratory. The first of these was that presenting the toothpaste for many trials under neutral conditions would reduce the effect of pairing it with the pleasant slides later, something known to conditioning theorists as *latent inhibition*. This is indeed what happened. A third study presented the pleasant slides immediately before the toothpaste, setting the scene for *backward conditioning*, which is known to be much weaker than *forward conditioning*; as predicted, the level of acquired pleasantness was much less, suggesting that conditioning might indeed provide a suitable model for this aspect of advertising. However, conditioning does not seem to be a good way of presenting complex information such as radio wavelengths. Acquisition of such detailed information is likely to demand explicit learning, which demands attention, rather than implicit learning, which is much more automatic.

Meaning and memory

As the results of the BBC study suggest, a crucial factor in deciding whether something will be learnt and remembered is its meaningfulness to the learner. Ebbinghaus explicitly tried to avoid the complicating effects of meaning by adopting a strategy of rattling through nonsense material at a rapid rate, and sternly refusing to think about meaningful associations. He was probably justified in believing that he had at least reduced the role of meaning in his memory experiments. However, those who followed him were less zealous in dissuading their subjects from using whatever meaning they could find in material presented to them. A little thought about the list of nonsense syllables given on page 72 will, I think, convince you that even though they were selected as being peculiarly devoid of meaningful content, nevertheless they do have associations.

By the 1930s all the available nonsense syllables had been classified on the basis of how likely they were to give rise to meaningful associations, and it was shown that the greater the probability of an association, the greater the probability of learning a given syllable.

It can be argued that very little of our learning in real life involves meaningless material and that the psychology of memory for nonsense is therefore of limited value. In recent years there has been much more interest in using real words rather than nonsense syllables for experiments on memory. Needless to say, not all words are equally easy to remember. Words that refer to concrete objects of which the memorizer can form a visual image are on the whole more easily remembered than abstract words for which imagery is difficult. Try to memorize the following two lists:

List A *virtue history silence life hope value mathematics dissent idea*

List B *church beggar carpet arm hat teapot dragon cannon apple*

Now count how many you got right from each list. Most people find the words in List B more memorable than the abstract words in List A. Although the lists are made up of words which are themselves highly meaningful, the lists as a whole are meaningless, merely comprising a random selection of words. As such they are much less meaningful than a list made up of the following sequence of words: *large grey elephants terrified by roaring flames trampled tiny defenseless rabbits*. Such a list would obviously be even easier to remember than the random sequence of highly imageable words in List B.

Learning and predictability

Wherein lies the difference between sentences and unrelated word strings? One obvious difference stems from the fact that strong relationships exist between the words in a sentence but not between the words in a list. The structure of English is highly constrained and during the 1950s there was great interest in attempting to measure and understand this constraint. The theoretical underpinning of this analysis of language was *information theory*, a statistical approach to the understanding of language. Its influence on psychology was primarily through its emphasis on the importance of *redundancy,* or predictability. Language is redundant in the sense that successive words are not equally probable and not independent; adjectives tend to precede nouns and pronouns are generally followed by verbs. The topic being written or spoken about further constrains the selection of words. All of these constraints are reflected in the tendency for each word in a sentence to be predictable on the basis of surrounding words. Hence, if I were to ask you to play a guessing game in which I presented parts of sentences and asked you to guess the next word, you would do reasonably well.

It is possible to produce sequences of words that more or less approximate English prose by playing a guessing game of this sort. Suppose, for example, I give you a single word *the* and ask you to create a sentence incorporating it. You might produce 'The cats sat on the mat'. Suppose I then take *cats* and give it to a second person; he or she might produce 'Cats catch mice'. *Catch* would then be passed on to another person, who might produce the sentence 'If you are not careful you will catch a cold.' *A* could then be presented to someone else, who might come up with 'A stitch in time saves nine.' If we put all the words together we then get a sequence 'The cats catch a' and so on.

If I had given you two words rather than one, then the possibilities for sentence creation and meaning would have been more constrained. If I had given four or five words, the sequence it was possible to generate would have been extremely constrained. Using this procedure one can generate passages that range from random selections from a dictionary, through words selected according to their frequency in English, to passages in which relationships extend over quite long sequences of words, giving a much higher degree of constraint. Some examples of such passages generated by university students are given below.

First order
Pomegranates mouthful handle man superhero perhaps hippopotamus amazing sex stored fircones plausible happy twinkle underestimated sun boggling joint beard mauve axolotl lewd freak-out exhausted

Second order
would that although children like groovy scene one for goldilocks bears like werewolf virgins ten tickles hairy nostrils flapping voluptuously trailing walruses tusks emancipated suffragettes suffer little bogs oozing cataclysmic climax came cunningly consummated

Third order
was growing beyond hope and glory hallelujah to unnerve destroy people is groovy mind-blowing freak-out unfortunately ending hysterically bubbling bath giggling hysterically underneath sparsely populated wasteland escalating into doom irretrievably obnoxious and placated

Fifth order
by their example incalculable risks degradation for Xerxes while grovelling horribly amid decaying garbage was heaped disgustingly sideways beside bulging perverted earthworms lay mouldering silently in acid putrefied thoughts Henriette fainted through excitement

If subjects are given such passages to remember, they find that the closer the approximation to normal English, the more words are recalled correctly. Redundancy affects a range of other tasks in a similar way. Hence if you attempt to read out the various passages you will find that it takes less time to read the higher order approximations to English than the lower, and if you were to try to type them you would find a similar advantage.

Even within textual material quite marked differences occur in the degree of redundancy or predictability. One way of measuring this is the *Cloze technique* whereby a group of people are presented with a passage from which every fifth word has been deleted. Their task is to guess the missing words. Try it yourself on the two passages shown below.

'The sly young fox — to eat the little — hen for his dinner. — made all sorts of — to catch her. He — many times to — her. But she was — little hen. Not — of the sly fox's — worked. He grew quite — trying to catch the — red hen. One day — sly young fox said — his mother, 'Today I — catch the little red —. I have made the — plan of all.' He — up a bag and — it over his back. '— shall put the little — hen in this bag,' — said to his mother.' (Extract from *The Sly Fox* by Vera Southgate)

In the first place, — had by that time, — the benefit of his — education: continual hard work, — soon and concluded late, — extinguished any curiosity he — possessed in pursuit of —, and any love for — or learning. His childhood's — of superiority, instilled into — by the favours of — Mr. Earnshaw, was faded — . He struggled long to — up an equality with — in her studies, and — with a poignant though silent —: but he yielded completely; — there was no prevailing — him to take a — in the way of — upward, when he found — must, necessarily, sink beneath — former level.' (Extract from *Wuthering Heights* by Emily Bronte)

The missing words from the first passage were *wanted, red, he, plans, tried, catch, a, one, plans, thin, little, the, to, will, hen, best, picked, slung, I, red, he*. From the second passage the words omitted were *he, lost, early, begun, had, once, knowledge, books, sense, him, old, away, keep, Catherine, yielded, regret, and, on, step, moving, he, his*. Most people find the children's text rather more predictable and fill in considerably more words. Redundancy as measured by the Cloze technique is a reasonably good predictor of the rated readability of material and of its memorability. The more redundant and predictable a piece of prose, the easier it is to recall.

We have come some distance from the original Ebbinghaus experiments, limited as they were to learning, under rigidly controlled conditions, material stripped of all meaning. Yet, using such unpromising material, Ebbinghaus made the enormously important discovery that human memory can be studied systematically and objectively. By throwing out meaning, however, he left out what is probably the most significant feature of all human memory. The importance of meaning was the main interest of the second great pioneer of the study of human memory, Sir Frederick Bartlett, whose work is discussed in the next chapter.

Implicit learning

Thus far we have mainly concentrated on the use of explicit learning to feed memory, a process that depends on the active use of attention. However, as we saw in Chapter 1, there are aspects of learning that appear to operate according to somewhat different principles. Since our main concern in this book is explicit rather than implicit learning, we shall not be giving particularly close attention to this type (or these types) of learning. However, since this is a particularly active area of current research, some of the work that is currently emerging deserves brief attention. Once again I shall use the neuropsychological evidence to structure my brief account, considering in turn a number of types of implicit, or non-declarative, learning that appear to be preserved in amnesic patients. The categorization follows that proposed by Squire, who identifies four types of non-declarative learning, namely the acquisition of skills, priming effects, classical conditioning and non-associative learning.

Cooking by computer. If you have used recipe books all your life, learning how to use a computer keyboard to call up recipes is quite a challenge. In this case learning is largely by doing (implicit learning) rather than deliberately recalling previous experience.

Skills

It has frequently been observed that amnesic patients are capable of acquiring new skills. Reports have included a pianist learning a new tune, motor skills such as pursuit tracking, perceptual skills such as reading script in mirror writing, and cognitive skills such as solving puzzles. In one case two boys who had become amnesic after encephalitis were given a pursuit tracking task which required them to keep a pointer in contact with a rotating target. The better they became at tracking, the greater amount of time they spent in contact with the target. They learned to do this just as well as two normal boys would have done and retained their skill just as well too, even after an interval of one week, although they denied having encountered the equipment before.

Priming

When an object has just been perceived or processed, there is a tendency for that object to be perceived more easily the next time, a temporary facilitation that is something like a warm-up effect. Such priming operates across a wide range of sensory and motor systems, occurring at a range of different processing levels. For example, presenting a picture of an aeroplane will make it easier for a subject to identify a highly fragmented version of the picture as an aeroplane when it is presented shortly afterwards. In general, priming tends to be very specific, as though some aspect of the perceptual system has been facilitated by being used recently.

As mentioned earlier, priming is usually preserved in amnesic patients. In one experiment amnesic subjects were presented with words (e.g. *apple, robin*) and then tested for retention. Explicit or declarative memory was tested by means of a recognition test in which the words that had been presented were mixed in with new words; subjects were required to classify them as 'new' or 'old' (e.g. *robin* — old, *label* — new). Implicit memory was tested by presenting words with missing letters, and requiring subjects to identify the word (e.g. *a-p-e*). What happened? Performance on the recognition test was very poor, but performance on the fragmented word tests was much better, showing that some implicit learning had taken place. In their ability to fill in the letters missing from the fragmented words they had already seen, amnesic subjects performed nearly as well as control subjects.

Priming is not limited to already familiar material. In a study by Daniel Schacter and his colleagues, amnesic and control subjects were shown a series of drawings and required to decide whether the objects depicted were possible or impossible to construct (some of the objects contained structural violations which would have prevented them existing in three-dimensional space). Clear priming effects occurred for both groups, but only for the possible objects, suggesting that the process of perception involves attempting to create structure. When the attempt is successful its effect persists, allowing that structure to be recreated more rapidly the next time. This process appears to be intact in amnesic patients. Schacter suggests that a whole range of perceptual processes occur that involve the temporary storage of information as part of the processes of object and word perception. These processes appear to depend on parts of the brain that are often preserved in amnesic patients, and are not dependent on the hippocampus and related areas that are crucial for explicit learning.

Unless you had specifically noticed this house, you would probably have a general impression that it was pink and green, with a tower and a verandah . . . A great deal of information gets logged in memory without conscious effort or intention.

While we have emphasized evidence from amnesic patients, much of the recent work in this area has been based on normal subjects. Here the emphasis has been on demonstrating that factors that lead to good explicit learning do not influence implicit learning, and vice versa. For example, requiring a subject to make a judgement about the meaning of a word leads to better explicit recall or recognition of that word than making a judgement about its visual appearance or rhyming characteristics; this is the *levels of processing effect* which will be discussed further in Chapter 9. However, such deeper processing does not enhance implicit or non-declarative memory, as measured by the capacity for identifying a word from a fragment.

Another feature of implicit learning is the way in which it appears to bypass conscious awareness. This was demonstrated very neatly by Larry Jacoby in a study in which subjects were first required to listen to a series of sentences, then went on to take part in what purported to be a different experiment concerned with judging the loudness of noise. The subjects listened to a mixture of new and old sentences against what was, in fact, a constant background noise. When subjects were listening to sentences they had heard before, they consistently judged the background noise to be quieter than when hearing a new sentence. The priming effect allowed them to hear the old sentences better, an effect they attributed to a lower noise level rather than to their own implicit knowledge.

In another ingenious demonstration of implicit memory Jacoby had his subjects read a series of names. In a second and apparently unrelated experiment subjects were required to make judgements about a new set of names, deciding in each case whether the name was or was not famous. The subjects were not aware that some of the non-famous names came from the earlier list. There was a clear tendency for these names to be wrongly judged to be famous. In another study Jacoby showed that even when subjects were explicitly told that any name they had encountered in the previous test was not famous, they were still inclined to judge repeated names as famous, again indicating the unconscious nature of implicit learning.

Classical conditioning

As the great Russian physiologist Pavlov demonstrated in his experiments on salivation in dogs, if a bell is always associated with the presentation of food, eventually the bell alone will cause salivation.

Some indication of conditioning in amnesic patients comes from the description by the Swiss neuropsychiatrist Claparède of a rather curious experiment he carried out in the early years of this century with an amnesic patient in his charge. On one occasion, while doing his morning rounds, he secreted a pin in his hand when he shook hands with this patient. The next day the patient refused to shake hands, although having no recollection of the actual incident.

Classical conditioning has since been confirmed in amnesic patients using eyeblink conditioning in which a sound is followed by a light puff of air causing the subject to blink. Densely amnesic patients proved quite capable of conditioning — they blinked on hearing the sound — but had no recollection of the conditioning experience.

Non-associative learning

There are other types of learning that may well be implicit and preserved in amnesia. For example, there is a general tendency for people to favor the familiar over the unfamiliar. Hence, if a listener hears a melody from an unfamiliar culture, it will at first be judged as not very pleasant, but will improve on subsequent hearing. In one study the investigators played a series of Korean melodies to amnesic patients and control subjects. On a later occasion they were played a mixture of old and new melodies, and required to judge each one for pleasantness. Both the amnesic and the control subjects showed a clear tendency to prefer the melodies they had heard before, although the amnesic subjects had no recollection of this prior experience.

Implicit or non-declarative memory is an area that has seen an enormous amount of research over the last five years. As we have seen, the manifestations of implicit learning range from classical conditioning to problem solving and from word completion to esthetic judgements. While it is possible that all of these phenomena may ultimately prove to depend upon a single system, in my opinion this is unlikely. It seems much more probable that what they have in common is their non-dependence on declarative or explicit memory. In implicit learning, performance is measured by actually doing a task. Learning is demonstrated by doing the task more rapidly or more effectively. Adequate performance does not depend upon being aware of previous learning. In con-trast, declarative memory is concerned with recalling or recognizing a prior experience or fact. It is this declarative or explicit aspect of memory that forms the bulk of what will be discussed in the rest of the book, but it is important to bear in mind that memory tests are rarely, if ever, pure measures of the various underlying systems. Consequently many experimental results are likely to reflect at least some component of implicit non-declarative memory. However, as we have seen, such learning tends not to be influenced by attentional and processing factors, and these are the factors that we will be concentrating upon in the chapters that follow.

5 Organizing and remembering

The psychological study of human memory has, over the last 100 years, been dominated by two distinct traditions. One of these stems from the work of Ebbinghaus, who emphasized careful measurement of a simplified memory task under rigorously controlled conditions. The great advantage of such an approach is that it reduces the problem of understanding the enormously complex and subtle human memory system to a series of sub-problems of manageable size. This was essential for the start of the empirical study of memory, and it continues to be an important feature of the scientific study of memory; without the willingness to concentrate on tractable questions about human memory, we are unlikely to make progress. The danger that always underlies such an approach, however, is that we may be excluding from our experiments just those aspects of human memory which are the most important and most characteristic. If we understood everything about remembering lists of nonsense syllables, we still would know very little about human memory as it functions outside the laboratory. This was the view argued by the founder of the second great tradition, Sir Frederick Bartlett.

In his book *Remembering,* published in 1932, Bartlett attacked the Ebbinghaus approach to memory, which had dominated psychology for 50 years. He argued that the study of nonsense syllable learning merely told one about repetition habits; by excluding meaning Ebbinghaus had excluded the most central and characteristic feature of human memory. Bartlett reacted against the Ebbinghaus tradition by studying rich and meaningful material, learned and re-called under relatively naturalistic conditions. His subjects were asked to remember pictures and stories, of which the following is a well-known example. If you had been one of Bartlett's subjects, you would have been asked to read the story quietly to yourself, and then recall it later.

A cellar master tests a maturing wine. Wine connoisseurs organize and remember sensations of taste and bouquet by grape variety, producing region, producer, and taste.

The War of the Ghosts

One night two young men from Egulac went down to the river to hunt seals, and while they were there it became foggy and calm. Then they heard war-cries, and they thought: 'Maybe this is a war-party.' They escaped to the shore, and hid behind a log. Now canoes came up, and they heard the noise of paddles, and saw one canoe coming up to them. There were five men in the canoe, and they said: 'What do you think? We wish to take you along. We are going up the river to make war on the people.'

One of the young men said: 'I have no arrows.'

'Arrows are in the canoe', they said.

'I will not go along. I might be killed. My relatives do not know where I have

gone. But you' he said, turning to the other, *'may go with them.'*

So one of the young men went, but the other returned home. And the warriors went on up the river to a town on the other side of Kalama.

The people came down to the water, and they began to fight, and many were killed. But presently the young man heard one of the warriors say: 'Quick, let us go home: that Indian has been hit.'

Now he thought: 'Oh, they are ghosts.'

He did not feel sick, but they said he had been shot.

So the canoes went back to Egulac, and the young man went ashore to his house, and made a fire. And he told everybody and said: 'Behold I accompanied the ghosts, and we went to fight. Many of our fellows were killed, and many of those who attacked us were killed..They said I was hit, and I did not feel sick.'

He told it all, and then he became quiet. When the sun rose he fell down. Something black came out of his mouth. His face became contorted. The people jumped up and cried. He was dead.

Sir Frederick Bartlett, (1886–1969) stressed the importance of meaning in memory. His willingness to take the study of memory out of the laboratory provided an alternative to the more rigid Ebbinghaus tradition.

Now close the book and attempt to recall the story as accurately as possible.

While different subjects recalled the passage in their own characteristic way, Bartlett detected a number of consistent tendencies. The remembered story was always shorter, more coherent, and tended to fit in more closely with the subject's own viewpoint. This shows up particularly clearly with material like *The War of the Ghosts,* in which a number of features of the Indian story were incompatible with European expectations. Hence the supernatural aspect of the story was often omitted. Alternatively, puzzling features might be rationalized so as to fit into the rememberer's expectations. Hence 'something black came out of his mouth' becomes 'foamed at the mouth'. The rememberer often selects certain features of the passage and uses these to anchor the whole story. In *The War of the Ghosts* the death scene often serves this role. Detail is often changed so as to become more familiar, for example 'canoes' often become 'boats'.

Bartlett observed that in the process of remembering a passage the first thing the subject tends to recall is his attitude towards it: 'The recall is then a construction made largely on the basis of this attitude, and its general effect is that of a justification of the attitude.' In short, what you remember is driven to some extent by your emotional commitment and response to the event. In a laboratory experiment this may not be too important, but it may be a crucial feature of much remembering outside the laboratory. Try, for example, asking two participants in a quarrel for an objective account of the dispute, or even ask the supporters of two opposing football teams for a summary of a particular game. Under such conditions two rather different versions are likely to emerge.

The classic study on this effect was carried out by two American social psychologists following a very violent college football game between Dartmouth and Princeton. Princeton had had a particularly successful season and one of their players, Kazmaier, had appeared on the cover of *Time* magazine. Within minutes of the start, the game was already getting very rough, with the Dartmouth players concentrating on Kazmaier, who left the field with a broken nose at the beginning of the second quarter. During the third quarter a Dartmouth player was carried off with a broken leg, and there were fights, lost tempers and injuries on both sides. The accounts given by the Princeton and Dartmouth newspapers are reproduced below. It is not hard to guess which is which!

'This observer has never seen quite such a disgusting exhibit of so-called "sport". Both teams were guilty but the blame must be laid primarily on Dartmouth's doorstep. Princeton, obviously the better team, had no reason to rough up Dartmouth. Looking at the situation rationally, we don't see why the Indians should make a deliberate attempt to cripple Dick Kazmaier or any other Princeton player. The Dartmouth psychology, however, is not rational itself.'

'However, the Dartmouth-Princeton game set the stage for the other type of dirty football. A type which may be termed as an unjustifiable accusation. Dick Kazmaier was injured early in the game . . . after this incident (the coach) instilled the old see-what-they-did-go-get-them attitude into his players. His talk got results. Gene Howard and Jim Millar (from Dartmouth) were both injured. Both had dropped back to pass, had passed, and were standing unprotected in the back field. Result: one bad leg and one leg broken. The game was rough and did get a bit out of hand in the third quarter. Yet most of the roughing penalties were called against Princeton.'

Newspaper reports are of course unlikely to give the most unbiased view, and do not necessarily reflect even the writer's actual opinions. The investigators therefore decided to show a film of the game to Dartmouth and Princeton students, instructing them to be as objective as possible and to note any infringements of rules, and to classify such infringements as 'mild' or 'flagrant'. The two groups of students were roughly in agreement as to how many infringements were made by Princeton, with Princeton students judging 4.2 infringements and Dartmouth students 4.4. In the case of Dartmouth infringements, however, there was a huge difference; the Dartmouth students reporting a mean of 4.3 infringements while the Princeton students reported 9.8. Both sets of students rated the violations made by the opposing team as more flagrant than those made by their own.

If an observer's perception and memory of a football game can be as distorted as this, what about eyewitness testimony in the case of a frightening crime, where a judgement of guilty or innocent may hang on its reliability? To what extent will the witness recall what really happened, and to what extent will his recall be determined by his attitude to the accused and to the crime? We shall be returning to this important question in Chapter 10. The essence of Bartlett's approach is its emphasis on our struggle to impose meaning on what we observe and what we recall of our experience. While this can lead to error, the fact that the world is, on the whole, a lawful and structured environment makes such a strategy a useful one, as we shall see.

The role of organization

It is not uncommon for certain chess masters not only to play a large number of amateur players simultaneously, but to do so while blindfolded. This would seem to imply an amazing feat of memory, since the master must simultaneously keep accurate track of several complex and ever-changing patterns of pieces. A few years ago a Dutch psychologist with an interest in chess, Adriaan de Groot, decided to study the memory of chess masters, comparing their performance with that of average club players. In one experiment he set out a chess board in a position selected from a game, allowed his chess players a series of five-second glimpses of the board, and after each glimpse required them to attempt to reproduce the position on another board. The masters correctly placed 90 per cent of the pieces after a single five-second glimpse, whereas the weak players positioned only 40 per cent of the pieces correctly after one glimpse, and needed eight glimpses before they could equal the initial performance of the masters. De Groot argued from this, and from a number of other experiments, that the superior playing skills of chess masters stem from their ability to perceive the chess board as an organized whole rather than as a collection of individual pieces.

Similar effects have been shown when expert bridge players attempt to recall bridge hands, or when electronics experts are shown and asked to remember well-designed circuits. In each case the expert is able to organize the material into a meaningful and

Garry Kasparov, world champion chess player, considers his next move. The computer program has not yet been designed that can beat the world's top players. Although a computer has a faultless memory, it cannot match the strategic skills of the world's best players.

lawful pattern. In order to do so the chess player, bridge player or electronics expert brings to bear a rich background of experience.

There have of course been many laboratory demonstrations of the importance of organization for memory. In some of these memory for relatively unstructured material has been compared with the recall of material with built-in structure. Try to remember the items in the two panels below. In each case read the material through at a steady rate twice then look away and write down as many words as you can remember in any order you like.

A place for everything and everything in its place allows a rapid purchase, for the regular customer at least.

		minerals		
	metals		stones	
rare	common	alloys	precious	masonry
platinum	aluminum	bronze	sapphire	limestone
silver	copper	steel	emerald	granite
gold	lead	brass	diamond	marble
	iron		ruby	

pine   elm   pansy   garden   wild   banyan   plants delphinium   conifers   dandelion   redwood   palm   ash violet   daisy   tropical   chestnut   flowers   spruce   lupin buttercup   trees   deciduous   mango   willow   rose

Most people find that the items organized as a hierarchy (top panel) are much easier to remember than the others, although it is in fact quite possible to organize the second collection of items in the same way as the first.

Another approach is to take material which is not designed to fit a particular organization, but to instruct the subject to organize it in some particular way. For example, the subject might be instructed to take the words in a list and attempt to weave them into a story. Consider, for example, List B on page 85, which might be elaborated as follows: By the *church* was a *beggar* on a *carpet*. Clutched in a withered *arm* he held a dusty black hat. He held his good hand out for money which he put into an old *teapot* which was decorated with a coat of arms comprising a *dragon* flanked by two *cannon*. In the *teapot,* together with a few pennies he collected was his lunch, an *apple*.' There is good evidence that linking words in a story makes them more memorable, but creating your own story, doing your own organizing, leads to even better recall. Try it for yourself with the following words: *tree, arrow, cake, castle, chariot, princess, bedstead, shoe, musket, star*. When you are satisfied that you have created a story linking these words in the appropriate order, read on.

One of the most common techniques for organizing material is that of *visual imagery*. Suppose you were trying to associate two unrelated words like *rabbit* and *steeple*, so that whenever one of the words is given you can come up with the other. A good strategy would be to imagine a rabbit and a steeple interacting in some way; you might, for example, imagine a rabbit clinging to the top of a steeple. It does not matter how unlikely or strange the image is provided the two components interact to form a single unitary image; imagining the rabbit and the steeple side by side, for example, will not be very helpful. Having created an interactive image, you will find that if you are prompted with one word of the pair, the other will pop up too.

Visual mnemonics

You will no doubt have come across invitations to improve your memory either in the small advertisement section of magazines or perhaps on station bookstands. Such memory training courses involve a number of techniques, but visual imagery almost invariably plays an important role. One popular mnemonic system is a technique for allowing you to remember sequences of ten unrelated items in the appropriate order. It requires you first to remember ten pegwords. Since each pegword rhymes with a number from one to ten, it is not a particularly onerous task. Try it for yourself.

One = *bun*	**Two** = *shoe*	**Three** = *tree*	**Four** = *door*	**Five** = *hive*
Six = *sticks*	**Seven** = *heaven*	**Eight** = *gate*	**Nine** = *wine*	**Ten** = *hen*

4	9	2
3	5	7
8	1	6

A magic square. However you add the numbers — across, down or diagonally — they come to 15. There are at least half a dozen ways of remembering the correct positions of the numbers. One, depending on verbal, visual and auditory memory, would be: 'For nine to free five, seven ate one six .' How many others can you think of?

Having mastered this you are ready to memorize ten unrelated items. Suppose these are *battleship, pig, chair, sheep, castle, rug, grass, beach, milkmaid, binoculars.*

Take the first pegword, *bun* (rhyming with one), and form an image of a bun interacting in some way with *battleship*; you might, for example, imagine a battleship sailing into an enormous floating bun. Now take the second pegword, *shoe*, and imagine it interacting with *pig*, perhaps a large shoe with a pig sitting in it. Pegword three is *tree*, and the third item is *chair*, so you might imagine a chair wedged in the branches of a tree. Pegword four is *door* and that has to be associated with *sheep*, so you might imagine a sheep on its hind legs tapping at the door with its hooves. Number five is *hive*, and this has to be associated with *castle*, so you might imagine a beehive shaped like a medieval castle. Pegword six is *sticks* and has to be associated with *rug*. You might imagine a bundle of sticks with a rug wrapped around them. Seven is *heaven*, to which you are to associate *grass*, perhaps the long lush grass of the Elysian fields. Pegword eight is *gate*, and you want to associate this with *beach*, so a gate-way opening onto a beach would be a possible association. Nine is *wine* and here you need to form an association with a *milkmaid*, perhaps a milkmaid milking a cow and getting wine instead? Ten is *hen*, which needs to be associated with binoculars, perhaps by just imagining a hen peering through binoculars. Having generated these images I should be able to come up with an accurate list of the ten words, as should you. See if you can.

Somewhat to my relief I was successful and I hope you were too. If you were not, it may be because it is much more effective to create your own images than to accept those created by someone else.

There are a number of other mnemonics based on imagery of which perhaps the most common are *location mnemonics*, where the items to be remembered are imaged at some specified location — in particular parts of a room or particular points along a walk through a familiar city or large building. This is a technique we will return to later.

If you lived in Moscow, the public buildings around Red Square might be convenient visual 'pegs' on which to hang material you wished to remember.

Supernormal imagery

One should not leave the topic of mental imagery without some reference to the Russian mnemonist Shereshevskii, who had a truly amazing memory which relied heavily on imagery. This remarkable man was studied over a period of years by the Russian psychologist, A.R. Luria, who has written a fascinating book about him, *The Mind of a Mnemonist*. Shereshevskii was first discovered when, as a journalist, his editor noticed that however complex the briefing instructions he was given before he went out on a story, he never took notes. Despite this he could repeat anything that was said to him word for word, a feat he simply took for granted. His editor, realizing that he was a somewhat unusual case, sent him along to see Luria, who gave him a series of increasingly demanding memory tests. There appeared to be no limit to the amount of information he could commit to memory — lists of more than a hundred digits, long strings of nonsense syllables, poetry in unknown languages, complex figures, elaborate scientific formulae . . . He could repeat such material back perfectly, even in reverse order, and even years later!

What was the secret of Shereshevskii's amazing memory? He proved to be someone who had quite remarkable imagery. Not only could he rapidly and easily create a wealth of visual images, he also had an amazing capacity for synesthesia.

This is the term used to describe the capacity for a stimulus in one sense to evoke an image in another. A mild degree of synesthesia is very common; most people have a slight tendency to associate high-pitched sounds with bright colors and low-pitched sounds with more somber hues. Nor is it uncommon for people to associate days of the week with colors. However, for most people any tendency for one modality to spill over into another is slight and of little practical significance. In Shereshevskii's case the amount of overlap was quite enormous. For example, when presented with a tone with

Alexander Luria, the Russian neuro-psychologist who gave the classic account of the amazing memory of Shereshevskii.

a pitch of 2,000 cycles per second, he said: 'It looks something like fireworks tinged with a pink-red hue. The strip of color feels rough and unpleasant, and it has an ugly taste — rather like that of a briny pickle . . . you could hurt your hand on this.' In talking to a colleague of Luria's he commented: 'What a crumbly yellow voice you have.' For him, numbers tended to have shapes and colors: 'One is a pointed number — which has nothing to do with the way it's written. It's because it's somehow firm and complete. Two is flatter, rectangular, whitish in color, sometimes almost a gray.' Numbers also resembled people, with one being 'a proud well-built man' and two 'a high-spirited woman'. Anything he was asked to remember was immediately encoded in this very rich and elaborate way. In general this meant that even the driest and most unpromising material created a vivid experience not only visually but in terms of sound and touch and smell as well.

Shereshevskii became a professional mnemonist, giving demonstrations of his extraordinary memory on the stage. He would supplement his amazing synesthesia by means of a number of mnemonic techniques, including imagining objects located along a familiar route and constructing stories to link them together. This was his way of remembering an extremely complex meaningless formula, part of which went like this:

$$\sqrt{N \cdot d^2 \cdot x \cdot \frac{85}{vx}} \quad \sqrt{\frac{276^2 \cdot 86x \cdot n^2 b}{\pi^2 v \cdot \pi 264}}$$

'Neiman (N) came out and poked with his stick (.). He looked at a dried-up tree which reminded him of a root ($\sqrt{\ }$) and he thought: "It is no wonder that this tree withered and that its roots were lain bare, seeing that it was already standing when I built these houses, these two here (d^2)", and again he poked with his stick (.). He said "The houses are old, a cross (x) should be placed on them." This gives a great return on his original capital, he invested 85,000 roubles in building them.

The roof finishes off the building (———), and down below a man is standing and playing a harmonica (x). He is standing near the Post Office and at the corner is a large stone (.) to stop carts bashing the corner of the house . . .'. This bizarre and lengthy anecdote not only allowed him to recall the formula faultlessly at the time, but also 15 years later!

Although this remarkable synesthesia ·was obviously extremely advantageous for Shereshevskii, it also presented problems. For example, if someone coughed while the material to be remembered was being read out, the cough would impress itself on his memory as a blur or a puff of steam which threatened to get in the way of subsequent recall. His synesthesia also created difficulties when remembering material that had been spoken to him, since a slight difference in inflection of the speaker's voice would completely change the image; this sometimes got in the way of his understanding even relatively simple prose. 'Each word calls up images; they collide with one another, and the result is chaos. I can't make anything out of this. And then there's also your voice . . . another blur . . . then everything's muddled.' His rich capacity for association also made reading difficult. He gave the following account of his attempt to understand the phrase *the work got under way normally*: 'As for *work*, I see that work is going on . . . there's a factory . . . but there's that word *normally*. What I see is a big, ruddy-cheeked woman, a *normal* woman . . . Then the expression *get under way*. Who? What is all this? You have industry . . . that is a factory, and this normal woman — but how does all this fit together? How much have I to get rid of just to get the simple idea of the thing!'

As a professional performer Shereshevskii was very successful. However he had enormous difficulty in forgetting and consequently would find that his memory was cluttered up with all sorts of information which he did not wish to recall. Eventually he hit on a very simple solution; he imagined the information he wished to remember written on a blackboard and then imagined himself rubbing it out. Strange to relate, this worked perfectly.

Mnemonists and supernormal memory

Since the publication of Luria's book there have been a number of other investigations of people who can perform amazing feats of memory, but to the best of my knowledge no one has proved to have the remarkable visual memory capacity of Shereshevskii. I myself was fortunate enough to study the memory performance of Rajan Mahadevan, who has a remarkable facility for remembering numbers. Until recently he held the world record for memorizing the maximum number of digits of *pi*. The record then passed to a Japanese mnemonist, although his learning rate was slower that that shown by Rajan.

We were interested in the extent to which Rajan's expertise was based on an outstanding general capacity for phonological learning, possibly resulting from a particularly capacious phonological loop. We therefore tested his performance not only on digits, which was remarkable, but also on verbal memory for unrelated words, and recall and recognition memory for both verbal material (people's names) and visual material (pictures of doors and drawings of crosses). He proved to have a good short-term verbal memory, but his performance was not outstanding. Rajan is a graduate student in psychology, and his performance was equivalent to the best, but not substantially better than that of his fellow graduates.

Wherein lay Rajan's amazing success with numbers? Discussing the question with Rajan himself, he pointed out first of all that he grew up in India where rote memorization is highly regarded, and that he is a member of a family that has produced a number of very good mathematicians. He describes how, at the age of five, he felt somewhat neglected at his sister's first birthday party and passed the time by memorizing the license plates of the visitors' cars. He was greatly praised for the feat, and appears to have been remembering numbers ever since! It appears then that Rajan has good native memory ability, but has coupled this with strategies and expertise acquired as a result of many years of practice. Ericsson, who has made a particular study of outstanding performance in the mnemonic, athletic and musical fields, argues that it is always associated with huge amounts of practice — the perspiration rather than the inspiration theory of genius.

Outstanding performance in any field tends to be associated with many, many hours of practice. A little natural ability helps, but after that it's mostly perspiration.

6 Forgetting

What did you do yesterday? What did you do on the same day last week? A year ago? Ten years ago? For whatever reason, it is highly unlikely that you recall what you were doing on a specific date ten years ago. You have presumably forgotten. To understand our memories, clearly we need to know not only how to get information in but also how information is lost.

The forgetting curve

Once again the classic study was done by Ebbinghaus· using himself as the subject and nonsense syllables as the material to be learned. He learnt 169 separate lists of 13 nonsense syllables, then relearned each list after an interval ranging from 21 minutes to 31 days. He always found some forgetting had occurred and used the amount of time required to learn the list again as a measure of how much had been forgotten. He found a clear relationship.

You will recall that the relationship between learning and remembering was more or less linear (see page 72), with the long-term memory store behaving rather like a bath being filled by a tap running at a constant rate. But how about forgetting? Is it simply like pulling the plug out of the bath, causing information to be lost at a constant rate, or is the relationship less straightforward? The results obtained by Ebbinghaus are shown overleaf. Forgetting is rapid at first but gradually slows down; the rate of forgetting is more logarithmic than linear. As with Ebbinghaus's other work, this result has stood the test of time, and has been shown to apply across a very wide range of material and learning conditions. Another way of describing the relationship is in terms of Jost's Law, named after a nineteenth-century psychologist, which states that if two memory traces are equally strong at a given time, then the older of the two will be more durable and forgotten less rapidly. It is as if, in addition to decaying, memory traces become tougher as they age, resisting further decay.

Memory for events

Memories get fainter as they recede in time. Is this because the memory trace fades, or do more distant memories become obscured by more recent ones?

Most studies of forgetting have, like Ebbinghaus's, concerned themselves with highly constrained sets of material such as lists of nonsense syllables or unrelated words, and have rarely investigated retention intervals of more than a month or so. What happens when more realistic material is recalled over longer intervals?

Answering such a question presents a major problem. Consider my question about what you were doing ten years ago. If you were to give me an answer, how would I know whether the information was correct? How would I go about

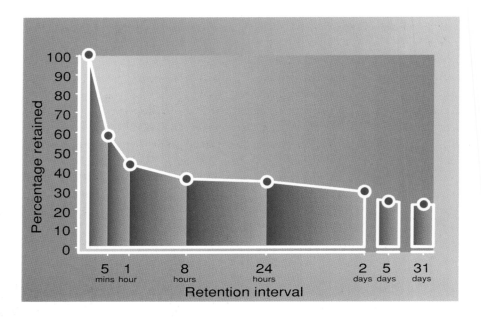

This is the dramatic curve that Ebbinghaus obtained when he plotted the results of one of his forgetting experiments. His finding, that information loss is very rapid at first and then levels off, holds good for many types of learned material. (Ebbinghaus, 1885)

checking? It is extremely unlikely that the necessary information is still available. One solution is to question respondents about events which were sufficiently noteworthy to attract the attention of virtually everyone at the time they happened. This strategy was followed by Warrington and Sanders, who selected items that were headline news in Britain for each of a series of years extending from the previous year to more than 30 years before. They then tested their respondents' memory for these events either by recall or recognition.

The results obtained by Warrington and Sanders showed that substantial forgetting of public events does occur, but that contrary to popular belief younger people have a better memory than the elderly for both recent and distant events. Broadly similar conclusions were arrived at by Squire in the United States, using

The Braer, *driven onto the rocks of the Shetlands in January 1993, sheds her 85,000 tons of oil. In what year did the* Exxon Valdes *run aground? When was the Chernobyl disaster? Bhopal? Three Mile Island?*

memory for the winners of classic U.S. horse races or the names of TV programs presented for only a single run.

The forgetting curves we have discussed so far have been concerned mainly with memory for relatively poorly learned material. What of information that has been much more thoroughly and deliberately learned? Light was thrown on this by an intriguing study by Bahrick, Bahrick and Wittlinger, who traced 392 American high school graduates and tested their memory for the names and portraits of classmates. Their study showed that the ability to *recognize* a face or a name from among a set of unfamiliar faces or names, and the ability to match up names with faces, remained at a remarkably high level for over 30 years. In contrast, the ability to *recall* a name either unprompted or in response to a person's picture was less good and showed much more extensive forgetting. In both conditions the performance of those tested after nearly 50 years was impaired, implying that there may be an aging effect possibly associated with more general intellectual impairment.

It seems that our ability to recognize faces lasts much longer than our ability to put a name to them. If you have an old school photograph, see how many faces you can recognize and how many you can put a name to.

Harry Bahrick is a Professor at Ohio Wesleyan University, which in common with many American colleges has an annual reunion for alumni. Bahrick has made ingenious use of this tradition to study the retention by alumni of a wide range of material, from the geography of the small town where the University is located to the vocabulary of foreign languages learned at college. The graph overleaf shows the effect of delay on memory for a foreign language (Spanish in this case). The most striking feature of the graph is the way in which forgetting levels out after about two years, with very little further loss up to the longest delay, virtually 50 years later. It is as if forgetting occurs only up to a certain point, beyond which memory traces appear to be frozen. By analogy with the permanently frozen ground in polar regions, known as permafrost, Bahrick has suggested the term *permastore* for this stable level of language learning performance. The second point to note is that the overall level of the permastore is determined by the level of initial learning, or at least as far as learning a foreign language is concerned.

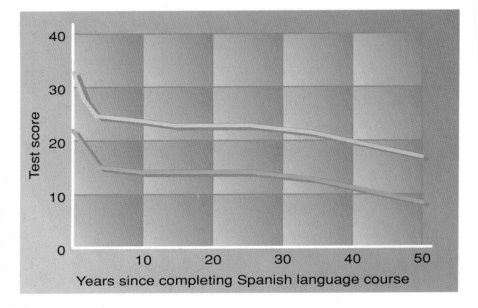

People who learned Spanish in college showed rapid forgetting over the first three or four years, followed by remarkably little forgetting over the next 30 years. Those who had a good knowledge (the upper curve) continued to have a clear advantage over those with poorer knowledge even 50 years later. Frequent Spanish speakers were excluded from this analysis. (Bahrick and Phelps, 1987)

A more detailed analysis of the retention of Spanish vocabulary suggested that two factors determined which words were well remembered and which were not. First of all, those words which were easy to learn were more likely to be well retained. Secondly, those items that were learned over spaced learning sessions were better retained than those learned under massed practice, providing further evidence for the value of distributed practice described in Chapter 4.

Bahrick's observation of a permastore effect in language learning differs from his finding for recall of names of classmates, which tended to show a steady decline over the first 30 years, followed by a rather steeper decline between 35 and 50 years. The observation that different types of material are forgotten at different rates also comes through strongly in a recent study carried out among students of psychology at Britain's Open University. Differences in retention of material occured between topics, with statistics appearing to be particularly well retained. The researchers speculate that this might have been because statistical techniques involve the performance of skills rather than the retention of facts. Perhaps statistics contains a higher proportion of procedural or implicit learning, whereas the other topics principally comprise explicit declarative knowledge.

Do we forget skills?

I seem to remember that I found learning to ride a bicycle a rather slow and frustrating business; having once learned, however, I have had no trouble riding a bicycle again since, even after several years without cycling. Similarly, once we learn to swim, we appear always to be able to swim. Does this mean that skills, once acquired, are never forgotten? To answer this question we need rather more information. We could probably afford to forget quite a lot about cycling and swimming before being in danger of falling off a bike or drowning. One area of skill acquisition that is of considerable practical importance concerns the training of aircraft pilots. Typically much of this is done by simulator, since it is very much cheaper to spend an hour in the most expensive simulator than to fly an actual plane; it is also considerably safer. In one study subjects were trained on a flight simulator and then retested for retention of the skill some 9 to 24 months later. Their level of performance was virtually unchanged, indicating an almost complete absence of forgetting.

Unfortunately, however, this lack of forgetting is not true of all skills. Flying a plane or riding a bicycle involves a continuous or *closed-loop skill,* in which each action provides the cue for the next action, in contrast to a discrete or *open-loop skill* such as typing, where each keypress involves a separate response to a discrete stimulus.

Many skills are in fact a mixture of open- and closed-loop skills, often combined with the need for accurate declarative knowledge. A good example of this is provided by the skill of cardiac resuscitation studied in 215 shop and office workers who had acquired the skill as volunteers. They were trained and tested on a life-size manikin, which also recorded each volunteer's performance and provided feedback. A number of measures of performance were tested from three months to three years after successfull completion of training. As

Once a punter, always a punter? Some skills, especially purely physical skills, are not easily forgotten once mastered.

the graph below shows, a great deal of forgetting took place, with the estimated survival rate of a resuscitable patient dropping from 100 per cent to 15 per cent within the first year. Clearly the skill requires regular resuscitation by some form of regular refresher course!

As this graph clearly demonstrates, first aid skills need frequent brushing up. In this study, level of performance after only three months would have been inadequate to ensure the survival of more than two in ten people requiring resuscitation. (McKenna and Glendon, 1985)

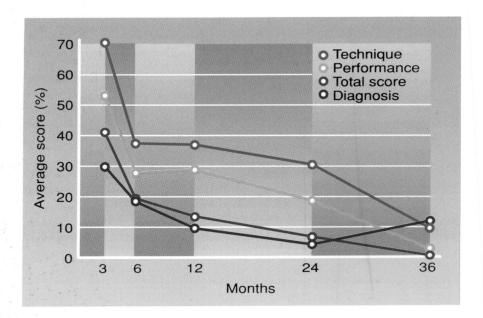

What principles need to be followed if learning is to be maintained as efficiently as possible? How much relearning is necessary and how often? This will clearly depend upon the nature of the material. With continuous motor skills the need for maintenance is very small, but with complex skills such as re-suscitation the need for maintenance may be quite substantial. Indeed it is probably necessary to answer such questions in order to decide whether it is sensible in the first place to try to teach resuscitation to a large number of volunteers, rather than concentrate on a smaller number who have a higher rate of expertise. Understanding the principles of maintenance of skill and knowledge offers a challenge that has been largely neglected in the past. Fortunately, following on from Bahrick's pioneering work, more extensive research in this area is now beginning to emerge.

Resistance to forgetting

Although recall of information from many years before is generally poor, people are able to recall some incidents many years later, particularly if the event was especially unusual or vivid. A particularly good example of this comes from a study of an East Anglian fishing community. In June 1901 the following report appeared in the local newspaper.

STRANGE TRAGEDY AT WINTERTON
Body found in the Sandhills

Late on Tuesday, a gruesome find was made on the sandhills at Winterton, a large fishing village eight miles north of Yarmouth. It appears that a fisherman with his dog, accompanied by a Yarmouth gentleman, was walking along the cliff, when they came across the body of a man hanging from a post driven high up in the sandhills and partially covered with sand. The body was hanging by a piece of stout cord, which had been neatly fastened to the post, evidently driven into the sands by the deceased's own hand. The features were quite unrecognizable, and covered with fungus. From the clothing the body was believed to be that of a fisherman named Gislam, who had been missing from home for about five weeks, and who was supposed either to have been drowned or to have gone to sea. So it was subsequently identified. The spot is a very wild and lonely one, and very rarely visited by Winterton people, and the body would probably not have been discovered now had it not been that the dog in question called the attention of his master to it . . .

The inquest was held the next day and reported in the local newspaper: 'The inquest was held on Wednesday afternoon by Mr Coroner Chaston, acting as deputy for the liberty of the Duke of Norfolk The first witness called was deceased's brother-in-law, Albert Robert George, also a fisherman, living at Winterton. Deceased, he said, was thirty-six years of age. He was at times very strange in his manner, and witness could not say whether on those occasions he was wholly responsible for his actions. He last saw him alive on the 8th of May near his own home. Deceased then put his arms round his little three-year-old son Stanley, said "Good-bye" and walked away. Witness supposed he was going to sea. He did not know that anything had occurred to upset him. The deceased's widow, Susannah Boulton Gislam, concurred with the evidence given by the previous witness, her brother. Her late husband's life, she said, was insured in the Prudential. There was no quarrel between him and her before he left home on May 8th, which was the last occasion on which she saw him alive; but he had been upset by being served with a County Court summons. She did not think that he fully knew what he was doing at times, though she had never heard him threaten to commit suicide, or even mention such a thing . . . The Coroner having summed up, the jury retired to consider their verdict. After a few minutes the Foreman announced that they could not agree as to whether it should be *felo de se* or temporary insanity. The Coroner further addressed them and pointed out that it might be his duty, in case they could not agree, to bind them over to the Assizes. On this they retired again, and returned in a few minutes with a verdict "That deceased committed suicide whilst temporarily insane".'

Then, in 1973, one man's memories of the events of that distant summer were revived by an interviewer.

Interviewer   We've been told that in some villages years ago if someone did something which the rest of the village disapproved of . . . a man might be a wife beater or a wife might be unfaithful to her husband . . .

Respondent   Yes. Uh huh.

Interviewer   That people would gather round at night and bang tins and this sort of thing?

Respondent   Not for that reason, not for that reason, but they'd . . . yes, they'd do it, yes. I know one.

Interviewer   What was that? Could you tell me about that?

Respondent   Well — long story, 1910 this was. This woman wanted her husband to get away to sea or be earning some money — they'd none. Well, you could understand the woman a' being — getting on to him about getting of a . . . At the same time, if he couldn't he couldn't. He went on the beach one day, and he was last seen at a — at an angle — and he went — as people saw him, to the south. But he was artful. When he knew people were all down . . . down home after their dinners, he turned and went north. They . . . ransacked the hills . . . they went to Yarmouth to see if he went on a boat. And nobody found him. No one. And they gave it up. Well, his poor wife didn't hardly get — well she didn't go out of doors . . . The result was — a man one evening — this happened in May, and six weeks following, so that'd be in June — perhaps the fore-part of July, I won't say exactly, a man was . . . well, like they used to go walking along the water's edge . . . He had a dog with him, perhaps he'd got — come out to give this dog a good run. And this dog would not leave this place. That got up on the hills. And he kept barking and yapping, barking and yapping, good way from Winterton, toward the north. And he thought to himself, whatever on the earth's that. He called him several time. The result was he had to go see — and there was this here man, tied to a post, about that high. And he — well, he was picked by the birds. Awful. Weren't fit to look at. Of course he got the dog away . . . Well he had to come home to Winterton and got the coastguard and report it. And of course that was — soon a — well, hullaballoo. There was some people were against her, so much as if they dressed up an effigy, lit it up — didn't do it 'til it got dark at night, ten or eleven o'clock, and went round against where they lived. I don't know what they sung now, I was only ten. I forget . . . But that poor old girl went — well she didn't go mad but she had to go to the hospital, so she died there.

Interviewer   People felt she'd driven, nagged him into it?

Respondent   Yes. Yes.

Interviewer   You said it happened in 1910 and you just said you were ten years old?

Respondent   Well, I was ten years old.

Interviewer   You were born?

Respondent   1890.

Interviewer   If you were ten that would be 1900.

Respondent   Well, didn't I tell you 1900?

Interviewer   I think you said 1910.

Respondent   Ah well, 1900 might be. Just into the nineteenth-twentieth century. That was June, that . . . May when he done it and — I can't tell you the exact date — but he was buried — in Winterton churchyard.

The stormy East Coast of England, scene of the Winterton tragedy.

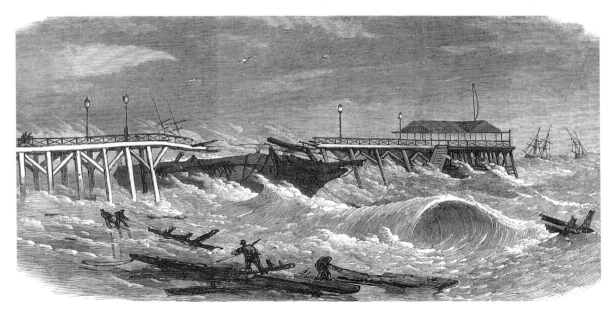

Bearing in mind that the event had occurred over 70 years before, the old man's account is surprisingly accurate, even to the date, given the appropriate prompting by the interviewer. The remembered account provides a good deal of additional detail, the barking of a dog, what the man thought, and so forth, which may or may not be an accurate memory of the man's account. It seems likely that the excellent recall stems from the very striking and macabre nature of the incident, which might well of course have made it into the sort of local story that would be recounted from time to time over the years, hence helping to preserve the memory.

It is tempting to assume that because we remember an incident that happened 20 years ago, we are accessing a 20-year-old memory. That can only be concluded if we have not recalled the event in the meantime. If we have, then at the very least we will have practised and rehearsed the memory, and at worst we may be remembering not the event itself but our later reconstruction of it.

The importance of this factor showed up very clearly in a study by Marigold Linton using herself as a subject. Every day for a five-year period she would note down in her diary two events that had occurred on that day. At pre-determined intervals she would randomly select events from her diary and judge whether she could in fact recall the event in question. Given the fact that she was sampling in this way, a particular event could crop up on a number of occasions. She was therefore able to re-analyze her results to find out what effects such earlier recalls had on the later memorability of an event. Her results are shown below; the items that were not retested showed quite dramatic forgetting over a four-year period (65 per cent forgotten). Even a single test was enough to reduce the amount of forgetting, while items which had been tested on four other occasions showed a probability of forgetting after four years of only

The probability of remembering something depends on the number of times it has been 'rehearsed' or called to mind. Recalling an event acts as a rehearsal and reduces the rate of forgetting. (Linton, 1975)

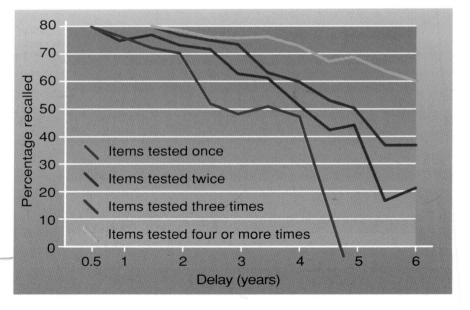

about 12 per cent, providing further evidence for the effectiveness of regular reminders in maintaining learning and memory. When this factor is taken into account, the forgetting curves look broadly similar to what one might have expected from the original Ebbinghaus experiments.

Theories of forgetting

There are two traditional theories of forgetting. One argues that the memory trace simply *fades* or decays away rather as a notice that is exposed to sun and rain gradually fades until it becomes quite illegible. The second suggests that forgetting occurs because memory traces are disrupted or obscured by subsequent learning, in other words that forgetting occurs because of *interference*. Which of these two interpretations of forgetting is right? If the memory trace decays spontaneously, then the crucial factor determining how much is recalled should simply be the amount of time that has elapsed. The longer the delay, the greater the forgetting. If forgetting results from interference, however, then the crucial factor should be the events that occur within that time, with more interpolated events resulting in more forgetting.

It is often difficult to separate the importance of time from the importance of events, but it is occasionally possible. In one study by Graham Hitch and myself, rugby football players were asked to recall the names of the teams they had played earlier in the season. The graph below shows the probability of their recalling the name of the last team played, the team before that, and so forth. It proved to be the case that most players had missed some games either due to injury or other commitments, so that for one player the game before last might have taken place a week ago and for another it might have been two weeks or even

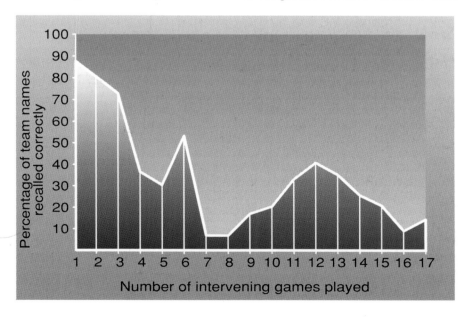

This graph, showing rugby players' memory for the names of teams recently played, demonstrates the general tendency for recent events to interfere with memory of similar but less recent events. (Baddeley and Hitch, 1977)

a month before. It was therefore possible to ascertain whether forgetting depended on elapsed time or on the number of intervening games. The result was clear. Time was relatively unimportant, whereas the number of games was critical, suggesting that, in this situation at least, forgetting was due to interference rather than trace decay.

If forgetting only occurs when some similar event intervenes, it presumably means that if one asks only about the last time a given event has occurred, and avoids the occurrence of any intervening events which might interfere with the memory trace, then no forgetting should be observed. A number of attempts have been made to test this prediction, some of them using animals and attempting to immobilize the animal during the interval. For example, one study used cockroaches, taking advantage of the fact that if induced to crawl into a cone lined with tissue paper, a cockroach will apparently lie quite inert, as if asleep. The experimenters therefore taught their cockroaches to avoid turning into a previously attractive darkened compartment by giving them an electric shock whenever they did so. They then retested the insects after varying intervals of time ranging from ten minutes to 24 hours. The immobilized cockroaches showed relatively little forgetting (25 per cent), but their colleagues, who had been allowed to crawl about and do whatever cockroaches like to do in the intervening time, showed forgetting of 70 per cent.

Immobilizing human subjects is rather more difficult, but a number of experiments have attempted to study forgetting under conditions of reduced interference. It has been shown, for example, that subjects who learn material immediately before going to bed show better retention 24 hours later than subjects who learn in the morning and then indulge in a normal day's activities. However, although lack of interference may be one factor here, it is almost certainly not the only one, since subjects who learn a list of words in the morning and then sleep before recalling it later in the day show as much forgetting as those who remain awake and active during the interval. One possible reason why learning in the evening might lead to better retention than learning earlier in the day is because the physiological process of consolidating the memory trace may operate more effectively at night. The human body has a number of cyclic rhythms that vary through a 24-hour period. The most obvious one is the sleep/wake cycle, but associated with it are a number of others, including body temperature, which rises during the day and drops at night, and the production of a range of hormones, some of which may possibly be important in allowing the development and consolidation of the physiological trace that presumably underlies learning.

Sleep and memory

A number of people have suggested that sleep may be important in learning because of some form of reorganization that takes place while we are dreaming. It has been suggested that the process of dreaming serves the purpose of organizing the events experienced the previous day, relating them to what has gone before and discarding what is irrelevant. While this is an intriguing idea, there is little evidence to support it. One can identify the period during which a sleeper is dreaming by recording the electrical impulses put out by the brain during sleep, and by monitoring eye movement. From time to time the eyes move rapidly around beneath the closed lids. This can be monitored through the electrical potential given off by the eye muscles and is found to be associated with a particular brain rhythm. If the sleeper is woken up during this period he will report that he was in the middle of a dream. Rapid eye movement (REM) sleep occurs throughout the night, but predominantly towards morning. By presenting material at different times during the night it is possible to ensure a greater or smaller amount of dreaming between presentation of material and testing. So does dreaming enhance memory or does it do the opposite? The same question can be asked when dream-inhibiting drugs are given to sleep volunteers.

There have been a number of experiments conducted in this area and the results are frankly disappointing. Some show a slight tendency for dream sleep to be more helpful than deep sleep without dreams, whereas some show the opposite; the result seems to depend not only on the method of manipulating sleep but also on the type of material the person is learning.

Despite their differing results, most workers in the area seem to interpret their results in terms of *consolidation* rather than referring to some process of *sorting out* the previous day's experiences. Whatever interpretation is made of these results, the observed effects are small and give little support to the view that dreaming plays a central role in the process of learning, attractive though this idea might seem.

Why do we remember so little of what we dream? Perhaps our low level of arousal during sleep means that the memory traces never consolidate. Or is waking so different from sleeping that when we are awake we cannot retrieve the memories laid down in sleep?

Interference and forgetting

A more fruitful way of investigating the effect of interference in forgetting is to abandon the idea of producing a forgetting interval that is completely devoid of interfering activity and study instead the effect of different types of interfering material on recall. A good example of this was a study carried out 50 years ago by McGeoch and MacDonald in which subjects were asked to learn and relearn lists of adjectives. They studied the effects of interference by varying the activity between the original learning and the subsequent recall. They found that the amount of forgetting was least when subjects merely rested during the interval, and was somewhat more when they learned unrelated material (such as three-figure numbers or nonsense syllables) during the interval. Forgetting increased when the subjects were required to learn other adjectives, being greatest when the interpolated learning involved adjectives that were similar in meaning to those originally learned. This result shows the characteristic feature of interference, that the more similar the interfering material, the greater the amount of forgetting.

Some idea of the importance the role of similarity plays in producing interference can be gained from the material below. This comprises two lists, A and B, with five nouns and adjectives in each. Read through List A, trying to commit to memory the adjective associated with each noun. When you have done so, cover up the list and try to remember the adjective associated with each of the nouns listed again beneath. Repeat the procedure until you get all five adjectives right and note the number of learning trials required. Then go on to List B and repeat the process.

List A	**List B**
sailor—tipsy	vicar—cheery
actor—pompous	curate—merry
politician—crafty	parson—happy
lawyer—noisy	rector—jovial
singer—doleful	priest—jaunty
Test	**Test**
politician ?	parson ?
sailor ?	priest ?
singer ?	vicar ?
lawyer ?	curate?
actor ?	rector?

You probably found it easier to learn List A, where the five nouns and the associated adjectives are fairly dissimilar, than List B, where they are virtually synonymous. This particular exercise demonstrates the interference effects of similarity. Very comparable effects occur if you learn one item and then try to learn something else that is highly similar. You will be slower to learn the second item, and in doing so will tend to forget the first to a much greater extent than would have been the case if the two items were unrelated.

There are of course few situations where the amount of potential confusion between initial and later learning is as great as this. Indeed, in general, the learning of one set of facts tends to help the learning of another. The world is a structured and coherent place, not a collection of purely arbitrary relationships. So although interference can certainly be demonstrated, there is some disagreement as to how important it is outside the laboratory.

In one study two groups of subjects were given a piece of prose about Buddhism; one group was then asked to read a passage on another form of Buddhism, while the other was given a neutral passage about libraries. Both groups were then required to recall the original piece of prose. There was little difference between the two groups, indicating that no serious interference had taken place. Since that time, however, more carefully designed passages have shown that interference *can* be demonstrated in prose recall. For example, a study by Crouse required subjects to learn a passage concerning the life of a fictitious poet, John Payton. The passage began as follows: *Payton was born in Liverpool at the end of October 1810. When he was only five years of age his father, who was a servant, was killed by a robber . . .* It continued in this vein, finally concluding: *Soon after this, however, he began to suffer haemorrhages in the lungs and after much misery, he died in Geneva on April 12th 1859.* After studying and recalling such a passage, subjects went on to learn two further passages of a similar nature, each having the same biographical framework and containing

New information can obscure old and make it difficult to retrieve, particularly if the new information is similar to the old.

detailed 'facts'. One such passage concerned an imaginary poet, Samuel Hughes: Hughes was born in Paddington at the end of October 1805. When he was only nine years of age his father, who was a weaver, was killed in a swimming accident. The passage ended: *Soon after this, however, he began to suffer haemorrhages of the lungs, and after much misery he died in Paris on March 18th 1846.*

Subjects were then asked for individual pieces of information about the first passage, such as where John Payton was born, how his father died, and so on. They proved able to recall only 54 per cent as much as subjects who, instead of reading other similar biographical passages, had been given unrelated material to read, indicating that substantial interference had occurred.

It must be admitted that such experiments go to extreme lengths to maximize interference. To my mind at least, they demonstrate just how well the memory system manages to cope with a continuous stream of often similar infor-

mation without becoming clogged by interference. Consider the car driver who changes from driving in Britain to driving in the United States, or vice versa. In my own case, having spent all my driving life on the left-hand side of the road, I found remarkably little difficulty in switching to driving on the right. One would clearly be unwise to assume that no interference occurs in this situation, yet the amount of interference is remarkably small.

Retroactive interference

The forgetting of old information caused by new is normally termed *retroactive interference* (RI). The term 'retroactive' implies that the interference works backwards, which of course is not strictly true. What does happen is that the new material somehow supersedes the old. In general this type of interference increases as the amount of new learning increases, and is most dramatic when it is interfering with a relatively weak older memory trace.

Retroactive interference was very extensively studied during the 1940s and 1950s, when a whole range of experimental means of producing interference effects were explored. These typically used the technique of *paired-associate learning* whereby one item, the stimulus, is associated with another, the response. Hence if you have learnt to associate the word *tipsy* with *sailor*, and are then required to associate *cautious* with *sailor*, the learning of the second adjective will tend to weaken recall of the first (*tipsy*). It is as if two competing associations are being set up, in which the stronger the initial association, the more resistant it will be to interference from later learning. Similarly, the greater the degree of later learning, the greater the amount of interference there will be with the initial association. There has been a much controversy as to whether forming the second

Factors influencing the recall of a paragraph of prose. The more times the paragraph has been read, the better it is recalled, but when another paragraph intervenes, it will hinder recall, the so-called 'retroactive interference' effect. (Slamecka, 1960)

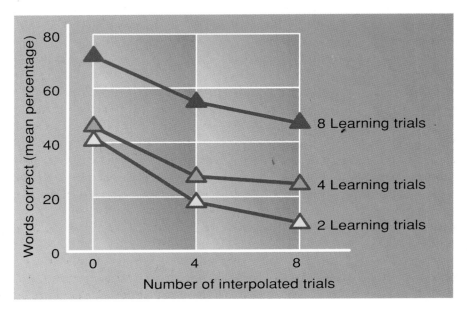

association (*sailor — cautious*) actually weakens the first, or overshadows it by its greater strength. Whichever occurs, there is no doubt that whatever strengthens recall of one association minimizes the recall of the other.

Proactive inhibition

So far we have concentrated on the phenomen of later learning interfering with earlier. But what if the old response suddenly breaks through and wins out against the new? This phenomenon is termed *proactive inhibition*. It is as if the old trace, having been displaced and suppressed by the new one, strikes back, often when one least expects it. An example of this occurred to me recently. One of my local pubs sells beer brewed by a company called Wells, who used to make a very strong beer called Fargo. They subsequently replaced it with a weaker beer which they called Bombadier, to which I reluctantly converted. About a year later, on returning to my local after a month's absence, I went in and ordered a pint of Fargo, and it was only after being asked where I had been for the last twelve months that it dawned on me that I was the victim of proactive inhibition (or should it be called 'inactive prohibition'?).

The first person to suggest that proactive inhibition, or PI, might be a major source of forgetting was the American psychologist Benton J. Underwood. He was interested in explaining why subjects who had learned a list of nonsense syllables should show so much forgetting when tested 24 hours later. It was assumed at the time that most forgetting was the result of retroactive interference, and that substantial interference would depend on the subject learning similar material in the intervening period. Since it seemed unlikely that Underwood's subjects went home and swotted up yet more nonsense syllables, it was far from clear where the interference was coming from. It occurred to Underwood that while retroactive interference from similar material might be implausible, proactive interference was a real possibility. The reason for this was that almost all work on human learning at the time was being done in a relatively small number of laboratories, all of which traditionally used undergraduate subjects. If you happened to be a student in one of these departments, you were likely to be required to serve a substantial number of hours in the verbal learning laboratory as part of your course. It occurred to Underwood that it might be interference from the many *previous* lists of nonsense syllables learnt by his long-suffering subjects that was causing forgetting. Fortunately it was possible to find out how many previous lists each subject had learnt and to plot the amount of forgetting in a 24-hour period as a function of this prior experience. He was able to obtain similar data from a range of other studies and, putting everything together, concluded that the more lists of nonsense syllables one has learned previously, the more likely one is to forget the most recent list!

In essence, PI and RI reflect the fact that our experiences tend to interact, to run into one another, with the result that our memory for one experience is unlikely to be completely insulated from our memory of others. The more similar two experiences are, the greater the probability that they will interact. In many cases this interaction is helpful, since the new learning builds onto the old. However, when it is important to separate the two memories, problems occur, exaggerating the amount of forgetting that would otherwise have happened. We should be aware of the potential dangers of such forgetting. For instance, designers of surveys and questionnaires may be tempted to rely on our memories to a greater extent than is wise, asking about the frequency and incidence of events and expecting us to respond with a degree of detail that is totally unrealistic. Perhaps more seriously, eyewitnesses to crimes may be assumed to have a much better recall of the incident than is at all reasonable.

Accessing the memory trace

The very fact that PI occurs, with earlier memories supplanting more recent ones, implies that the effect of interference is to make earlier traces less accessible, not to destroy them. If intervening material can disrupt access to earlier memory traces, are there ways in which access can be regained? The general problem of access to a memory trace, or retrieval, will be discussed in Chapter 9.

Knowing something, but not being able to access it, is a very common experience. This occurred to me when my wife referred to a visit we had made to the town of Aldeburgh on the Suffolk coast before we were married. I simply could not recall the incident, although I was sure that I had been to Aldeburgh and could conjure up a vivid visual image of a long-sweeping, rather gray pebbly beach with strong associations to Benjamin Britten and his gloomy and romantic opera *Peter Grimes*. To what extent I was actually remembering something I had experienced or something that had been conjured up by reading or watching television, I found it hard to judge. And I confessed no, I could not remember the visit. 'You remember, it was when you sat in the seagull dung!' my wife said. Immediately the memories came flooding back — not at all like the mournful romantic image of Aldeburgh I had previously been scanning!

Clearly, we store far more information than we can retrieve at any given time. Indeed some would claim that we store every piece of information we have ever experienced, and that it is all lying there in our memory banks simply waiting for the appropriate key to be turned for it to come flooding back. One piece of evidence that is often cited in favor of this view is the report by the eminent neurosurgeon Wilder Penfield of memories evoked by direct electrical stimulation of the brain. Penfield performed over a thousand brain operations in which a portion of the skull was lifted and part of the cortex removed. The purpose of this operation was to reduce epilepsy by removing from the brain areas of scar tissue which facilitate seizures. In carrying out these operations it was routine for the patient to be conscious. Before removing any brain tissue, the neuro-surgeon would stimulate the brain electrically in order to plot the function of the suspect area. The purpose of this process was to avoid removing crucial portions of the brain, in particular those involved in language and speech where a comparatively small lesion may dramatically impair the ability to speak.

A total of 40 patients reported 'flashbacks' when Penfield stimulated areas of the temporal lobes. These flashbacks appeared to be memories of previous incidents and often occurred in great detail. Blakemore gives the following account: 'One of Penfield's patients was a young woman. As the stimulating electrode touched a spot on her temporal lobe, she cried out: "I think I heard a mother calling her little boy somewhere. It seemed to be something that happened years ago . . . in the neighborhood where I live." Then the electrode was moved a little and she said: "I hear voices. It is late at night, around the carnival somewhere, some sort of travelling circus. I just saw lots of big wagons that they use to haul animals in." ' Both Blakemore and Penfield seem to assume that what was being evoked were accurate memories of real events 'with no loss of detail, as though a tape recorder had been receiving it all.'

Taken at face value these observations seem to suggest that all experience is stored in great detail somewhere in the brain. However, such an interpretation of Penfield's results is open to a number of objections. First, the incidence of reported flashbacks was extremely low, occurring in less than 4 per cent of patients tested.

A more fundamental objection comes from the fact that no evidence is given that what was being reported were indeed actual events. As we shall see later on, even under normal conditions it is possible to have a clear and very detailed image of an incident you were sure you

A flight of steps, a child with a red balloon . . . a memorable image. But not all 'vivid memories' are real. Some 'memories' we cobble together from photographs, films, family anecdotes . . .

experienced, which turns out never to have occurred. There is no doubt that Penfield's electrodes did cause items to be retrieved from memory, and that these items were associated in patients' minds with feelings of familiarity. There is, however, no evidence that these feelings of familiarity were justified; they could have been artificially induced *déjà vu* sensations, unjustified feelings of familiarity. As we shall see in Chapter 11, where we discuss amnesia, the temporal lobe and hippocampus are certainly implicated in long-term memory, but there is considerable evidence to suggest that damage to these areas produces memory disturbances, which may themselves involve a disruption of ability to judge the familiarity of material. In short, intriguing though they are, the flashbacks reported by Penfield's patients do not represent very strong evidence for the proposition that nothing is ever forgotten.

7 Repression

Sigmund Freud (1856–1939) theorized that thoughts highly toned by anxiety, guilt or pain are excluded from consciousness and therefore from conscious memory. We repress such thoughts because they are too threatening.

Sigmund Freud, the originator of psychoanalysis, put forward an interpretation of forgetting which has been popular for many years. In his book *The Psychopathology of Everyday Life* he suggested that many of the processes characteristic of the mental life of his neurotic patients also occurred in normal behavior. One such process is the 'Freudian slip' whereby a slip of the tongue or of the pen results in the speaker or writer making an error which reveals his true opinions. On one occasion the President of the Austrian House of Deputies opened a session of which he expected very little, by declaring the session closed! A *British Psychological Society Bulletin*, in a list of forthcoming events, made reference to 'the Fraud Memorial Professorship'. Freud would probably not have been amused, but he would not have been surprised. Over the years his views have evoked a great deal of controversy and opposition.

Freud suggested that a good deal of everyday forgetting might have its origin in the repression of events associated with anxiety. He gives an example of a man who, when attempting to recall a poem, blocked on a line describing a snowy pine tree as covered 'with the white sheet'. When asked to free associate to this phrase, the man remarked that it reminded him of the sheet that would be used to cover a corpse, and through this it was associated with the recent death of his brother from a congenital heart condition which he feared would eventually cause his own death. While such cases do have plausibility, most of the examples given by Freud are much more tortuous and questionable. A skeptic could argue that, given a little ingenuity and imagination, virtually any word can be linked with any experience.

Forgetting what is unpleasant

There have been a number of attempts to produce repression in the laboratory. Some experimenters have tried to teach subjects lists of nonsense syllables and then been thoroughly nasty to them with the purpose of causing them to repress anything associated with the experiment. Sure enough, subjects treated in this way perform badly, but they do much better in subsequent sessions when experimenters remove 'repression' by telling them that the nastiness is all part of the experiment! Unfortunately, apart from being ethically dubious, the results of such experiments might just as plausibly be ascribed to subjects' natural reluctance to try very hard in response to an unpleasant and rude experimenter.

Another experiment designed to test the repression theory required subjects to produce associations to a series of words, some of which were neutral

The Scream by Edvard Munch, 1893. Unpleasant events are less willingly recalled than pleasant ones.

(tree, cow, window), while others had emotional overtones, *(fear, angry, quarrel)*. Immediately afterwards subjects were given the same words over again and asked to recall the associations they had made. There was a clear tendency for them to remember fewer emotional associations than neutral ones. On the surface this appeared to support the Freudian view of repression; presumably the words associated with anxiety produced responses associated with anxiety, and were therefore repressed. However, the situation is more complex than this since there is a good deal of evidence to suggest that highly arousing words will be poorly remembered when tested after a short delay, but well remembered after a longer period.

Do most of us have more pleasant than unpleasant childhood memories because we forget what is unpleasant, or do most of us have generally pleasant childhoods?

Two University of Cambridge undergraduates, Brendan Bradley and Beverley Morris, and I decided to test this interpretation. We asked our subjects to produce associations to neutral or emotional words, tested half of them immediately and the other half 28 days later. As in the original study, we found that associations to emotional words were poorly recalled initially, but that after 28 days they were consistently better remembered than associations to neutral words. If the cause of the initial poor retention had been repression, then one would have expected subjects to continue to have difficulty recalling emotional words; exactly the opposite happened, indicating that arousal rather than the repression of anxiety was the true cause.

In short, Freudian repression has not proved at all easy to demonstrate under laboratory conditions. However, one area in which it has been claimed that it can be easily demonstrated is in the recall of life events. Try it for yourself. Write down as many events as you can from the first eight years of your life. Give yourself a few minutes to dig them up since they are unlikely to spring to mind that easily. When you have written down as many memories as you can, try to categorize them as pleasant, unpleasant, or neutral. According to a study carried out by Waldfogel and cited by Hunter, pleasant memories should total about 50 per cent, unpleasant about 30 per cent, and neutral about 20 per cent. This preponderance of pleasant over unpleasant memories is also characteristic of memories from later life. Repression of unpleasant memories may be the reason, but it is always possible that most of us have more pleasant than unpleasant experiences.

Freudian theory suggests that incidents associated with pain are forgotten more readily than those associated with pleasure. A related question is whether pain is remembered as being less intense than it really was. Some interesting information on this point came from a study by Robinson and his colleagues, who were investigating the effectiveness of analgesics in childbirth. The women in this study were asked to rate the pain they experienced during childbirth using a line with the ends defined as 'no pain' and 'as much pain as you can possibly imagine'. They marked the line during childbirth, and again after delays of 24 hours, 5 days and 3 months.

Robinson and his colleagues were interested in comparing three methods of pain relief during childbirth. The graph below shows the pain ratings obtained in the delivery room and later from memory. In all three conditions memory for the pain seemed to fade over time. Is this characteristic of all memories of pain, or is it limited to the pain experienced during childbirth? One can certainly imagine good biological reasons why a species which forgot how painful childbirth was might be more likely to flourish than a species in which memory of pain was very vivid and long-lasting.

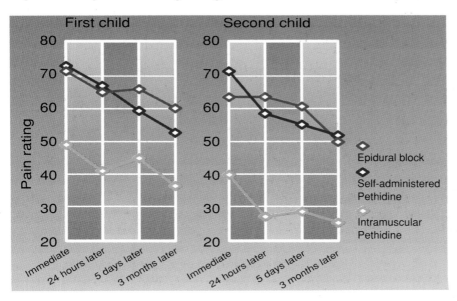

This graph not only shows the relative efficacity of three different methods of pain relief during childbirth, but also how quickly and substantially memory for pain fades. (Robinson et al., 1980)

In fact the evidence which supports the Freudian interpretation of forgetting most convincingly comes not from normal forgetting but from the pathological forgetting associated with neurosis. This shows up particularly clearly in cases of hysterical amnesia.

Hysterical amnesia

Occasionally one hears of people who have 'lost their memory' and are found wandering around apparently totally unaware of who they are, where they come from, or how they got there. With a little care and attention memory usually comes back within a few days, although cases exist of much longer amnesias. Almost invariably such people are undergoing an emotional crisis in their life. It is as if life has become intolerable and the only way of coping is to cease to be themselves, at least temporarily.

The term *fugue* is used to describe this pathological loss of memory. The pattern demonstrated varies, and seems to depend more on the person's assumptions about how memory works than on the actual working of memory. In this respect one is reminded of 'glove anesthesia', hysterical loss of all sensation in a hand, the pattern of numbness following the shape of the hand and bearing no relation whatsoever to the underlying nerve distribution. The cause is psychogenic and not based on dysfunction of the nerves themselves. While hysterical symptoms clearly differ from straightforward physical symptoms, they are not necessarily any less genuine to the patient or any more under conscious voluntary control.

In general a patient suffering from fugue recovers relatively rapidly, confronts the source of his or her anxiety, and is unlikely to relapse. However, there are hysterical patients who alternate between different states of mind, being completely unaware in one state of their personality and actions in the other state. The French psychiatrist Pierre Janet, who was a contemporary of Freud, gives the following case history: 'Irene was a girl of 20 years, who was greatly disturbed by the long illness and death of her mother. Her mother had reached the last stage of tuberculosis, and lived alone in abject poverty with her daughter, in an attic. The girl watched her mother during 60 days and nights, working at her sewing machine to earn a few pennies to sustain their lives. When finally her mother did die, Irene became very much disturbed emotionally. She tried to revive the corpse, to call the breath back again. In her attempts at placing the limbs in an upright position, the mother's body fell to the floor, whereupon she went through the strain of lifting her back into bed, alone.

'Certainly, such experiences cannot be forgotten in the ordinary course of things. Yet in a little while Irene seemed to have grown forgetful of her mother's death. She would say, "I know very well my mother must be dead, since I have been told so several times, since I see her no more, and since I am in mourning; but I really feel astonished at it all. When did she die? What did she die from? Was I not by her to take care of her? There is something I do not understand. Why, loving her as I did, do I not feel more sorrow for her death? I can't grieve; I feel as if her absence was nothing to me, as if she were travelling and will soon come back."

'The same thing happened if you put to her questions about any of the events that happened during those two months before her mother's death. If you asked her about the illness, the mishaps, the nightly staying up, anxieties about money, the quarrels with her drunken father — all these things seemed to have quite vanished from her mind.

'What had happened to her? Had something happened to her nervous system to wipe away all traces of the horrible events she had experienced? Was she simply pretending she did not remember? Or did she remember without being able to recall, owing to some powerful inhibitions?

'Some light is thrown on this question by a study of the crises (or fits) which she began to experience some time after her mother's death. These would last for hours at a time, and during them she would lose contact with her immediate surroundings and perform scenes with the skill of an actress. She would re-enact all the events that took place at her mother's death, as well as other unpleasanter episodes in her life, all with the greatest detail. She would carry out with words and acts different events, and when death finally came to her mother would prepare for her own suicide. She would discuss it aloud, seem to speak to her mother, and to receive advice from her. She fancied that she would try to be run over by a locomotive. She acted as though she were on the way, and stretched herself out on the floor of the room, waiting with dread and impatience for death to come. Finally, when it came, she would utter a terrible shriek, and fall back motionless, as if she were dead. Then she would get up and begin acting over again one of the previous scenes. After a time the agitation would seem to die down and she came back to normal consciousness, took up her ordinary business, seemingly quite undisturbed about what had happened, and with a concomitant loss of memory for the events she had so faithfully dramatized.'

We continue to be fascinated by the bizarre phenomen of multiple personality, in which one body is inhabited by two minds, each appearing to forget the other.

Multiple personality

An even more extreme example of repression occurs in multiple personality, in which one person will on different occasions adopt two, and sometimes even more, mutually exclusive personalities. The situation is that dramatized by Robert Louis Stevenson in *Dr Jekyll and Mr Hyde*. While such cases are relatively rare, well over 100 have been reported, and some 20 or more of the people concerned have possessed more than two distinct personalities. The best-known case is that reported in the book

The Three Faces of Eve by Thigpen and Cleckley, published in 1957. The patient originally had two contrasting personalities — Eve White, who was modest, gentle, hardworking and kind, and Eve Black, who was irresponsible, flashy and selfish. Eve Black was aware of Eve White, but this awareness did not work in reverse. During treatment a third and much more balanced personality emerged, Jane, who was aware of both Eves, and who eventually succeeded in producing a balanced amalgam of the two.

There is no doubt that repression does occur in cases such as this. It probably also plays an important role in neurotic behavior of a less flamboyant kind. At a crude level a person may simply refuse to report what he does not wish the listener to know. At a more subtle level it is likely that when he is thinking about certain events or people that are remotely related to the source of his anxiety, he will find this unpleasant and direct his memory search elsewhere. Such a simple expedient is likely to keep the source of anxiety well away from the focus of attention. Freudian psychoanalysts use techniques such as free association and dream interpretation to uncover these hidden sources of anxiety and help patients to learn to cope with them. The validity of such methods has come under close scrutiny in recent years, with many claims of child abuse following the uncovering of 'repressed' memories during therapy.

Child abuse

In the early years of the development of psychoanalysis Sigmund Freud frequently observed that his patients reported childhood memories of sexual advances from parents. Although he initially accepted these claims, he subsequently decided that they were fantasies, and built this assumption into his subsequent theorizing. According to Freud, a child feels sexually attracted to the parent of the opposite sex, and the repression of these socially unacceptable feelings plays an important role in the development of neurosis and is also responsible for infantile amnesia, an inability to recall anything of any significance from the first two to three years of life. (See Chapter 12 for a more detailed discussion of infantile amnesia.)

In recent years it has become tragically clear that child abuse is much more than a fantasy in the minds of patients undergoing therapy. By the mid-1980s the number of child abuse cases in the United States was reported to be in excess of 1.7 million. After decades of denying the reality of child abuse, therapists now appear to be actively searching for evidence of abuse, often with more zeal than wisdom. The comments that follow rely heavily on the text of a lecture given by Elizabeth Loftus to the centennial meeting of the American Psychological Association in August 1992. As will become clear from the chapter on eyewitness testimony, Loftus has carried out classic work on the application of the psychology of memory to the evaluation of legal testimony. As a result of this she is heavily in demand as an expert witness, which in turn has stimulated her interest in developing methods whereby current practice can be evaluated and improved.

The concept of repression moved from the consulting room to the court-room with a landmark case tried in Redwood City, California, in 1990. In this case the key witness claimed to have recovered a previously repressed childhood memory of her father sexually abusing and then killing one of her friends. Despite inconsistencies in her testimony on different occasions, the jury believed the witness and her father was found guilty of murder.

Other similar cases have begun to appear, including cases in which people have sued for recovery of damages for injury suffered as a result of childhood sexual abuse. In a number of states the Statute of Limitations, which normally specifies that a crime must be prosecuted within some specified time period, now allows victims to prosecute at any time within three years of *remembering* a previous incident. The popular press has also begun to publicize cases in which memories of child abuse have been repressed. A former Miss America did not remember sexual violation by her father until she was 24 years old, by which time her father had died.

How plausible are such claims? While it is inherently difficult to estimate the frequency of child abuse, there does seem to be agreement that it is far from rare, with estimates ranging from 10 per cent to as high as 50. Up to three-quarters of women involved in therapy groups have been reported as providing 'some confirmation' of sexual abuse. This frequency does not necessarily imply that either repression or abuse has necessarily occurred. However, an indication of the possible frequency of repression comes from a survey of 450 abuse victims; when asked if there had been any period in which they had demonstrated amnesia for the abuse, 59 per cent of them reported that this was the case. While this is clearly a very difficult judgement to make after the fact, it certainly does support the possibility of repression.

It is perhaps worth mentioning here evidence for repression from another source. Two British psychiatrists, Taylor and Kopelman, report that 30–40 per cent of criminals convicted of violent crime, and in particular homicide, are unable to recall the crime. This is particularly likely to occur when the victim is a close relative or lover killed in a crime of passion. A similar psychogenic amnesia is also reported in the case of Sirhan Sirhan, who assassinated Senator Robert Kennedy in 1968. He was able to recall the incident under hypnosis, however: 'As Sirhan became more worked up and excited, he recalled progressively more, the memories tumbling out while his excitement built to crescendo leading to the shooting. At that point Sirhan would scream out the death curses, "fire" the shots, and then choke as he re-experienced the Secret Service body-guard nearly throttling him after he was caught.'

However, it should be borne in mind that the Taylor and Kopelman study is based on the recollection of violence by the perpetrator. Another study based on children who had seen a parent killed reported that none showed evidence of repression; on the contrary, the experience tended to be recalled all too frequently.

A study of reports of ritual child abuse uncovered during therapy contacted

6,000 practising American clinicians. Of the 2,700 who responded, 30 per cent reported dealing with at least one case where ritual abuse was claimed. Of this group, over 90 per cent believed that physical harm had been done and that their clients had indeed experienced the ritualistic aspects they reported. In a smaller study carried out by Loftus, 80 per cent of clinicians expressed a belief in the authenticity of such reports, with comments such as 'If a woman said it happened, it happened', or 'I have no reason not to believe them'. The supporting evidence presented was typically that of symptomatology, poor self-esteem, sexual dysfunction and self-destructive behavior. Many of the clinicians resented the use of the term 'authentic', feeling that it was not the clinician's job to question the authenticity of patients' reports.

Which of these 'memories' is authentic? While the scale and reality of child abuse cannot be ignored, the nature of memory is such that remembered events can be distorted by persistent questioning and suggestion.

At one level such a non-judgemental approach is admirable; the therapist's first job is surely to help the patient. However, when it comes to instituting legal proceedings, the validity of the original claim becomes of paramount importance. The damages awarded by courts in such cases can be substantial. A recent case in Los Angeles resulted in the jury awarding $500,000 to a 39-year-old woman who sued her father. A Michigan judge assessed damages of over 1 million dollars in a case where an adult daughter sued her father, itemizing them as follows: past counseling and hospitalization — $18,600; future damages (counseling 7 years) — $165,000; future damages (hospitalization) — $30,000; past bodily injury (pain, suffering) — $67,500; fright, shock — $268,500; humiliation — $250,000; future mental distress damages — $97,222.22; lost earnings and earning capacity — $252,065.18. Since the father had no insurance, no money, and was not even represented by counsel, this represented a pyrrhic victory but to the daughter the judgement represented some form of 'emotional justice'.

Even when child abuse is not enmeshed in the more rapacious aspects of the American legal system, accusations of child abuse can be sufficiently damaging to those concerned to suggest that they should not be automatically regarded as true. Loftus reports receiving letters from parents who have been accused by their children. Here is an excerpt from one such letter, from a mother in California: 'One week before my husband died after an eight-month battle against lung cancer, our youngest daughter (aged 38) confronted me with the accusation that he had molested her and I had not protected her. We knew who her "therapist" was: a strange young woman . . . In the weeks, months that followed, the nature of the charges altered, eventually involving the accusation that my husband and I had molested our grandson, for whom we sometimes cared while our daughter worked at her painting. This has broken my heart: it is so utterly untrue. The daughter has broken off all relationship with her four siblings. She came greatly under the influence of a book, *The Courage to Heal*.'

The Courage to Heal presents itself as a guide for women survivors of child sexual abuse, taking a very strong line on evidence: 'If you are unable to remember any specific instance . . . but still have a feeling that something abusive happened to you, it probably did' (page 21) and 'So far no one we've talked to thought she might have been abused, and then after discovered that she hadn't been . . . If you think you were abused and your life shows the symptoms, then you were' (page 22). The 'symptoms' referred to are low self-esteem, suicidal or self-destructive thoughts, depression and sexual dysfunction.

This tendency to suggest very strongly to the patient that sexual abuse might have occurred if memories are missing or hazy also features in a number of complaints about therapists. In one case, for example, an attorney went to a therapist to try and deal with his feelings about his father's suicide. He became increasingly depressed at the lack of progress, while his therapist kept saying that there was something else. When he proved unable to find this something else, the therapist amazed him by saying: 'I don't know how to tell you this, but you display the same kinds of characteristics of some of my patients who are victims of satanic ritualistic abuse.' The attorney denies saying anything that might reasonably have justified such a conclusion.

Satanism and claims of ritual abuse are a strange feature of many claims of child abuse. Although there is considerable evidence that child abuse itself exists, the evidence for satanic rites appears to melt away whenever it is thoroughly investigated. In one case, for example, the child of an alcoholic and violent father was treated for depression by a Catholic psychiatrist. After months of treatment involving hypnosis, the girl began to have 'memories' of being imprisoned by her mother and of seeing a band of satanists when she was five. The memories included bizarre ceremonies featuring black candles, goblets, dismembered bodies and sexual abuse; she was endlessly imprisoned in snake-infested cages and dismembered baby limbs were rubbed on her. She even developed physical symptoms, a rash on her neck that supposedly developed when Satan wrapped his tail around her. Her therapist believed her, and indeed subsequently married her and co-authored her published story, but there appears to be no concrete evidence to corroborate the authenticity of her story or her memories.

Woodcut from a compendium of witchcraft published in Milan in 1626. Claims of child abuse as part of satanic rituals may owe more to manufactured 'memories' than to fact.

It is of course very difficult to evaluate claims that refer to events that occurred many years before. Alleged memories produced over many hours of therapy may well involve strong suggestion. There are, however, a few cases in which remembered events have been recorded in a way that allows more objective evaluation. In 1988 Paul Ingram, who held a high position in the Sheriff's office and was Chairman of the County Republican Committee, was arrested for child abuse in Olympia, Washington, at a time when rumors of satanic ritualistic abuse were common in the media. The police, aided by a psychologist, interrogated Ingram for many hours, suggesting acts of abuse such as the raping of his daughter. Ingram eventually admitted that he had abused his daughter and that he was also a member of a satanic cult. The prosecution brought in a professor of sociology from the University of California at Berkeley, Richard Ofshe, to help them find out more. In order to test the truth of Ingram's confessions Ofshe invented an incident in which he said that two of Ingram's children, a son and daughter, had been forced to have sex in front of him. After initially reporting no memory of such an incident, Ingram reported recalling vague pictures of such a scene. Over the next day Ingram prayed for the scene to be revealed to him and shortly afterwards it was, at which point he wrote a three-page detailed account of it.

In the same case the son of the accused was interviewed, again by the psychologist with the help of a detective. In the recorded interview the son reported on his dreams:

Son   I've had dreams of uh little people . . . short people coming and walking on me . . . walking on my bed.

Psychologist What you saw was real.

Son   Well, this is a different dream . . . every time a train came by, a whistle would blow and . . . which would come in my window . . . I would wake up, but I couldn't move. It was like blankets were tucked under and . . . I couldn't move my arms.

Psychologist You were being restrained?

| **Son** | Right, and there was some-
body on top of me. |
| **Psychologist** | [Son's name], these things
happened to you. It's real,
not an hallucination. |

Sure enough, before long the son 'remem-bered' witches holding him down and joining his father in abuse.

As we shall see in the chapter on eyewit-ness testimony, there is ample evidence that memories can be introduced and manipulated with far less extreme methods than those just described. As we saw earlier, evidence for re-pression itself is far from solid; we know far too little about it to uncritically accept the authen-ticity of many reported experiences. Even under ideal conditions, we can be mistaken about the 'reality' of our memories. Strength of convic-tion is certainly not a good guide to reliability or reality. To decide on the authenticity of a recollection we have to find some way of separating reality from dreams, delusions and confabulations.

There is no doubt that cases of child abuse do occur, and it seems probable that the memory of these is sometimes repressed. The evidence we have dis-cussed, however, suggests that there is a real danger of therapists 'suggesting' childhood traumas to patients, possibly as a way of explaining patterns of symptoms that might equally plausibly result from other causes. If such misdiag-noses do indeed occur, then they may well lead to endless and fruitless series of therapy sessions, draining patients financially and emotionally, and possibly establishing false beliefs which may be more destructive than the original symp-toms. If false accusations of child abuse are made, the effect on the patient's family can be devastating and the patient's distress may be amplified many times.

Finally, there is the more general point that one can cry 'Wolf!' too often. If accusations are repeatedly proved to be false, there is a real danger that those who have genuinely been abused will cease to be believed. The very real problem of child abuse will once again be denied by society, as it was for so many years.

What then should the therapist do? It is important to recognize that our capacity for distinguishing genuine repressed memories from inventions or confabulations is at present extremely limited, particularly where therapeutic suggestion is involved. The therapist should probe with care and circumspection, bearing in mind the point made by Loftus, that zealous conviction is a dangerous substitute for an open mind.

John Dean testifying during the Watergate hearings in 1973. He 'remembered' conversations with President Nixon in such detail that he became known as 'the man with the tape recorder memory'. But his testimony turned out to be inaccurate. Did the pressure of a public hearing cause him to embroider facts only half remembered?

Chapter

8 Storing knowledge

W hat is the capital of Italy? How many months are there in a year? Who is the current President of the United States? Do rats have wings? What is the chemical formula for water? Is *umplitude* an English word? What does a seismologist do? Is New York south of Washington?

I'm sure you found all those questions relatively easy to answer, and answered them very rapidly. It would not be too difficult to fill the whole of this book with such questions — all of us possess an enormous store of general knowledge which we take for granted. The division of memory that stores all this information is generally referred to as semantic memory.

All of us have an extensive semantic memory. If you were to stop the first woman you saw and tested her vocabulary, you would discover that she knew the meaning of anywhere between 20,000 and 100,000 words. She might also know a foreign language. She would certainly know a great deal, in geographical terms, about her own neighborhood and about the wider world. Because she has learnt to drive a car, make telephone calls, use credit cards and so on, she functions well in her environment. She also has a great deal of specialist knowledge acquired in connection with work, hobbies and pastimes. In addition, she has the usual interesting but non-vital mental baggage, much of it media-related, that most of us carry around in our heads — facts and images to do with politics and sport, films and music, TV programs and advertising. It is not until one starts to think about designing a store of similar capacity, accessible with similar speed and accuracy, that one realizes what a phenomenal memory system we possess.

Hieroglyphics from a pyramid at Saqara, Egypt. If you knew that these pictograms represented an inventory of weapons or the story of a hunting expedition you would be much better equipped to translate them than if you knew nothing at all about their context. Inference plays a large part in semantic memory.

If one had a computer with a very large store, and keyed in all the necessary information, would it do the job that human memory does? To find a piece of information one would simply scan the store until the answer appeared. But how exactly would the store be scanned? Early computer models used a serial search strategy, systematically examining each potential storage location in turn. Using such a system, if one wished to retrieve the meaning of a word, one would have to go through all the words in one's brain serially until one came up with the right word. Suppose one had a rather small vocabulary, a mere 20,000 words. With a serial search system the understanding of each word would require the searching of an average 10,000 memory locations, which would be extremely laborious. Understanding fluent speech requires the sort of speed of search that is well beyond current computer science.

Clearly the human memory system does not operate by scanning all possible memory locations. It takes advantage of the fact that language is predictable, first at the level of the individual word, where 'the' is almost always followed by an adjective or a noun, secondly in terms of meaning, where a sentence such as 'The boy was bitten by the . . .' allows one to narrow down the range of things that might plausibly have bitten the boy, and thirdly in terms of our general knowledge of the world. This knowledge is structured, just as the world itself is structured and organized. In general, the more we know the more complete our organization of that knowledge will be, and the easier it will be to incorporate new information. The expert chess players we discussed in Chapter 5 found it easy to take in information about a new chess position because they could map it onto an already existing knowledge of chess that was rich and flexible.

An interesting example of expert chess memory occurred in a study carried out by myself and colleagues. We were investigating memory for chess positions, and using positions from actual games. Although we avoided classic games, one of our subjects, a chess journalist, was not only able to identify one of the positions as coming from a specific game between Kasparov and Karpov, but also pointed out that we had introduced a slight modification.

At a simpler level, an avid bridge player is likely to have a much more complex and rich perception of the strengths and weaknesses of a given hand, and because of this is likely to be much better than a novice player at remembering it after the game.

Storing simple concepts

Before you read this section, test yourself on the questions below and opposite, noting how long it takes you to answer each set of questions.

Set 1

Name a fruit BEGINNING with the letter p	_____
Name an animal „ „ „ „ d	_____
Name a metal „ „ „ „ i	_____
Name a bird „ „ „ „ b	_____
Name a country „ „ „ „ F	_____
Name a boy's name „ „ „ „ H	_____
Name a girl's name „ „ „ „ M	_____
Name a vegetable „ „ „ „ p	_____
Name a weapon „ „ „ „ s	_____
Name a flower „ „ „ „ p	_____
Time taken	_____

You probably found it much quicker to answer Set 1 than Set 2. What does this imply? Simply that the initial letter of a word is a much more effective cue than the terminal letter. This in turn tells us something about the way in which

Set 2

Name a fruit ENDING with the letter	h	_____
Name an animal " " " "	w	_____
Name a metal " " " "	r	_____
Name a bird " " " "	n	_____
Name a country " " " "	y	_____
Name a boy's name " " " "	D	_____
Name a girl's name " " " "	N	_____
Name a vegetable " " " "	t	_____
Name a weapon " " " "	w	_____
Name a flower " " " "	t	_____

Time taken _____

names are stored, since there is no logical reason why the above should be the case; logically, one could design a system where items were retrievable either by the first, last, second, fourth, or any other letter.

Elizabeth Loftus and her colleagues have carried out a number of experiments exploring the task of coming up with particular words, given a category and a first letter as cues. She found that giving the category (*fruit*, for example) first and the initial letter afterwards led to faster responses than the reverse. It seems easier to activate the category *fruit* in preparation for searching for the appropriate

An engraving of the library at the University of Leyden, as it looked in 1630. Categorization is crucial in a library. Without subject categories, access to specific pieces of information becomes a very tedious business.

initial letter than all words beginning with, say, *p*. This is probably because the category *fruit* is a reasonably coherent and manageable one, whereas words beginning with *p* represent far too large and diffuse a category to be useful. Evidence of this comes from a study in which the category used was *type of psychologist* and the initial letter that of the psychologist's surname. Hence a typical question might be 'Give me a developmental psychologist whose name begins with *P*' (Piaget) versus 'initial letter *P* — a developmental psychologist'. Students who were just beginning to specialize in psychology showed no difference between the two orders of presentation, but those who had already specialized were faster when the category was given first. Presumably they had already developed categories such as 'developmental psychologist', whereas the novices simply searched all 'psychologists', not having sufficiently developed their categories to operate otherwise.

Inference in semantic memory

Did Aristotle have feet? Was George Washington at the Battle of Hastings? What is Beethoven's telephone number? A support system that merely recorded and accessed information previously presented would be likely to answer 'Don't know' to all three questions. It is highly unlikely that you have ever specifically been told that Aristotle had feet, but nevertheless it seems a reasonable assumption that he did. A lack of feet is something one would almost certainly have known about, so one can infer that Aristotle had feet and respond 'Yes'. In the case of the George Washington question, while there were large numbers of people at the Battle of Hastings whose names we do not know, the fact that George Washington lived several hundred years later allows us to conclude reasonably confidently that he was not present. In the case of Beethoven's telephone number, a simple computer memory would search diligently through lists of telephone numbers and come up with the information that Beethoven does not possess a telephone or is perhaps a recent subscriber whose number has not yet been added to the directory. Once again, knowledge of the approximate date when Beethoven died and the probable date when the telephone was invented allows one to come to the conclusion that he did not possess a telephone and hence had no telephone number.

Psychologists began studying the process of accessing knowledge in the last century, then neglected the topic for virtually 70 years. Interest revived when attempts were made to produce computer memory systems with some of the richness and flexibility of human memory. One of the most influential of these was a computer program devised by Ross Quillian called *The Teachable Language Comprehender*. At the heart of this program is a system for representing and accessing knowledge. Knowledge is stored in terms of a network of interrelated concepts; more specifically, the relationship is hierarchical, with particular instances being linked together at a more abstract level. This system is best demonstrated if you look at the diagram opposite, which shows a sample of part of a network of this kind. Take the concept *canary*; this is linked to the more abstract concept of *bird,* which in turn is linked to the concept of *animal.* Attached to each concept are a number of attributes, hence *canary* is associated with its characteristic color, yellow, the fact that it can sing, and so on. This model has a further interesting feature, namely that it economizes on the amount of information directly stored by only storing at the level of *canary* information that is not characteristic of all birds, and only storing at the level of *birds* information which is not characteristic of *animals.* In order to decide that a canary can fly,

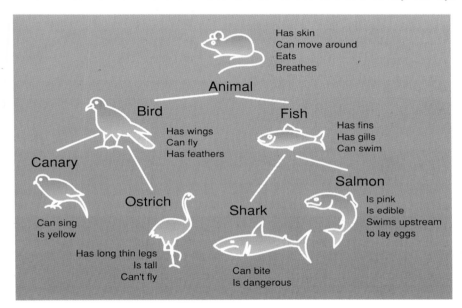

the program uses a process of inference, moving from the fact that a canary is a bird to the fact that birds can fly. A statement such as 'Canaries have skin' involves a further inference from 'A canary is a bird' to 'A bird is an animal' to 'Animals have skin'. On the basis of the model, Ross Quillian and psychologist Alan Collins predicted that it would take longer to verify sentences that involved moving further through the network than those that could be verified more directly. Hence verifying 'A canary is yellow' should take less time than deciding on the truth of the statement 'A canary breathes'. When volunteers were asked to verify such simple sentences, this proved to be so.

In order to get a feeling for this task try the examples overleaf, checking 'Yes' or 'No' to each statement. These are not the specific examples used by Quillian and Collins, but were devised by Neil Thomson and myself in order to look at the effect of various stresses on trying to access semantic memory. You may not be too surprised to learn that alcohol slows down the rate at which such sentences can be verified.

While Quillian and Collins obtained results which supported their view, other interpretations are of course possible. One might, for example, argue that

	Yes	No
Pork chops can be bought in shops.	___	___
Jamaica is edible.	___	___
Oranges drill teeth.	___	___
California is a state of America	___	___
London is a place.	___	___
Potatoes move around searching for food.	___	___
Drills are scientists.	___	___
Aunts are relatives.	___	___
Spaghetti is a dish.	___	___
Corporals can be bought in shops.	___	___
Beer is a liquid.	___	___
Gin is sold by butchers.	___	___
Fish and chips are an alcoholic drink.	___	___
Peas are edible.	___	___
Antarctica tends the sick.	___	___
Beefsteaks are people.	___	___
Chairs are furniture.	___	___
Priests wear clothes.	___	___
Flies carry disease.	___	___
Mayors are elected representatives.	___	___
Asia has high mountains.	___	___
Paris is a living creature.	___	___
Rattlesnakes move around searching for food.	___	___
Bees treat the mentally ill.	___	___
Knives are manufactured goods.	___	___
Trout have fins.	___	___
Squirrels are fish.	___	___
Lions are four-legged animals	___	___
Sharks have wheels.	___	___

yellowness is something that you specifically store about canaries, since it is one of their dominant features, whereas the possession of skin and a tendency to breathe is not something particularly characteristic of them.

Consider the following statements: 'A canary is a bird' and 'A penguin is a bird'. On the Quillian and Collins model both should take an equal amount of time to verify since they simply involve moving from *canary* or *penguin* to the level above, namely *bird*, but in actual fact it takes longer to decide that a penguin is a bird than that a canary is a bird. Why? It has been suggested that a concept like 'bird' is not a simple label attached to all instances of bird. Rather, it comprises a set of characteristics which birds tend to possess, but which are not possessed to the same extent by all birds. This was tested by Eleanor Rosch, who produced a series of sentences containing the word 'bird', such as 'Birds eat worms', 'I heard a bird singing', 'I watched a bird fly over the house', 'The bird was perching on the twig'. Now try replacing the word *bird* in each case by the following: *robin, eagle, ostrich, penguin*. It will be obvious that whereas *robin* fits all the sentences, *eagle*, *ostrich* and *penguin* fit progressively less well; in short, penguins and ostriches are less typical of birds than eagles, which in turn are less typical than robins. If you ask people to name as many birds as they can in a limited period of time, they tend to produce typical birds such as robins and blackbirds rather than atypical birds such as ostriches and penguins, even though they are in no doubt that all are birds. Similarly, if asked to verify a sentence such as 'An ostrich is a bird', they take reliably longer to do so than if asked to decide that 'A robin is a bird'.

What does this tell us about the structure of our knowledge system? It implies that the concepts we use do not comprise rigidly defined categories, but are much more loosely determined. This point was made by the philosopher Wittgenstein using the category *games*. What are the defining characteristics of a game? What, for example, do rugby, poker, tennis and chess have in common? It is very difficult to think of a single set of features shared by all games. Wittgenstein suggests that members of the category *games* (and other categories for that matter) are like members of a family who have certain characteristics which they tend to share; some members of the family may have several characteristics, while others may have only one or two, and often not the same one or two.

Sometimes an item falls on a category boundary. Is *tomato* a *fruit* or a *vegetable*? The conflict here comes from general appearance and manner of growth on the one hand, and the fact that tomatoes tend to be savory on the other, whereas most fruits are sweet. Another example is *dolphin*, which has the appearance of a *fish*, but which we have to learn specifically is a *mammal* in order to exclude it from the category *fish*. The particular boundary we draw around a category can vary with context. For example, in colloquial conversation we might refer to a spider as an insect, although we know that it is an arachnid and has too many legs to be an insect.

A given concept may have quite different boundaries in different situations. The term 'repression' suggests one set of meanings in a discussion of psychoanalysis and a different set in a discussion of dictatorship; although the two sets of meanings have a common origin, their contextual meaning is substantially different. Communication in such situations depends crucially on shared assumptions about concepts.

John Bransford describes an informal experiment in which experimenter E walked into the office of a colleague C and said simply, 'Bill has a red car'. Here is his description of C's reactions: 'He looked very surprised, paused for about three seconds, and finally exclaimed "What the h— are you talking about?" After a hasty de-briefing session C laughed and told E what had gone on in his head. First he thought that E was talking about a person named Bill that C knew. Then C realized that E could not in all probability know that person; and besides Bill would never buy a red car. Then C thought that E may have mixed up the name and really meant to say J (a mutual friend of C and E). C knew that J had ordered a new car, but he was surprised that it was red and that it had arrived so soon. C also entertained a few additional hypotheses — all within about three seconds. After that he gave up, thereupon uttering "What the h— are you talking about?" '

Schemata

The common ground necessary for understanding extends well beyond merely having the same interpretation of simple concepts. Consider the following passage taken from a study by Bransford and Johnson: 'The procedure is actually quite simple. First you arrange items into different groups. Of course one pile might be sufficient depending on how much there is to do. If you have to go somewhere else due to lack of facilities, that is the next step; otherwise, you are pretty well set. It is important not to overdo things. That is, it is better to do too few things at once than too many. In the short run this may not seem important but complications can easily arise. A mistake can be expensive as well. At first the whole procedure will seem complicated. Soon, however, it will become just another facet of life. It is difficult to foresee any end to the necessity for this task in the immediate future, but then one never can tell. After the procedure is completed one arranges the material into different groups again. They then can be put into their appropriate places. Eventually they will be used once more and the whole cycle will then have to be repeated. However, that is part of life.'

For one person to use a map to explain a route to another, both must share certain concepts. In this situation, knowing where you are is analogous to knowing the context of a story or conversation. Unless you know where you are, a map is of little use.

Asked to rate the comprehensibility of this passage on a scale ranging from 1 to 5, Bransford and Johnson's students rated it as pretty incomprehensible, with a mean comprehensibility of 2.29. As might be expected, when asked to recall it they performed rather poorly, scoring only 2.82 out of a possible 18 ideas. A second group, *after* reading it but *before* they recalled it, was told that the topic was washing clothes. This did nothing to enhance either the comprehensibility of the passage or the amount recalled. A third group, however, was told what the topic was *before they began reading*; their comprehension ratings averaged 4.5 out of 5 and they recalled over twice as many ideas. Try it yourself, bearing in mind that it is about washing clothes.

The problem in comprehending the description stemmed not from the writer and readers having different concepts, but from the fact that the readers were not keyed in to the appropriate situation. Once they were aware of the correct semantic context, the passage immediately made sense. A number of years ago the British psychologist David Bruce showed very similar effects in a task that simply involved listening to and repeating sentences spoken against a noisy background. Bruce showed that giving subjects the context made it much more likely that they would hear the sentence properly. If, for example, subjects were told 'sport', they were much more likely to correctly report a sentence such as 'Our center forward scored the winning goal'.

Cues of this kind give access to a whole complex of knowledge about a particular topic. Sir Frederick Bartlett used the term *schemata* to refer to such knowledge structures. Later theorists have either adopted Bartlett's terminology or occasionally devised their own, as in the case of *frames* or *scripts*. Both of these are essentially schema concepts developed by computer scientists attempting to produce computer programs that simulate comprehension of text.

A test for your restaurant script? When we move from one country to another, or even from one restaurant to another, the script subtly changes.

Scripts

Essentially a script is an integrated package of information that can be brought to bear on the interpretation or understanding of a given event. For example, a story involving a restaurant brings into operation a 'restaurant' script which involves all the information the comprehender already has about restaurants: that one normally sits at a table with others, that the food is cooked and then brought to the table by a waiter, that the waiter gets the food from a kitchen and expects to be paid and tipped, and so forth. This is the sort of information that is brought to bear in a statement such as 'Luigi's is a nice restaurant, but the waiters are slow'. If it were spelled out fully, it would involve statements to the effect that food is delivered by waiters, that one cannot order a meal until the waiter comes, that a second course is not served until the first has been cleared away, and that the speed with which all these operations proceed is variable. In contrast, a statement like 'Luigi's is a good gym but the waiters are slow' is baffling, because the 'gym' script and the 'waiters' script simply do not mesh; one can only make sense of the statement by assuming either that 'gym' is the name of a restaurant or that 'waiters' refers to some role analogous to but different from that of a waiter in a restaurant, perhaps involving handing out locker keys or equipment. The programs developed by Schank, the originator of the 'script'

concept, have information about the relevant scripts built into them, and are therefore able to go beyond the information explicitly given in the text and make inferences on the basis of previous knowledge. In this respect they resemble human comprehension.

Schank has produced a number of impressive demonstrations of the phenomenon of inference, but in doing so he raises the problem of exactly what should and should not be included in a script. Should a 'waiter' script include the fact that waiters normally wear socks? Presumably not, since most men, in Western countries at least, wear socks. If it did, would it contain information about what socks looked and felt like, and that in the case of a waiter they were more likely to be black than red? Such information is likely to be potentially available to the human reader, but is of course unlikely to be specified or utilized unless necessary. Similarly, the type of information specified in a Schank script is rarely explicitly used by a human. Take, for example, the following sentence: 'John went to New York by bus'. This is interpreted by Schank's program as 'John went to a bus stop. He waited at it a few minutes. He entered a bus. The driver got the ticket from John. He went to a seat. He sat down in it. The driver took John to New York. John got off the bus.'

It is certainly not necessarily the case that John sat down rather than stood. In fact he might have stood during his journey rather than sat down, or he might have caught a bus immediately or had a long wait. The script could presumably specify that John waited for the bus door to open before entering, or that he waited for the bus to stop before he got off.

Schank therefore went on to develop and elaborate his earlier ideas, suggesting that the memory structures involved in storing semantic knowledge are much more dynamic and interactive than his earlier concept of scripts. Furthermore, any given script is likely to have a number of elements that are common to many other scripts; these common elements he referred to as MOPs, short for Memory Organization Packets. Hence a particular bus trip might be encoded using a range of MOPs, including those concerned with travelling, weather conditions, general politeness to strangers and modes of interaction with officials. Anything that is not standard will be encoded separately, and these pointers provide the mechanism for *reminding*, a process whereby one person can attempt to convey to another the particular episode he or she had in mind: 'You remember! The time you almost forgot your umbrella on the bus, and the conductor got cross when you got back on the bus to retrieve it.'

Schank's system also incorporates higher level concepts which he terms TOPs, Thematic Organization Points. These refer to broader categories such as occasions in which family values take priority or occasions when one fails to achieve a goal. Schank's modified approach certainly seems to provide a more plausible representation of social knowledge and in a form that can be encoded within a computer program. To what extent such a model will generate empirically verifiable *new* information about the way in which human memory stores and acquires information remains to be seen.

The nature of semantic memory: words, images or propositions?

Thus far we have discussed the semantic memory system without saying anything about its constituent units It is, for example, easy to slip into the assumption that semantic memory is concerned with associations between words. In fact semantic memory is more concerned with *concepts* or *ideas,* which are in some cases clearly related to words but are not in themselves words. Semantics has been studied primarily by linguists and psycholinguists, whose goal has been to explore meaning in relation to language. Perhaps the most extreme view of the relationship of language to meaning is that put forward by linguist Benjamin Lee Whorf. He argues that language is not simply a way of expressing one's view of the world, but that language actually determines that view: 'We dissect nature along lines laid down by our native language. The categories and types that we isolate from the world of phenomena we do not find there because they stare every observer in the face; on the contrary the world is presented in a kaleidoscopic flux of impressions which has to be organized in our minds — and this means largely by the linguistic system in our minds.' This view of language is known as the *linguistic relativity hypothesis.*

Whorf argues that people who speak different languages will and do remember the world differently. He supports his view by offering examples of the difficulty of translating languages of very different cultures. One example he gives is from the Apache language, in which the English sentence 'It is a dripping spring' translates into 'As water, or springs, whiteness moves downward'. Eskimo languages have a large number of adjectives describing different snow conditions,

Of necessity an Inuit hunter has a subtle and detailed appreciation of ice and snow. A Bushman would perceive worlds of subtlety in sand and rock. Do our perceptions of things precede the words we invent to describe them, or do words preprogram our perceptions?

and there is little doubt that an Eskimo's perception of these differences would be greatly superior to that of someone from the Mediterranean. However, there is a chicken and egg problem here; while Whorf would argue that language structures the Eskimo's world, one could equally well argue that the Eskimo's language develops as a result of his different perception of the world. How can one test the validity of these two views? One way might be to show that different environments give rise to different perceptual capacities in non-verbal animals. One might predict, for example, that polar bears would be better at discriminating between different types of snow than Indian honeybears would! However, while such an experiment might present an interesting challenge to the comparative psychologist, it would be extremely difficult to carry out and to interpret. Fortunately there are other ways of tackling the question.

Many years ago two American psychologists, Roger Brown and Eric Lenneberg, showed that certain colors appear to be particularly easy to name and remember. Such 'focal' colors tend to be named very consistently, with many subjects giving the same name. The names given to these colors tended to be short, such as *red* and *green*; less focal colors such as vermilion and turquoise tend to have longer names. Initially these findings were interpreted along the lines of the Whorfian hypothesis, that colors which correspond to good verbal labels are easily perceived and well remembered. However, Eleanor Rosch has pointed out that the alternative interpretation, that language follows perception, is equally plausible. She also came up with convincing evidence for this view by testing a group of speakers of Dani, a language spoken until recently by a Stone Age people living in New Guinea. Dani has the interesting

Dani tribesmen prepare for a war ceremony. A lack of words to describe different colors does not mean that colors are not properly perceived.

characteristic of containing only two color terms, roughly corresponding to *dark* and *light*. Rosch argued that if Whorf were correct, Dani speakers should not show the normal tendency for focal colors to be consistently recognized and easily learned. She found that although the overall level of performance of Dani speakers was lower than that of American subjects, they nevertheless showed exactly the same tendency to find focal colors easy to discriminate between and to remember. Despite having no labels for red, green and yellow, the Dani found them easy colors to handle, suggesting that language is based on perception, not the reverse.

A less extreme linguistic argument suggests that, although the semantic system might initially be based on and driven by our perception of the world, it encodes that information in terms of a linguistic system. This cannot be true of all semantic information of course, since much of it is beyond our capacity to express in words. The particular color of a sunset, the taste of a particular wine, or the sound of a well played violin all represent much more than can be conveyed in words, which will not be fully understood unless one has experienced exactly those sensations in the first place.

In the case of language comprehension, it is clear that we interpret words within a general context of real-world knowledge. For example, a sentence such as 'The ham sandwich was eaten by the soup' might appear to be absurd, since soup is not animate and therefore should not be capable of eating. It is entirely interpretable, however, if you are a waiter; waiters sometimes use an order to label the person who has placed that order. Consider the statement 'A is on B's right; B is on C's right, therefore A is on C's right.' This would be true if A, B and C were seated down one side of a rectangular table, but it would not be true if they were seated around a circular table. In short, words need to be interpreted in the context of our real-world knowledge, which in turn is likely to be based on information that goes well beyond the meanings of individual words.

A semantic memory system that was only concerned with links between words would be locked into what Johnson-Laird has called the *symbolic fallacy*. He illustrates this by the imaginary example of aliens in space who are trying to work out the meaning of the languages of earth by listening to radio transmissions. Without being able to observe the link between words and the objects and events to which they refer, the aliens would have little chance of understanding the languages of earth.

One type of knowledge that is hard to represent adequately in words is spatial knowledge. Take knowledge of the shapes of countries, for example. This was investigated by Ian Moar using a technique he calls *mental triangulation*, based on the way in which surveyors construct maps. He gave each of his subjects a piece of paper with a vertical line marked North and a dot at the bottom of the line as a starting point, and asked them to draw lines representing the direction between pairs of British cities — London and Edinburgh, Edinburgh and Birmingham, Birmingham and London, and so on. By averaging out the directions of the various lines he was able to construct maps of his subjects' spatial concepts about Britain. Below are the composite maps produced by two of his groups, Cambridge housewives and Glasgow housewives. No prizes for guessing which group produced which map! The Glasgow group tended to exaggerate the size of Scotland and the Cambridge group did the same with England. Britain is roughly a triangle with a base that deviates quite a few degrees from the horizontal, but both groups 'straightened up' the triangle.

It is extrememly difficult to argue that spatial concepts are represented in memory in purely verbal form, and even more difficult to defend a purely verbal interpretation of our memory for faces, tastes, sounds, smells and so on. However, it is much easier to defend a linguistic interpretation of the types of semantic category we were discussing earlier in the chapter. However, are such categories as *fruit*, *carpenters' tools* and *birds* basically language categories, or are they categories which happen to have a linguistic label?

The first map here shows the correct relationship between all the towns shown. The map in the center, produced by the Cambridge group, exaggerates distances in the south of England, while the map on the far right, produced by the Glasgow group, shrinks everything south of Carlisle (Moar, 1978).

One experiment by Potter and Faulconer required student subjects either to name or categorize *pictures* of common objects or to read or categorize their *printed names*. They observed that their subjects were able to categorize a picture of a dog as an *animal* or a picture of a saw as a *carpenter's tool* just as rapidly as they could categorize their names, and *more* rapidly than they could produce the name when shown the picture. If one has to name a picture before it can be categorized, then categorization should always take longer than naming.

Is it possible then that semantic concepts are stored as images? There is no doubt that visual or spatial characteristics can be important. For example, one might have a concept of *round things* or *red things*, but it is much less easy to argue that a concept such as *justice* or *guilt* is primarily stored in terms of its visual characteristics. Of course one can come up with visual images that might in some sense represent *justice*, but such images would be of very little assistance in

Visual material can be coded verbally as well as visually. That is why the drawings below are more easily remembered than the corresponding word list (torch, bear, mousetrap, bath and so on). Dual coding increases one's chances of remembering. It also helps to explain why words which conjure up strong images are more memorable than abstract words.

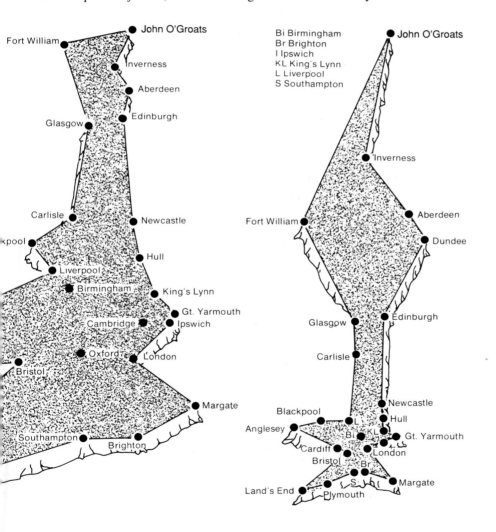

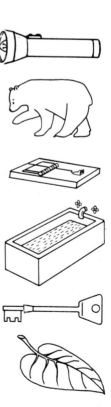

deciding whether justice had been done in a particular court judgement. The most plausible assumption is probably that concepts are stored in some abstract code which may be translated into a verbal or linguistic form or into an image when the need arises, just as information stored in a computer may, given the appropriate commands and peripheral equipment, be output as an image on the screen, as hard copy on a printer, as codes on a floppy disk, or as sounds over the telephone. In each case the information stored is the same, but the mode of display is different.

People vary enormously in the extent to which they claim to have vivid visual imagery. This is very rarely, if at all, reflected in what they actually recall, although, as Bartlett pointed out, people who use visual imagery may be more confident about their recall abilities than those who use verbal strategies. The reason for this lack of difference is presumably that what is recalled is determined by what is stored, not by the preferred method of display. Visual imagers may be using the equivalent of a screen and the verbalizers the equivalent of a printer, but since both draw on a single abstract store, the accuracy of what they recall will not differ.

Rubbish in, rubbish out? It seems reasonable to assume that information in semantic memory can be displayed in a variety of ways, just as data on computer can be output in a variety of forms. Different methods of display do not necessarily imply different methods of storage.

Learning new concepts

So far we have been concerned entirely with how existing knowledge is stored and accessed, but have said nothing about the crucial question of how new concepts are formed. Since this is the question that lies at the heart of all education, it is obviously a very important one, and yet it is very poorly understood. Much of the psychology of education has been concerned with episodic memory (recalling experiences) rather than semantic memory (the development of knowledge) and even now this is only gradually beginning to change.

The problem of concept formation has been of interest to psychologists for many years, but in the past the emphasis has been on identifying concepts rather than acquiring new ones. In a concept identification study the experimenter usually selects, on a somewhat arbitrary basis, a particular combination of features and asks the subject to work out what the combination is. Experiments carried out by Heidbreder in the mid-1940s are a good example of this approach. Heidbreder's subjects had to attach nonsense names, such as *RELK, FARD* and *LING*, to various categories of objects.

It can be argued that formation of concepts of this kind is analogous to the task confronting a child who is trying to learn a language or to understand the world. What sort of results have emerged from such studies? As might be expected, concrete concepts such as *building, animal,* and *face* seem easier to learn than more abstract concepts such as *twoness* or *roundness.* A concept based on an obvious characteristic, such as size or color, is more quickly acquired than one based on less obvious features, such as orientation on the page. Where two features are involved, conjunctive rules, whereby the concept demands both features (for instance, green *and* square), are easier to apply than disjunctive rules, where the target need only be green *or* square.

There is an extensive literature on concept identification, often associated with relatively complex models which attempt to predict how people will perform on such tasks. I myself remain to be convinced that concept identification tasks bear very much relation to the process whereby children learn about the world or their language. Although such tasks are occasionally of practical value, for example in deciding whether a brain-damaged patient has suffered frontal lobe lesions, I think they tell us very little about the way in which our extensive and rich store of knowledge is developed and accessed. A much more promising line of investigation is that developed by John Bransford and his colleagues at Vanderbilt University in Tennessee. This is described in more detail in Bransford's book *Human Cognition,* but some of the flavor of his approach is given by the following example, which comes from the doctoral dissertation of one of his students, K.E. Nitsch. Nitsch set out to teach his subjects a series of concepts which were applicable to social situations. Here are a few examples.

CRINCH   *To make someone angry by performing an inappropriate act*

MINGE   *To gang up on a person or thing*

RELL   *To rescue someone from a dangerous or problematic situation*

Nitsch was interested not only in how well such definitions would be learnt, but in how well they would generalize to new situations. In one experiment he produced six such concepts, and required one group of subjects to learn them so that they could come up with a definition whenever they were given the concept, while a second group was taught by means of examples until they could categorize each example correctly. Both groups were then tested on a series of examples which were entirely new to them. Those who had learnt the definitions did considerably worse than those who had learnt through example.

A second experiment was concerned with the range of examples used during learning. It was explained, for example, that the term *CRINCH* was originally used by waitresses and the term *MINGE* by cowboys. One group was given examples taken entirely from these two contexts, while a second group was given the same information about origin, but a wider range of instances. The definitions and examples are given overleaf.

Group 1 — Consistent context for new word

CRINCH   To make someone angry by performing an inappropriate act; originally used by waitresses. Usage: when a diner fails to leave a tip; when diners argue about the prices on the menu; when a diner deliberately spills ketchup; when diners complain about slow or inefficient service.

MINGE   To gang up on a person or thing; originally used by cowboys and cowhands. Usage: when three or more riders decide to converge on a single animal; when three or more work together to brand an animal; when three or more encircle a wolf or other marauder to prevent its escape; when three or more join forces against a rustler.

Group 2 — Varied context for new word

CRINCH   To make someone angry by performing an inappropriate act; originally used by waitresses. Usage: when a man does not remove his hat on entering a church; when a spectator at a public event blocks the view of those behind; when someone flicks ash over a beautifully polished table; when diners complain about slow waitress service.

MINGE   To gang up on a person or thing; originally used by cowboys and cowhands. Usage: when a band of dissatisfied sailors threaten their captain with mutiny; when an audience boos a mediocre act on stage; when someone is helpless to defend himself against attack; when a group of cowboys join forces against a rustler.

Having mastered the meanings of *CRINCH* and *MINGE* to the point where they were able to apply them accurately, both groups of subjects then moved on to an entirely new set of instances selected from social contexts that were different from any they had previously experienced. The correct application rate of both groups dropped. For Group 1, trained on consistent context examples, it dropped from 89 per cent in the old context to 67 per cent in the new context. But for Group 2, trained on varied context examples, it dropped from 91 to 84 per cent. Clearly the latter were better at generalizing their learning to new situations.

Nitsch's experiment makes the simple but important point that if one wishes to teach concepts that will generalize, then it is important to expose the learner to a wide range of examples. Unfortunately there is a price to be paid for this approach. Nitsch's single-context group found it quite easy to learn the new concepts within four trials, but the varied-context group had much more difficulty and required more training.

In his next experiment, therefore, Nitsch tried out a hybrid training scheme which aimed to obtain the benefits of varied training while avoiding the problems created by being presented with too wide a range of examples. In this study three groups were used, and all were given seven trials. The single-context group was trained entirely on examples drawn from the context in which the concepts were said to have originated, 'restaurant', 'cowboy', and so on. The varied-context group was given examples drawn from several different contexts. The hybrid-context group was trained with examples drawn from the context of origin, followed by three trials with varied contexts. All three groups were then tested on their ability to apply each concept to new social situations. Their performance is shown below.

Correct application of concepts	Old context	New context
Same-context group	90%	69%
Varied-context group	92%	82%
Hybrid-context group	90%	91%

As in the previous study, all groups performed at a level of 90 per cent correct when the initial context was used. As before, subjects trained on a limited context had more difficulty applying the concepts in new situations than those who had had varied training. What of the third group? The hybrid training system appears to have been extremely successful; subjects needed no more training than the same-context group, and transferred even better than the varied-context group. The conclusion is clear: it is easier to acquire new concepts if the range of examples learnt is limited, but if one wishes the information to generalize, then it is important to give broad experience in the training situation itself.

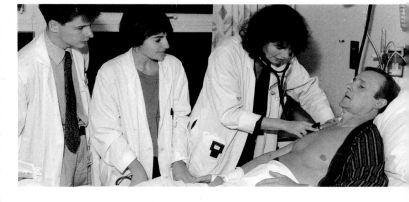

Real patients present junior doctors with varied context samples of dysfunction. Generalizing textbook concepts to real life eventually adds up to that precious commodity, experience.

Most professional training courses attempt something of this kind. A medical student will begin by learning in somewhat oversimplified fashion how the body works. Then he will learn about the effects of various diseases on normal function. During his clinical training he will be exposed to a range of illnesses within each of a number of hospital departments. Within any given department the number of possible illnesses will be constrained, so he will not need to be too worried about neurological factors while he is attached to a consultant gastroenterologist, or about skin diseases during his familiarization with obstetrics. As a junior doctor he will probably have to confront a much wider range of illnesses, and with much less direct supervision. By the time he emerges as, say, a general practitioner, he will have sufficient experience to allow him to bridge the gap between textbook examples of disease and diseases in real people. Real people are seldom textbook cases of anything.

Disorders of semantic memory

In 1888 the neurologist Lissauer described the case of GL, an 80-year-old salesman, who was blown against a fence by a strong wind. Afterwards he felt unwell and complained of visual problems. His visual acuity proved to be normal, as was his capacity to copy drawings. However, his ability to recognize objects was seriously disrupted. On one occasion he mistook pictures on the wall for boxes and attempted to take things out of them; on another he mistook his jacket for his trousers.

Agnosia, as this impairment in recognizing objects is called, can be seen as a disruption of the normal procedures for moving from perception of an object to apprehension of its meaning. The object recognition system can break down at a number of different points, hence there are patients who are able to name objects when they see them but not when they touch them, and other patients who have the opposite problem. There are also patients who show disruption for both vision and touch. One example is JR, a young woman who suffered a severe head injury on being thrown from her horse. This resulted in major problems in recognizing objects. She could not, for example, recognize an onion by sight or touch, but when asked 'What is the vegetable that makes you cry when you peel it?', had no difficulty in producing the correct response. She also had difficulty recalling visual information about named objects, despite obvious evidence that she recognized them. She was well able to describe an eagle as 'a bird of prey', but when questioned indicated that she thought it had four legs and teeth. Over the years her agnosia has gradually improved. Today she is reasonably good at identifying familiar everyday objects, but still has difficulty in identifying model animals, which presumably tend to be visually quite similar, and which are not realistic in terms of size, color or texture.

The organization of semantic memory

The evidence we have presented so far demonstrates the multi-faceted nature of retrieval of information from semantic memory. What do we know about storage of information in semantic memory? It has been known for a some years that patients suffering from aphasia (defects in the comprehension and expression of language) may have particular problems in producing words of certain categories — one patient may have a problem with colors, while another may have particular difficulty in naming foods or body parts. In recent years this phenomenon has been explored in much more detail, in particular by Elizabeth Warrington and her colleagues in London. They describe one patient, JBR, who appears to have great difficulty in understanding words that refer to living things, although he has few problems in dealing with inanimate objects. He can define *torch* as 'hand-held light' and *briefcase* as 'small case used by students to carry papers', but produces very impoverished definitions of plants and living things. For example, his definition of *daffodil* was 'plant' and *ostrich* he simply described as 'unusual'.

Disorders in naming can be quite specific to particular categories. One patient, for example, found it very difficult to name fruits and vegetables but had no trouble identifying animals and buildings.

It is commonly the case that patients who lose the capacity to define words precisely may still be able to produce the appropriate superordinate category name. They know that a deer is an animal or that a rose is a flower, but they may not be able to provide any further information about roses or pick out a picture of a rose from other flowers. This is broadly consistent with the hierarchical models of semantic memory described earlier. Such disruptions of semantic memory are sometimes observed following severe encephalitis. They can also occur in the later stages of Alzheimer's disease, where the breakdown of semantic memory is progressive. Initially deterioration may be specific to concrete rather than abstract concepts, or vice versa, then it tends to become more and more general. On some occasions specific categories may be differentially lost.

The areas of the brain particularly involved in storing information about the meaning of objects are the temporal lobes. Research is still at an early stage, but it seems that different subregions of the temporal lobes may specialize in information regarding shape, taste or associations between these modalities. Specific deficits of the kind just described probably occur because one region has deteriorated more than others. For example, impairment in the region that specializes in visual or tactile information might lead to problems in naming three-dimensional objects. On the other hand deterioration of an area that encodes verbal associations might lead to a deficit in dealing with abstract words and concepts. Differentiating *fruit* and *vegetables* may depend particularly on color and smell, while differentiating one animal from another may depend much more on shape. One day neuropsychologists will undoubtedly provide us with a richer and more adequate basis for psychological theories of semantic memory.

Chapter

9 Retrieval

I would like you to imagine you are a spy and that you are required to commit to memory the following coded message — time yourself, and see how long it takes to log it into your memory.

S E S H S A

R K I W T C

Memory is often likened to a vast library, full of rich information. For the library to be useful, however, the information must be accessible, and this means that it needs to be organized and cataloged. As we saw in Chapter 5, the process of organization is a crucial one, and the reason why it is crucial is that unless information is stored in an orderly and systematic way, it will not be accessible at the appropriate time. An unorganized memory would be just like a library with rooms full of books stored at random. An historian wanting to read about some aspect of the French Revolution might well have to search through thousands of books before finding anything relevant. Such a library would be relatively useless. The mode of organization is also critical. A library might store all books with red covers in one room, books with blue covers in another, yellow covers in another, and so on, but this would scarcely help our historian unless he happened to know that the book he was looking for had a particular color cover.

A more useful classification would be in terms of subject, with the subjects being classified in terms of initial letter. This at least would enable one to look under F for French or under R for Revolution. Suppose, however, I wanted to find Joseph Conrad's novel *Heart of Darkness*. Would I look under H, D or N for novel? Clearly one needs a cross-classification in terms of the author. Suppose I only knew the outline of the plot and that the author was Polish but wrote in English. At that point my only recourse would be to abandon the catalog and talk to the librarian, the human cross-classification system being much richer and more flexible, if less reliable, than most schemes so far devised for libraries.

The subject classifications that exist in human memory are infinitely richer and more flexible than any library or computer categorization system.

Is long-term memory really like a library with the vast amount of information we experience every day neatly coded and tucked away, ready to be brought out at the appropriate moment? Certainly, speaking subjectively, the amount we forget is much more impressive than the amount we remember. As I wrote this passage I could hear a large number of swallows chirping outside my window, and some cars passing on the road at the bottom of the garden. It is hard to believe that every chirp and every car was stored away in my memory. Similarly, as I looked out of the window I could see a field of wheat and behind it a wood. Was every ear of

wheat and every tree going to be stored just in case, at some time, perhaps 20 years hence, I might need that information? It seems highly unlikely. And yet logically we can never prove that all the information has not been stored. Probably it has not. Probably what is stored is some representation of my memory of looking out of my window, together with a representation of a cornfield and a wood based on my general knowledge of cornfields and woods, together with perhaps one or two features that are peculiar to this particular view. And if you take this line, does it not suggest that long-term memory is less like a library, accumulating information steadily through life, than like a scene where new events constantly displace old? Perhaps, when we forget, it is genuinely because the memory trace has been destroyed, not that it has become inaccessible.

However, this view must also be too simple. If all forgetting represents the destruction of the memory trace, then the sum total of our memories must be what we can recall at any given time. There is abundant evidence that this is not so. Obviously we know a great deal more than we can retrieve in any given instance. Although it may not be possible to recall a piece of information at a particular moment, it may be possible to retrieve it given a clue or cue. *Retrieval cues* allow one to locate information which is otherwise inaccessible. Read through the following list of 28 words carefully twice, then take a sheet of paper and, looking away from the list, try to write down as many of the words as you can in any order you wish.

hut, cottage, tent, hotel, cliff, river, hill, volcano, captain, corporal, sergeant, colonel, rose, violet, daffodil, peony, zinc, copper, aluminum, bronze, gin, vodka, rum, whisky, drill, saw, chisel, nail

The 28 words came from the following seven categories: *dwellings, natural features, military ranks, flowers, metals, alcoholic drinks* and *carpenters' tools*. Now write these categories on the back of your answer sheet and see how many words from each you can recall. Now compare the number recalled under the two conditions. Most people find that the category cues enable them to retrieve words previously left out. It is as if the cues direct you to search in the appropriate location in memory, and as such allow access to traces which would otherwise have been missed.

While there is no doubt that both cueing and recognition can reveal information which is not accessible using straightforward unaided recall, it could also be argued that the memory trace is present but not strong enough to allow recall. The cue provides extra information which, together with the weak trace, allows the item to be recalled. In terms of the library analogy, this is tantamount to saying that the problem is not one of locating the book but of recognizing it once it has been located.

Learning to retrieve

An experiment done by the Canadian psychologist Endel Tulving throws a little more light on the process of retrieval. In this experiment the normal procedure for learning lists of words was modified. A typical learning experiment involves presenting subjects with a list of words (36 in all), asking them to recall it, presenting it for a second time, asking for a second recall, and so on, until the list is mastered. Tulving modified this by following each learning trial with three successive attempts at recall. Subjects would read through a list of words, try to recall it, then try to recall it again, and again, and then go on to a second reading of the same list of words. This would be followed by another three recalls and then another presentation of the same words (i.e. learn, recall, recall, recall; learn, recall, recall, recall; learn, recall, recall, recall, and so on).

What effect did this procedure have on performance? Somewhat surprisingly, subjects under this regime learned just as rapidly as those who alternated learning and recall trials. It appears that the process of searching for and retrieving items actually contributes to learning — there seems to be a process of learning to retrieve a specific set of items.

When he looked in detail at the three successive attempts to recall, Tulving noticed that the total number of words retrieved did not differ within each of the three successive recalls; if the subject recalled five words on the first recall, he or she recalled about five on the second, and on the third. This is perhaps unsurprising in the absence of learning trials between recalls. What was surprising was that only about half of the words were recalled consistently on all trials; the rest popped up and disappeared again. Suppose a list contains the words *dog*, *cat* and *canary*; *dog* might be recalled on all three trials, whereas *cat* might be recalled on the first trial, lost on the second (when *canary* might be recalled), but might reappear on the third. Tulving's subjects were clearly not revealing on any given recall trial all that they knew; it was as if they were rummaging about in a box containing the items they had stored, sometimes pulling out one, sometimes another. This effect is not of course limited to newly acquired material. If you wish to observe it in yourself, try writing down the names of as many countries in Africa as you can in three minutes. Then repeat the exercise. You will find that on the second occasion countries that were not included in the first instance pop up, but that some of the previously recalled ones are forgotten.

Is your memory like this, a vast accumulation of fact to be rummaged through on the off-chance?

'On the tip of the tongue'

From a subjective viewpoint perhaps the most convincing evidence that our memory contains information which we cannot access comes from the experience of being asked a question to which we are sure we know the answer, although we cannot produce it at that precise moment; we feel we have it 'on the tip of the tongue'.

A few years ago two Harvard psychologists, Roger Brown and David McNeill, decided to try and see whether this feeling was based on genuine evidence or was simply an illusion. They set up a 'tip of the tongue' situation by reading out a series of definitions of relatively obscure words to their subjects and asking them to name the object being defined. Take for example 'a musical instrument comprising a frame holding a series of tubes struck by hammers'. Subjects were instructed to indicate if they were in the 'tip of the tongue' state (convinced that they knew the word although they were unable to produce it). When this occurred they were asked to guess at the number of syllables in the word and to provide any other information, such as the initial letter. They were consistently much better at providing such information than one would have expected by chance. Other studies have shown that giving the subject the initial letter, in this case x, frequently tends to prompt the correct name, *xylophone*.

The task of trying to remember the names of capital cities of countries is a good way of evoking this effect. Read rapidly through the list of countries below, covering up the initial letters of their capital cities. Eliminate those countries for which you can immediately produce the answer, and also eliminate those for which you feel you do *not* know the answer. Concentrate on the rest. Any luck? If not, see if the letter cues jog your memory. Check your answers on page 164.

	Country	First letter of capital city
1	Norway	O
2	Turkey	A
3	Kenya	N
4	Uruguay	M
5	Tibet	L
6	Australia	C
7	Saudi Arabia	R
8	Romania	B
9	Burma	R
10	Bulgaria	S
11	South Korea	S
12	Syria	D
13	Cyprus	N
14	Sudan	K
15	Nicaragua	M
16	Ecuador	Q
17	Colombia	B
18	Cameroon	Y
19	Thailand	B
20	Venezuela	C

In general the feeling that you know something is a reasonably good indication that you do . . . given the right prompting. In a capital city recall test similar to that shown above, recall was over 50 per cent when cues were given for the cities people thought they knew, but only 16 per cent for those they thought they didn't.

We have established then that even if everything we experience is not stored, our memory store nevertheless contains more information than we can access at any given moment. What therefore determines the accessibility of this information? To return to our library analogy, good retrieval depends on good encoding; the way in which a book is classified on entering the library determines the ease with which it can be accessed later. Suppose we go back to the code that you committed to memory at the beginning of this chapter. How well can you remember it? Try writing it down.

If, like the redoubtable Dr Ebbinghaus, you rehearsed it rapidly and frequently without recourse to anything as artificial as a mnemonic aid, then you can probably remember the first line moderately well, but what about the second? If you have the twisted mind of a crossword puzzle addict, you might have noticed that if you start with the C in the bottom line and zigzag up and down between the two lines the sequence spells *catswhiskers*. If you noticed this, you probably reconstructed the code extremely accurately. But if I had asked you to reel off verbally the sequence of letters in the top row, you would probably have fared less well than if you had simply committed it to memory in a straightforward way — although, given pencil and paper, you could probably have produced them reliably and reasonably quickly. In short, the method of retrieval depends on how the material is encoded during the learning.

Classifying incoming material

Are all methods of encoding or classifying incoming information equally useful, provided they are systematic and logical? Clearly not. Returning to the library analogy, if the librarian has classified Shakespeare's *Julius Caesar* under 'History', we are likely to have difficulty finding it if the cue given is 'Drama'.

There are in fact substantial variations in the after-effects of different methods of classifying material. Try categorizing the words given opposite, checking each one as a 'Yes' or 'No'. When you have finished, do the addition sum that follows and then read on.

Now try to recall as many of the 30 words you have just classified as possible. Write them down in any order you like. You will have noticed that giving the answer 'Yes' or 'No' required three separate types of word processing: first, you had to decide whether the words were printed in upper or lower case; second, you had to make decisions about the sound of the words when pronounced; and, third, you had to process their meanings.

Score how many of each type of word you recalled. The words classified

Capital cities of countries listed on page 163: **1** Oslo **2** Ankara **3** Nairobi **4** Montevideo **5** Lhasa **6** Canberra **7** Riyadh **8** Bucharest **9** Rangoon **10** Sofia **11** Seoul **12** Damascus **13** Nicosia **14** Khartoum **15** Managua **16** Quito **17** Bogota **18** Yaoundé **19** Bangkok **20** Caracas

		Yes	No
Is the word in lower case?	*prince*	——	——
Does the word rhyme with dog?	*FOG*	——	——
Is it the name of an animal?	*tiger*	——	——
Does the word rhyme with pin?	*STYLE*	——	——
Is it the name of a fruit?	*BOTTLE*	——	——
Is the word in upper case?	*SCISSORS*	——	——
Does the word rhyme with castle?	*battle*	——	——
Is it the name of a game?	*FLOOR*	——	——
Does the word rhyme with stump?	*skunk*	——	——
Is the word in upper case?	*lamp*	——	——
Is the word in lower case?	*TABLE*	——	——
Is it the name of a piece of furniture?	*desk*	——	——
Does the word rhyme with grave?	*SLAVE*	——	——
Is it the name of a unit of time	*statue*	——	——
Is the word in lower case?	*oak*	——	——
Is it the name of a vegetable?	*carrot*	——	——
Is it the name of a building?	*MOUNTAIN*	——	——
Does the word rhyme with locket?	*rocket*	——	——
Is it the name of an insect?	*COCKROACH*	——	——
Is the word in lower case?	*GUN*	——	——
Does the word rhyme with wheat?	*WHEEL*	——	——
Is the word in upper case?	*book*	——	——
Does the word rhyme with wrote?	*coat*	——	——
Is the word in upper case?	*TOMB*	——	——
Does the word rhyme with hot?	*YACHT*	——	——
Is it the name of a disease?	*measles*	——	——
Is the word in lower case?	*typist*	——	——
Is it the name of a country?	*SHOE*	——	——
Is the word in upper case?	*COACH*	——	——
Does the word rhyme with simple?	*dimple*	——	——

Addition sum

$4 + 6 + 3 + 7 + 9 + 1 + 5 + 8 + 3 + 2 =$

according to case were *prince, scissors, lamp, table, oak, gun, book, tomb, typist* and *coach*; those classified on the basis of rhyme were *fog, style, battle, skunk, slave, rocket, wheel, coat, yacht* and *dimple*; and those classified according to semantic category were *tiger, bottle, floor, desk, statue, carrot, mountain, cockroach, measles* and *shoe*.

Typically, people find that superficial processing of a word, processing it purely in terms of its appearance, leads to very poor recall or recognition. Paying attention to its sound leads to slightly better recall. But the best processing results from attending to a word's meaning. The graph below shows the results of an experiment similar to the one you have just performed. Encoding on the basis of meaning has a very clear advantage over encoding on the basis of visual appearance or sound.

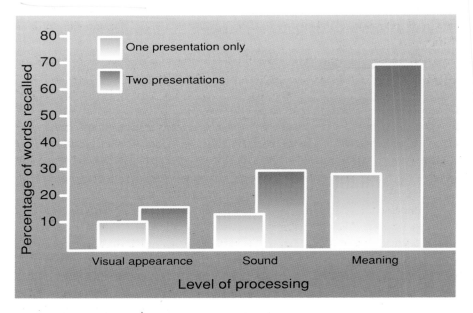

Processing incoming information according to meaning appears to leave a stronger memory trace than processing on the basis of sight or sound. (Craik and Lockhart, 1972)

Depth of processing

In an influential paper written in 1972 Fergus Craik and Robert Lockhart suggested that the amount of information retained in long-term memory depends on how 'deeply' it is processed during learning. This concept of 'depth' was based on a perhaps oversimplified view of the way in which we process information. It assumed, for example, that written words are first processed purely in terms of their visual characteristics, that these are then turned into a representation of the sounds of the words, and that these subsequently evoke the appropriate meaning. In judging whether a word is written in upper or lower case letters, there is no need to process information at any other than the purely visual level; such 'shallow' processing is assumed to give rise to a relatively impoverished memory trace which will be of little assistance in the task of recalling the words. In order to decide what the word sounds like, however, it is necessary to go beyond this superficial visual analysis and attend to its sound; this is assumed to give rise to a rather more robust and useful trace. However, processing the word in terms of its meaning requires one to go beyond this stage, creating a richer and more durable memory trace.

Craik and Lockhart do not of course claim that only meaning is stored. If that were so, we would never learn to talk or to understand speech, since both of these processes require the learning of 'shallow' auditory features. There is also evidence to suggest that we do, sometimes at least, remember incidental physical features of visually presented information; for example, one can sometimes remember where on a printed page one read some particular fact. There is, however, a problem in specifying exactly what is meant by 'depth'. Without a means of independently deciding how 'deep' a given type of processing is, it is difficult to test the theory.

An alternative concept to that of 'depth' is probably that of 'richness' or 'breadth' of processing. Let us go back to the librarian classifying books. He or she could categorize them in terms of their size, but merely knowing the size of a book one is looking for is not particularly helpful. In the same way, trying to access a word on the basis of its visual characteristics is not much use either. Most libraries of course classify books in terms of their content, such a classification system being rich and flexible enough to allow one to track down. with equal ease, a book on Swahili, Ming pottery, mole catching, or the sonnets of William Shakespeare

The essence of such a system is that it is structured and organized but also rich and flexible. These are the characteristics which make semantic coding so widely used in long-term memory — the structure is built in through our knowledge of a structured world, and because it is so rich and contains so many different but related dimensions it allows us to lay down very precise but nevertheless retrievable codes. In general, information that is encoded in terms of a rich and detailed representation of the world is likely to be more accessible than material that is processed in terms of a simpler or more impoverished scheme.

What other stratagems might help to classify new material so that it can be easily retrieved? As one might expect, enriching and elaborating the encoding process tends to make material more memorable. Hence someone who is asked to make up a story about a word is more likely to remember it than someone who is simply asked to decide whether it is a meaningful word or not. Similarly, if you are trying to associate the words *man* and *watch*, a simple sentence such as 'The man dropped the watch' is less likely to lead to good learning than a more elaborate effort such as 'The old man hobbled rheumatically across the courtyard and dropped the gold watch down the castle well'. Generally, putting a lot of effort into encoding leads to better recall. You are more likely to remember later the solving of a difficult problem than an easy one.

Retrieval cues

Suppose that you have logged a certain piece of information in your long-term memory, categorizing or classifying it in an appropriate way. How do you access it when you need to? One way of calling up a memory is to present all or part of the code that was laid down when it was classified. Again, going back to the library analogy, if the play *Hamlet* has been classified under 'Shakespeare', 'Drama', 'Verse', 'Prince' and 'Denmark', then some subset of these would be enough to allow you to locate a copy of it. These are what are known as *retrieval cues*, snippets of information that allow one to access a memory trace.

The retrieval cue concept was introduced into the current study of memory by Endel Tulving, who has contributed most to our understanding of the process of retrieval. In one experiment he presented subjects with a series of words to be retained and then recalled; each word was accompanied by a cue word which had some association, but not a very strong one, with the word to be retained. An example might be the word *city* accompanied by the cue word *dirty* in one case, or *village* in another. Subjects were asked to recall the original words, either unaided or prompted by the cue word. Cue words substantially increased recall of the target words. Tulving argues that for a retrieval cue to be useful it has to be presented at the same time as the target word. For example, although *busy* is a valid associate of *city,* it will not act as an effective retrieval cue if it has not been presented during learning. Not being part of the classification process, it cannot be used to evoke the *city* memory trace. Tulving has gone on to show that this effect is a very powerful one. In a series of ingenious demonstrations

Three simple visual retrieval cues. The circled features prompt an image of the whole edifice, which in turn prompts images or ideas about Paris, London and New York.

he has shown that learners can be induced to produce target words but fail to recognize them as such, and yet be quite able to recall them when given the appropriate retrieval cue.

In order to understand how this can happen it is necessary to understand something about *word association*. In word association the subject is given a word and asked to respond as quickly as possible with the first word that comes to mind. Some responses are extremely common. If, for example I give you the word *hot*, you are likely to respond with *cold*; *bread* is likely to evoke *butter, black* usually elicits *white,* and so on. Tulving began by taking a set of such common response words and presenting them as a list to be learned, each one accompanied by a low-frequency associate; for example, *cold* might be given a fairly uncommon associate such as *ground*. Having learned the list of target words, subjects were asked to recall as many of them as possible. Only a few of the target words were successfully recalled.

Next, subjects were given the high-frequency associates of the target words and asked to produce the list of target words. This they did without much difficulty; *hot*, for example, readily elicited the target word *cold*. Then Tulving asked his subjects to go through the target words they had just produced and say if any of them had been on the original list. Recognition of the original words was very low. Subjects readily produced the word *cold* in response to *hot,* but denied that *cold* had been on the original learning list.. Finally, Tulving presented the original retrieval cues, *ground* and so on, and invited his subjects to recall the original target words. In a substantial proportion of cases these (*cold* and so on) were recalled, despite the fact that subjects had previously produced them and failed to recognize them as words they had originally learned. Since recognition is almost always easier than free or uncued recall, this presents a genuine paradox. What is the reason for it?

In fact such a result is mysterious only if you assume that what the subject is learning is literally the word *cold*. If you think about it, however, this is clearly not what one is asking the subject to remember; he already knows the word *cold*, so what we are asking him to do is to remember that the word *cold* occurred during a particular part of our experiment. In short, we are asking him to remember an experience, but to indicate his memory of the experience by responding with the word *cold*. If I present him with the word *cold* together with the associated word *ground,* then the experience that he has conjured up is likely to be one that is a composite of these two words, perhaps *burial* or *camping on a cold groundsheet*. If I ask you to respond with the first word that comes to mind when I give you the word *hot*, then once again the word *cold* will appear, but it is very unlikely to be associated with the type of experience that has accompanied the *cold ground* encoding. It may simply be classified at a superficial level as 'the opposite', or perhaps as the labelling on the control of a shower. Consequently presenting *cold* in that context evokes an experience which has little overlap with the original experience and as such it does not serve as a good retrieval cue. When the word *ground* is presented, however, it reminds the subject of the experience, or perhaps an image generated during learning, which in turn evokes recall of *cold*.

There are other ways of showing the same effect. For example, if I give you a sentence such as 'The man tuned the piano', but give another person the sentence 'The man lifted the piano', then the cue *something heavy* is likely to be a very poor retrieval cue for you, but a very good one for your colleague, who is likely to find it an even better cue than the word *piano*. Thus we remember what we experience, and we access our memory by using a fragment of that experience as a key to the whole.

Smells as retrieval cues

Can you conjure up the smell of a fish market and a tea rose? Generally speaking, odors are difficult to forget but difficult to recreate in the 'mind's nose'.

Smells and tastes are a particularly powerful source of recollection for many people. Probably the most famous literary example comes from the beginning of Proust's great novel *Remembrance of Things Past*, where he describes how the taste and smell of a madeleine cake soaked in lime tea brings back with enormous vividness memories of his childhood: 'I had recognized the taste of the crumb of madeleine soaked in her concoction of lime-flowers which my Aunt used to give me . . . immediately the old gray house upon the street, where her room was, rose up like the scenery of a theatre to attach itself to the little pavilion,

opening on to the garden, which had been built out behind it for my parents . . . and with the house the town, from morning to night and in all weathers, the square where I was sent before luncheon, the streets along which I used to run errands, the country roads we took when it was fine.'

It certainly seems to be the case that smells show virtually no forgetting. In one study, for example, Engen and his colleagues had their subjects smell a cotton swab impregnated with any one of a hundred different smells. After an interval ranging from 3 to 30 seconds, subjects were asked to smell a second swab and decide whether the odor was the same or different. While performance was certainly not perfect, it was well above chance and showed no evidence of forgetting over the 30-second interval. A similar result was observed when a slightly different technique was used. Subjects were asked to remember five different odors, then presented with a sixth and asked whether it was one of the previous five or not. Again, no forgetting occurred over a 30-second interval.

Having observed no short-term forgetting, Engen and Ross went on to study long-term memory for odors. In one experiment subjects were asked to remember 48 different odors and then tested 30 days later with 21 pairs of odors (each pair comprised one odor from the original 48 and one new odor). The old odors were correctly identified 67 per cent of the time, and when subjects were required to remember only 20 odors rather than 48, their recognition rate increased to 77 per cent. However, Engen and his colleagues found that performance could be reduced by pairing an old odor with a new one that was similar (onion with garlic, for example); this sent the detection rate down from 77 to 64 per cent.

From the admittedly scanty evidence available, therefore, it seems that smells are remarkably resistant to forgetting. In this respect they resemble continuous motor skills. Why should this be? We can only speculate, but one possibility is that smells are relatively isolated from the rest of our memory experiences. The words of a verbal request or comment are repeatedly used in other language contexts, while most of the visual stimuli we perceive are followed by large numbers of similar visual experiences. Furthermore, in the case of verbal or visual information we can imagine and recreate the experience. I suspect that our ability to imagine smells and tastes is much more limited. It is comparatively easy for me at least to evoke the visual image of a rose, but much harder to imagine its scent. That may be peculiar to me, but I suspect not. Try imagining both the visual appearance and odor of the following: a raw onion, white mice, scotch whisky, burning leaves. In most cases I can create some representation of the odor, but it is not nearly so vivid as the visual image I can create.

Having a durable memory for tastes and smells may once have been of survival value to our species. Recognizing a particular taste or smell and remembering that it was associated with sickness would have guarded us against eating poisonous or putrefying foods. A wide range of experiments involving non-humans has shown that many species are particularly good at detecting associations between taste and nausea, whereas associations between tastes and electric shocks are more difficult to learn. In the United States this particular piece of psychology has been applied to the practical problem of discouraging coyotes from attacking young sheep. The bodies of young sheep are impregnated with a substance that makes coyotes sick. The coyote eats the sheep, becomes ill, recovers, and thereafter has a lasting aversion to lambs.

Multiple cues

It was discovered a few years ago that memory performance is excellent when instead of merely reading words or seeing objects, subjects are required to perform some activity as well. For example, they might be required to scribble with a pencil, invert an egg cup, remove a cork from a bottle, and so forth, in addition to seeing the words or objects named. Under such circumstances recall is excellent. Adding the action dimension seems to make recall far more resistant to the effects of time and aging. It seems likely that the robustness and retrievability of the memory trace stems from the fact that it is particularly richly encoded — in terms of vision, semantics and action.

The power of multiple cueing is shown up particularly clearly in the recall of verse, a point made by novelist Anthony Burgess in praising the joys of spouting verse on bibulous pub crawls: 'What is wrong with prose is that it is not

learnable by heart and faults of memory in trying to recite it do not seriously impair its rhythms . . .'. However, since he also says 'A return to heroic couplets might save British civilisation', we should perhaps search for rather better evidence.

David Rubin and Wanda Wallace have made an extensive study of various kinds of oral recall, including some intriguing work on the memory for ballads shown by Appalachian folk singers. Work many years earlier on the recitation of epic poetry by Yugoslavian traditional bards had suggested that the epic poems they recited were not so much reproduced verbatim on each occasion as regenerated. Given the constraints of story and rhythm, each re-telling was very similar, but differed in small details. Similarly in the case of the folk singers, Rubin and Wallace found that different versions might be sung on different occasions, but were heavily constrained by the story and the rhyme. For example 'She cried bold captain tell me true' might become 'She cried brave captain tell me true'. Even when changes of meaning did occur, they were not great. Hence 'She had not sailed far over the deep/Till a large ship she chanced to meet' became 'She had not sailed far over the main/She spied three ships a'sailing from Spain'.

The singers showed great skill in producing material within the standard framework. Given five minutes to study a newspaper story on a train disaster, for example, they were able to produce a song in the standard style of train disaster songs of the Appalachians. As Rubin points out, material such as counting rhymes and folk songs which have stood the test of time have done so because they combine the richness of semantic coding with the rhyming and rhythmic constraints of verse.

Despite the apparent chaos, this old shoemender knows where to find every shoe brought in for repair.

Context-dependent memory

So far we have been talking about the active process of categorizing or classifying experiences and how important this is for long-term memory. But what about those features of our experiences which are only incidental to our interpretation of them? Consider the case cited by the seventeenth-century British association-ist philosopher, John Locke, who tells the story of a young gentleman who developed a strange association between dancing and a particular piece of furniture: '. . . there happened to stand an old trunk in the room where he had learned [to dance]. His idea of this remarkable piece of household stuff had so mixed itself with the steps of all his dances, that though in that chamber he could dance excellently well yet it was only while that trunk was there; nor could he perform well in any other place, unless that or some other such trunk had its due position in the room'.

The idea that reinstating the environment in which an event has been experienced will bring the memory of that event flooding back has of course played an important part in detective fiction, at least since Wilkie Collins' *The Moonstone*. It was also a popular theme in detective films of the 1950s. In a typical situation the key witness, who has seen the crime while frying his breakfast on the fatal morning, fails to recall some crucial details. He is taken back to his kitchen by the artful sleuth one morning, and with the crackling of the eggs and the sizzling of the bacon the crucial piece of evidence comes flooding back, allowing the crime to be solved and the hero saved. Do we have any solid evidence that reinstating the environment of learning enhances recall?

There is in fact a great deal of evidence that such effects occur. It is as if new learning is isolated from old, reducing the possibility of the one interfering with the other. Take people who have lived in a foreign country for a number of years and acquired the language; they return home and after a couple of years feel that they have forgotten most of what they learned of the second language. Fortunately, on returning to the foreign country, the language rapidly comes back, suggesting that it was merely inaccessible, not lost.

Some years ago Duncan Godden and I had the opportunity of exploring *context dependency*, as it is called, in connection with an applied problem, namely that of training deepsea divers. Earlier experiments of my own on the effect of cold on divers had suggested quite incidentally that the underwater environment might induce strong context dependency. This suggestion was supported by the observations of a friend who was in charge of a team of divers attempting to watch the behavior of fish about to enter, or escape from, trawl nets. Initially he relied on debriefing his divers when they surfaced, only to find that they had apparently forgotten most of the fishy behavior they had seen. Eventually he had to send his divers down with underwater tape recorders so that they could give a running commentary on the fishes' activities; the tapes were then transcribed.

Intrigued by this, Godden and I set up an experiment in which divers listened to 40 unrelated words either on the beach or under about 10 feet of water. After the 40 words had been heard, our divers were tested either in the same environment or in the alternative one, and then asked to recall as many of the words as possible. The results were very clear: material learnt underwater was best recalled underwater, although underwater recall of material learnt on land and land recall of material learnt underwater were about the same. In a subsequent experiment Duncan Godden trained divers in a simple manual task which involved transferring nuts and bolts from one brass plate to another. In all conditions the divers were required to work entirely by touch, a very common situ-

ation for commercial divers who often have to operate in water so muddy that they can see nothing. One group began work underwater immediately, but the other was given a practice trial on land first. The question that concerned Godden was the relative efficiency of land training versus underwater training. His results showed that the dry land training actually hindered underwater performance to the extent that the first underwater run was reliably poorer than it would have been had no prior training whatsoever been given.

What are the theoretical implications of the context dependency effect? Some light was thrown on this by a later experiment in which Duncan Godden and I repeated our verbal memory experiment, except that, instead of testing by free or uncued recall, we used a recognition test. Under these conditions we observed no trace of context dependency. Our subjects recognized the same number of words whether or not they were remembered in the environment in which they were learned. This seems to suggest that environmental cues may be important in helping to locate the relevant memory trace, but are not used in evaluating whether it is the appropriate trace or not. In a recognition test, where presenting the target word makes access to the relevant trace very probable, there is no need for the extra help of environmental cues.

What is learnt in one environment is best recalled in that environment. In one study involving fish observation divers had be be equipped with underwater tape recorders to supplement their fallible memories.

State dependent memory

We have shown that reinstating the *external* environment in which an item is learned makes it easier to recall that item. A similar effect occurs when the learner's *internal* environment is changed by means of a drug such as alcohol. This effect is known as *state dependency*. Goodwin and colleagues cite clinical evidence of this. Heavy drinkers who hide alcohol or money when drunk are unable to remember where it is hidden once they are sober; when they become drunk again, they remember (and are therefore able to get even more drunk). Goodwin studied this effect using a whole range of tests and found, in general, that what is learned when drunk is best recalled when drunk. Similar results have been shown with a wide range of other drugs, with nitrous oxide, sometimes used to anesthetize patients, and with marijuana.

In a recent review of this subject Eich convincingly showed that state dependency is only observed when memory is tested by recall; it disappears when recognition testing is used, as it does in the case of context dependency. Once again it appears that the subject's internal state helps him to access the memory trace, but that when access is made easy by presenting an item for recognition, this initial search stage is not necessary. When deciding whether or not a particular item has been presented earlier, it does not seem to matter whether the context during testing is the same as that during learning.

This last conclusion suggests that retrieval has at least two components, the first involving *finding* the memory trace, the second involving some form of *evaluation* of it. In short, retrieval is much more than a process of setting up the appropriate retrieval cue to guarantee the correct response.

Mood congruent memory

When depressed people are asked to recall autobiographical memories, they tend to recall unhappy incidents; the more depressed the individual, the more rapidly the unpleasant experience is recalled. One problem in interpreting this result of course is that depressives may indeed lead less pleasant lives; perhaps that is why they are depressed. One study avoided this problem by selecting patients whose level of depression fluctuated systematically throughout the day, as sometimes occurs in depression. During sad times of the day they were consistently less likely to produce happy memories than at other times. Similar results have also been obtained with normal subjects, using a procedure known as the Velton technique, after its originator. A happy or sad mood is induced by encouraging subjects to ponder sets of sad or happy statements. In the sad mood, subjects were consistently slower at evoking positive memories.

At one point it was believed that such demonstrations indicated mood-dependent memory, implying that mood operates in exactly the same way as external environment in the diving study just described; an item learnt in one mood is likely to be best recalled in that mood. Support for this came from a series of experiments in which subjects were hypnotized and induced to adopt one or other mood during learning, after which they were required to recall the learned items in the same or in a different mood. The original results looked promising, but it has subsequently proved difficult to show the effect of mood on learning and subsequent recall of *neutral* material — mood dependency. On the other hand, there does appear to be strong evidence of *mood-congruency*. This refers to material that is not neutral, but positively or negatively emotionally

When we feel 'down', it can be difficult to remember what it feels like to be happy. Not being able to access happy memories seems to be part of depression.

toned. In particular, as we saw earlier, subjects in a depressed mood have difficulty retrieving pleasant memories, a phenomenon that may well be part of the problem of depression. If a person is depressed, he or she will be likely to recall unpleasant incidents from the past, further lowering self-esteem and deepening the depression. Cognitive approaches to the treatment of depression involve helping the person to access less depressing memories and revalue the more positive aspects of their lives, aspects that tend to be hidden in the vicious circle of depressive thoughts.

Recollection

While much of our retrieval from long-term memory is effortless and automatic, this is clearly not always the case. When we are trying to retrieve something which is on the fringe of accessibility, something much more like searching or even problem solving goes on. I shall use the term *recollection* to refer to this active and interactive aspect of retrieval. Some of the flavor of recollection is given by the following account, produced a few days after the experience had taken place.

Thursday 16 November, 1978
On Tuesday I travelled to London. On the platform I notice a vaguely familiar face. I am preoccupied and since the person in question shows no obvious signs of recognizing me I assume that it is someone I have perhaps seen on other occasions on the train or around Cambridge, and forget about it. As I get off the train I notice him again, since he has been sitting in the same carriage. Again he seems familiar. As I have been thinking about processes of memory and retrieval, I decide to see if I can remember who he is. Two associations occur, the name Sebastian and something to do with children. Sebastian seems to me to be a specific and useful cue, but unfortunately all it calls up is the name of a friend in another city, the schoolboy son of a friend in Cambridge and an association with teddy bears through Evelyn Waugh's *Brideshead Revisited*. I also sense there are some vague associations with a darkish room with books, but nothing clear enough to suggest any useful further search.

A little later, for no apparent reason, the association 'babysitting' pops up and I immediately recall that we were both members of a mutual babysitting group, that his name is indeed Sebastian, although I cannot remember his second name, and that he lives in a road whose location I am quite clear about and in a house which I could visualize relatively easily. A very clear image of his sitting-room appears, together with the fact that it contains a large number of very finely printed books, and that he himself is by profession a printer. I remember noticing in fact that he has a printing press in one room of his house. I have no doubt that I have successfully identified him.

Two days later, thinking about this as an illustration of a certain type of remembering, it occurs to me that I still have not remembered his name or the name of the street in which he lives. I have no clues about his name, but know that he lives in either Oxford Road or Windsor Road. The two are linked, one running at right angles to the other, and I have a colleague who lives in the one that Sebastian X does *not* live in. If I have to guess, I would say that he lives in Oxford Road, and if I have to guess as independently as I can, I would say that my colleague lives in Windsor Road. I therefore plump for Oxford Road, though without any of the certainty which I feel about identifying him. I am however certain that he does not live in Richmond Road (since I don't *think* I know anyone who lives in Richmond Road). I also try again to re-member his surname. Sebastian . . . Nothing. And then for no obvious reason the name 'Carter' appears. It feels right, although not overwhelmingly so. There are other Carters about! Then the association 'Penny Carter' appears as his wife's name. I am fairly sure that this is correct and it reinforces my belief that his name is Sebastian Carter. By now, about an hour later, I am quite convinced.

I go and check the babysitting list. There is no Carter. Undeterred, I go to the telephone directory. After all this effort I had better be right. 'Carter' is indeed in Oxford Road. That does not of course mean that it actually was Sebastian Carter. I resolve to ring and ask him. November 16th, evening: I ring Sebastian Carter. Was he on the 14.36 train to Liverpool Street on Tuesday, November 14th? He was.

No doubt you have had similar experiences, and will need no convincing that the process of recollection is an active if sometimes frustrating one. There certainly is an apparent unconscious process whereby information 'pops up' for no obvious reason. The name 'Sebastian' and the association with baby-sitting were examples of this. Many, if not most, of the things we remember come to us effortlessly without apparent search. But what if the appropriate in-formation does not spring conveniently to mind? We seem to take the fragments that do suggest themselves and use them rather in the way that a detective might use a clue. In the case of the clue 'Sebastian', I followed up a number of plausible associations, each of which could be rejected. On what grounds did I reject them? Usually because it was obvious why that association should occur, and equally obvious that it did not lead to any further clues. In contrast, the vague association with children produced babysitting and then a clear image of the Carters' house. This in turn produced other information, including the fact that Sebastian Carter is a printer and a clear visual image of seeing a printing press in his house. In short, the clue about children gave rise to a great deal of information which would not otherwise have been aroused by the simple prompt 'babysitting'; in any case the vast majority of houses in which I have babysat have not contained printing presses.

In one of the few experiments to explore directly the cues we use to decide whether we know something or not, Brown, Lewis and Monk gave their student subjects lists of town names to remember. They tested their memory for the names using a recognition test in which they included, in addition to the original towns, a number of other town names, and the name of the home town of the student in question. The students were virtually always right when they reported that the name of their home town had not been presented during learning. Presumably if it had been, they would have noticed it and remembered.

Suppose I ask you your own name. I assume you will remember it rapidly and be reasonably confident that you are correct. And yet I doubt if you indulged in very much of a search for confirmatory evidence that you were correct. How do people know when they are right? We can only speculate. A plausible interpretation might be that any question which elicits a rapid answer, and to which there are no realistic alternative answers, evokes a high degree of certainty.

In recent years there has been increased interest in different kinds of retrieval from long-term memory, in particular in the distinction between 'remembering' and 'knowing'. In a typical experiment subjects are given a list of words to remember and are then tested by free recall. As they produce each word they are asked to categorize it as a *remembered* word (in the sense that the experience of encountering the word in a list has been actively recollected) or a *known* word (the only information available being a feeling that the word did occur in the list). Typically, distracting subjects' attention during learning reduces the number of words categorized as 'remembered', but has no such influence on words categorized as 'known', which suggests that remembered words reflect the output of the explicit declarative memory system, whereas words that are simply 'known' appear to depend upon more implicit non-declarative sources, such as priming.

Direct access or retrieval by inference? While it seems plausible to assume that we combine direct access to information (the phenomenon of information appearing to pop up of its own accord) with more indirect inferential techniques when recollecting events in our lives, neither of these processes is easy to study. In particular it is often impossible to confirm incidents in detail, so how do we judge whether they are being recollected accurately? This question was studied by Camp, Lachman and Lachman.

Two types of question were created in their experiment. With the first type the subject was expected to access the information either directly or not at all. Examples of the first type of question were: 'Which man's wife was turned into a pillar of salt?' (Answer: 'Lot') and 'What was the name of the flying horse of mythology?' (Answer: 'Pegasus'). In general, if such information is available, it is likely to be *directly* available and thus unlikely to be accessed by inference from other more available information. With the second type of question, inference was the more likely source of information. Examples were 'What southern U.S. city is named after an ocean?' (Answer: 'Atlanta') and 'What horror character would starve to death in Northern Sweden in the summer time?' (Answer: 'Dracula'). You will get a better feel for this direct and indirect access process if you try the two sets of questions opposite. Work as quickly as you can, checking A, B, C or D in each case.

Type 1 Direct access questions

1   What was the name of the flying horse of mythology? (A) Pyramus, (B) Griffin, (C) Grisines, (D) Pegasus
2   Who was 'Old Hickory'? (A) Johnson, (B) Jackson, (C) Taylor, (D) Truman
3   Which person wrote Uncle Tom's Cabin? (A) Stowe, (B) Michaels, (C) Mitchell, (D) Stovall
4   What were the Ten Commandments kept in? (A) Temple of Joshua, (B) Ark of the Covenant, (C) Tent of David, (D) Aaron's Casement
5   What man's wife was turned into a pillar of salt? (A) Ezekiel, (B) Loca, (C) Ebenezer, (D) Lot
6   Who is responsible for the basic concept of inertia? (A) Newton, (B) Galton, (C) Nevell, (D) Galileo
7   What man wrote *Pygmalion*? (A) Shaw, (B) Wilde, (C) Shakespeare, (D) Winthrop
8   What creature was struck dumb when his riddle was answered? (A) Siren, (B) Sphinx, (C) Chaos, (D) Cyclops
9   What was the name of the girl who drowned in a 1969 car accident with Senator Edward Kennedy? (A) Harris, (B) Harrington, (C) Kopechne, (D) Kupchek
10 Who co-starred with Bette Davis in *Whatever Happened To Baby Jane?* (A) De Havilland, (B) Crawford, (C) Crandall, (D) De Winter

Type 2 Inference questions

1   Which celestial body besides the sun causes the earth's temperature to drop? (A) Capricorn, (B) comet, (C) Mercury, (D) Moon
2   Which liquid is most often used by a nurse while treating a patient? (A) mercury, (B) Manganese, (C) water, (D) wash soap
3   Which ingredient in gasoline does not come from plants? (A) lithium, (B) oil, (C) lead, (D) octane
4   What musical instrument is made only of leather and metal? (A) cyclephone, (B) cymbal, (C) viola, (D) violin
5   How many months of the year don't share their first letter with another month? (A) seven, (B) four, (C) six, (D) five
6   Which pet besides a bird lays eggs? (A) gerbil, (B) guppies, (C) German shepherd, (D) goldfish
7   Which southern city of the United States is named after an ocean? (A) Atlanta, (B) Ithaca, (C) Augusta, (D) Indianapolis
8   Which domestic animal continually wears man-made apparel? (A) hog, (B) horse, (C) cat, (D) canary
9   Which continent other than Antarctica is a natural habitat of penguins? (A) South America, (B) Australia, (C) North America, (D) Asia
10 What cake ingredient comes from beans? (A) coconut, (B) vanilla, (C) vermilion, (D) chamomile

The correct answers to the direct access questions were: D B A B D A A B C B. In the case of the questions requiring inference, the correct answers were: D A C B D D A B A B. Camp and his colleagues found that their subjects took slightly longer to answer the inference questions, as one might expect if a more elaborate search and verification procedure has to be used. Subjects also reported that the process involved in verification of their answers was different for the two types of questions; much more searching and hypothesis testing was needed for the indirect sentences. The two question types also produced a different pattern of errors. Camp and his colleagues divided these into errors that were phonetically similar to the correct answer (such as 'Pyramus' for 'Pegasus' or 'vermilion' for 'vanilla'), and those which were meaningfully related to the correct answer (such as 'Galileo' for 'Newton'). Inferential questions gave rise to considerably more semantically related answers than did direct access questions, whereas the two did not differ in the likelihood of making a phonetic error. It seems probable that semantic factors and semantic plausibility are much more important in the indirect retrieval of information than they are in direct retrieval.

What can we learn from computers?

Sherlock Holmes, the creation of Sir Arthur Conan Doyle, reconstructed whole crimes by inferring the meaning of tiny pieces of evidence.

As mentioned earlier, research on memory in recent years has been heavily influenced by analogy with the digital computer. Models of retrieval are no exception. Indeed the fact that retrieval is a major problem becomes particularly obvious if one is attempting to store information in a computer. In particular, it is clear that current programs are far inferior to human memory in their flexibility.

Computers store information in specific locations, so provided the storage location can be accessed, retrieval is perfect. Without precise access to the correct storage location, the memory search is completely fruitless. In contrast, human memory typically provides the more important features of an event, while losing the fine detail. Information in a computer is normally stored in one location, so that if that location is overwritten or destroyed, the information is lost. Human memory on the other hand tends to show a quality known as 'graceful degradation'. Retrieval becomes slower and less detailed as the brain deteriorates, but essential information, such as who you are and where you come from, is enormously resistant to quite severe loss of brain tissue.

Human memory has the valuable characteristic of *content addressability*; in other words, feeding in a fragment of a memory will tend to call up the rest of it. For example, if I tell you I am trying to think of someone who was an American president and who was assassinated in Texas, you would know I was talking about John F. Kennedy, and be able to provide considerably more information.

In recent years there have been a number of attempts to produce computer programs that can simulate some of these features of human memory. They typically also attempt to operate using *parallel distributed processing* (PDP), in which information is stored within networks that operate in parallel rather than serially, as is the case with most current computers.

In the 1960s psychological models of retrieval tended to mimic the operation of computers of the period, assuming that memory locations were scanned serially until the target was finally located. One example of such a theory was developed by Saul Sternberg to explain the results of an experiment on speed of retrieval from short-term memory. Subjects were presented with strings of between one and six digits. Immediately after each string a 'probe' item would be presented; the subject's job was to decide as rapidly as possible whether the probe had been contained within the string. Hence, if the string *719382* was followed by the probe *1*, the subject would press a 'Yes' button; if the probe was *5*, the 'No' button would be pressed.

As the graph below shows, response time increases in a linear fashion with the number of items in the memory set, regardless of whether the response is 'Yes' or 'No'. Sternberg interpreted this result as meaning that subjects scan the location associated with each of the digits presented, deciding at the end of the string whether a match has occurred between the probe digit and one of the locations. The counter-intuitive assumption that subjects do not respond as soon as a match is detected, but wait until the end, derives from the fact that 'No' responses (which necessarily involve scanning all the digits) take just as long as 'Yes' responses for a given number of digits. However, other features of performance on speed of retrieval tend not to fit in with this 'serial scanning' model. For instance, when the probe corresponds to the last digit (e.g. *7914* — probe *4*), subjects respond particularly rapidly. Such findings have led to a search for alternative theories, of which several now exist. However, Sternberg's technique is still used since it tends to be sensitive to the effects of drugs and other

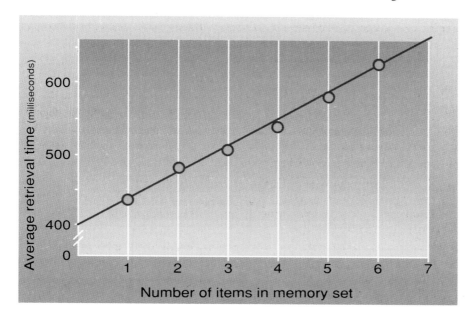

The time taken to retrieve items from memory is roughly proportional to the number of items in the memory set. (Sternberg, 1966)

stressors. Unfortunately, and despite a lack of good evidence that memories are serially scanned, investigators still tend to report their results as if they were directly measuring 'speed of memory scanning'. Theories are not destroyed by evidence so much as superseded by better theories.

Connectionist models of retrieval

As mentioned earlier, one important development in recent years has been the PDP approach to learning and memory. This involves storing information in the connections between units in a network hence the term *connectionism*. While a detailed account of such models goes beyond the scope of the present book, a brief description of one approach to the problem of content addressability will serve to give a flavor of these exciting new developments.

In 1981 J. McClelland described how a network model could be used to retrieve both general and specific information. He chose to store information about the fictitious members of two gangs in an insalubrious quarter of an imaginary American city. The table on the left shows the characteristics of the various gang members, and the diagram opposite shows how this information can be represented as a network. A double-headed arrow implies positive excitation between two units, while units within the same cloud mutually inhibit each other.

In the connectionist model, providing one piece of information will lead to the activation of other connected units. Thus the name 'Sam' will cause activation

Characteristics of individuals belonging to two gangs, the Jets and the Sharks

Name	Gang	Age	Education	Marital status	Occupation
Art	Jets	40s	J.H.	Sing.	Pusher
Al	Jets	30s	J.H.	Mar.	Burglar
Sam	Jets	20s	COL.	Sing.	Bookie
Clyde	Jets	40s	J.H.	Sing.	Bookie
Mike	Jets	30s	J.H.	Sing.	Bookie
Jim	Jets	20s	J.H.	Div.	Burglar
Greg	Jets	20s	H.S.	Mar.	Pusher
John	Jets	20s	J.S.	Mar.	Burglar
Doug	Jets	30s	H.S.	Sing.	Bookie
Lance	Jets	20s	J.S.	Mar.	Burglar
George	Jets	20s	J.H.	Div.	Burglar
Pete	Jets	20s	H.S.	Sing.	Bookie
Fred	Jets	20s	H.S.	Sing.	Pusher
Gene	Jets	20s	COL.	Sing.	Pusher
Ralph	Jets	30s	J.H.	Sing.	Pusher
Phil	Sharks	30s	COL.	Mar.	Pusher
Ike	Sharks	30s	J.H.	Sing.	Bookie
Nick	Sharks	30s	H.S.	Sing.	Pusher
Don	Sharks	30s	COL.	Mar.	Burglar
Ned	Sharks	30s	COL.	Mar.	Bookie
Karl	Sharks	40s	H.S.	Mar.	Bookie
Ken	Sharks	20s	H.S.	Sing.	Burglar
Earl	Sharks	40s	H.S.	Mar.	Burglar
Rick	Sharks	30s	H.S.	Div.	Burglar
Ol	Sharks	30s	COL.	Mar.	Pusher
Neil	Sharks	30s	H.S.	Sing.	Bookie
Dave	Sharks	30s	H.S.	Div.	Pusher

to spread to the various associated characteristics, indicating that he is in his 20s, a bookie, a member of the Jets, married, and has a college education. The same process will allow one to provide part of the information and come up with the person concerned. Who, for example, is in his 40s and a pusher? The spread of information along the arrows indicates that he is a member of the Jets, with a junior high school education, and is called Art.

A network has the advantage of graceful degradation, in that parts of the system can be destroyed without total breakdown occurring. The best available information will be provided. Misleading information also has a less than catastrophic effect. A network also has the characteristic of providing a default value, the best guess, for information that is not included. For instance, if we do not know whether Lance is a burglar, a bookie, or a pusher, the network would allow us to feed in his characteristics and come up with a best estimate based on the occupations of gang members who resemble him most closely.

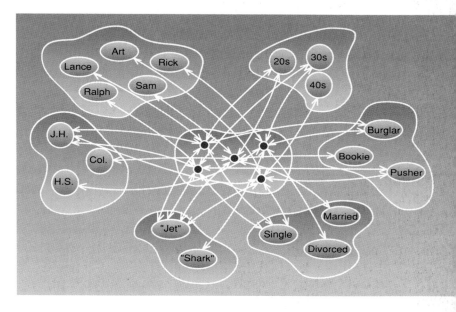

A related virtue of a network is that it can spontaneously generalize. For example, the network illustrated on the right could produce a stereotype of a Jet, who would tend to be single, in his 20s, and have only junior high school education, since these features characterize the majority of the Jet gang. Finally, it is important to note that these features fall naturally out of this type of architecture — they are not specifically built in. The connectionist approach to retrieval is considerably more plausible than earlier computer models with their serial scanning of memory locations.

Connectionist and PDP approaches to learning and memory remain controversial. Some claim that the analogy with parallel information processing within the brain is superficial and misleading, others object that such models are too powerful and unconstrained, while yet others argue that they run into massive problems of interference when they are required to operate under realistic conditions. My own view is that such approaches are providing us with valuable new tools for developing models of learning and retrieval. They provide a language and a technology for developing new theories. Many of these will no doubt prove inadequate, but in the long term they should give us better ways of conceptualizing the phenomenal power and flexibility of human memory.

This simplified representation of part of the computer model developed by McClelland represents information about the two gangs tabulated opposite. The units linked by double-headed arrows are able to excite each other, whereas all the units within the same cloud tend to compete so that if one is excited, the others will be inhibited.

10 Eyewitness testimony

A few years ago I received an unexpected telephone call. A London solicitor wanted to know whether I would be prepared to testify in court that a face seen once could not possibly be recognized 11 months later. Since I knew of no evidence on the durability of memory for faces I declined, but asked for more information on the case. It turned out to be an inquiry in connection with what was to become a famous case, that of George Davis, a professional criminal from the East End of London, who was being prosecuted for a shooting incident. The evidence rested crucially on the report of a police eyewitness who claimed to have seen Davis briefly and under far from ideal conditions 11 months previously, and who subsequently identified him in a police line-up. There were in fact many dubious features to the eyewitness testimony, including the fact that a photograph of Davis had been shown to the eyewitness before the line-up. However, the solicitor seemed less interested in these aspects of the case and, since I was not prepared to testify on the question of delay, all I could do was refer him to a colleague. The case went to court and Davis was convicted.

In the following months a vigorous and well-organized protest campaign was launched by George Davis' family and friends. They claimed that because of his previous record he had been framed for a crime of which he was entirely innocent. The campaign attracted a good deal of interest, particularly after an incident when the campaigners disrupted a cricket Test Match between England and Australia; they broke into the ground overnight and dug up the wicket.

In general, professional criminals appear to accept that they will be caught from time to time and do not make much fuss about it, so the vehemence and indignation shown by George Davis' family suggested that there might indeed be a case to answer. Eventually the case for retrial was conceded, the eyewitness evidence was interpreted as inadequate, and George Davis was freed. Shortly afterwards he was caught taking part in a robbery, tried and convicted. On this occasion there was no protest.

Violent incidents pose special memory problems for victims and witnesses. If a weapon is involved, it and not the person wielding it may become the focus of attention.

Innocent or guilty?

However reliable or unreliable, there is no doubt that eyewitness testimony carries a great deal of weight. In 1976 the Devlin Committee analyzed all the identification parades which had been held in England and Wales during the year 1973. There were over 2,000, with 45 per cent of them leading to a suspect being picked out. Of these, no less than 82 per cent were subsequently convicted. In all there were almost 350 cases in which eyewitness identification was the *only* evidence of guilt. Even here, 74 per cent were convicted, indicating the overwhelming weight given to eyewitness testimony.

Consider the following case, taken, as is much of this chapter, from Elizabeth Loftus' excellent survey of the issue of eyewitness testimony. On 15 May 1975 the assistant manager of a department store in Monroe, North Carolina, was forced into a car by two men, one of whom pointed a gun at him and told him to lie down in the back of the car. He got only a glimpse of the men before they pulled stocking masks over their faces. They then drove to the store and demanded that he open the safe. He convinced them that he did not know the combination. so they took 35 dollars from his wallet and let him go.

The victim, Robert Hinson, could say very little about his kidnappers other than that one of them looked Hispanic and that their car was an off-white 1965 Dodge Dart, but he also said that one of them resembled a man who had recently applied for a job in the store. On the basis of the fragmentary evidence available, a composite sketch was created of one of the suspects.

Some three days later the police stopped a 1965 white Plymouth Valiant and arrested the driver and passenger, Sandy and Lonnie Sawyer. Neither looked like the composite sketch, neither had applied for a job at the store and both denied knowing anything about the kidnapping. At the trial Robert Hinson positively identified the Sawyers as the men who had kidnapped him. Despite the fact that four witnesses testified that Sandy was at home at the time of the kidnapping and four others vouched that Lonnie was at a printing plant visiting his girlfriend, the jury found the Sawyers guilty. As they were led from the court Lonnie cried out: 'Momma, Daddy, appeal this. We didn't do it!'

The Sawyers were fortunate in having the support of a determined and persevering family, a tenacious private detective and a television producer who had become interested in the case. Their first real break came in 1976 when Robert Thomas, a prisoner at a youth center, admitted to being one of Hinson's kidnappers. Encouraged by this, the detective rechecked some of the earlier leads and discovered that Thomas had indeed applied for a job at the store shortly before the kidnapping. Furthermore, he had a friend whose mother owned a 1965 Dodge Dart. He went on to interview some of the jurors and a number admitted that, although the evidence did not seem very strong, they eventually became tired and simply went along with the majority.

The justification for a retrial seemed very strong, but the judge decided that, despite the new evidence, too much time had elapsed. The Governor was petitioned for a pardon and, while awaiting the outcome of this, Thomas confessed in writing, and then on camera; he subsequently recanted, but finally withdrew his recantation. On that day the Governor of North Carolina pardoned the Sawyers. They had spent two years in jail, had narrowly escaped sentences of 28 and 32 years, and the process of freeing them had cost their impoverished family thousands of dollars. And all this was due to the jury's willingness to accept the word of the victim, who admitted that he saw his assailants only briefly, and went entirely against the evidence of eight witnesses who testified to the fact that the accused could not have been present at the crime. Clearly there were powerful forces at work here — sympathy for the victim, outrage at the attackers, and a feeling that *someone* should be brought to justice. Given a plausible candidate, it is all too easy to persuade oneself that the crime is solved, particularly when the victim is prepared to point the accusing finger.

Suspect testimony

Psychologists have been interested in the accuracy of eyewitness testimony for at least 80 years. In 1895 the psychologist J. M. Cattell reported some investigations on the accuracy with which his students observed and recalled everyday events. He asked them what the weather had been like a week previously — it had in fact snowed and subsequently cleared. Of the 56 people who replied, only seven reported snow. As Cattell points out, it seems that people 'cannot state much better what the weather was a week ago than what it will be a week hence.'

Cattell then tried the following questions on his subjects:

Do chestnut trees or oak trees lose their leaves earlier in the autumn?
Do horses in fields stand with head or tail to the wind?
In what direction do the seeds of an apple point?

Cattell found that accuracy of observation was not very much better than one would have expected from pure guesswork. Chestnut trees lose their leaves first (59 per cent), horses stand with their tails to the wind (64 per cent), and apple pips point up towards the stem (39 per cent).

We also tend to be surprisingly bad at recalling details of objects we see or use daily. American psychologists Adams and Nickerson asked subjects to draw exactly what was represented on each side of a U.S. penny piece. On average subjects recalled only three of the eight critical features of the coin (head, In God We Trust, Liberty, date, building, United States of America,

Here are eight people's attempts at drawing a U.S. penny piece from memory. If familiar items such as coins are misremembered, what chance do we have of remembering sudden, unexpected events accurately?

È Pluribus Unum, and One Cent), and even the features correctly recalled were more often than not mislocated.

In a subsequent experiment two other American investigators asked their subjects to draw the full range of American coins. The drawings of the various coins tended to resemble each other, and all contained the features that most commonly occur on coins. When asked to design a new coin, subjects tended to come up with these same features, suggesting that they had a general schema for coins rather than specific memories of individual denominations.

One might plausibly suppose that an eyewitness, observing a novel event such as a crime, would notice much more and be in a much better position to remember it than when trying to recollect the incidental features of a coin or some other 'familiar' object. However, many factors work against the eyewitness, tending to obscure and distort his memory. Some are obvious. He sees the incident only once and is usually not expecting it. What he sees is often of very short duration, and criminals are usually careful to minimize the chances of their being recognized. However the influence of other factors may be less obvious and straightforward.

The influence of violence

In early 1989 I was telephoned one Sunday evening by a caller announcing himself as a detective with the San Diego Police Force. He was investigating a multiple throat-slasher whose seventh victim had escaped. The woman claimed that she would be able to recognize her attacker. What, the detective asked, was the likely effect of extreme emotion on the reliability and accuracy of her testimony?

This is an important and highly controversial issue on which both conventional and professional wisdom varies. A survey of 235 American lawyers found that 82 per cent of defense lawyers felt that high levels of emotion *would* impair facial recognition, while only 32 per cent of prosecution attorneys took this view. Who is right? Does extreme emotion brand the experience indelibly on the victim's memory, or does it reduce his or her capacity for recollection, possibly as a result of repression? A number of studies have attempted to answer this question, although even the most zealous experimenters fortunately do not attempt to convince their subjects that they are about to have their throats cut, so the findings are open to the objection that they may not generalize to very extreme levels of emotion.

The usual method of investigating recall of emotionally charged events is to expose subjects to a film or staged incident in which some crucial event occurs, an event that may be associated with violence, such as the apparent shooting of a child. Broadly speaking, the evidence seems to suggest that memory of a violent event is stronger than it would be for a neutral event, but that memory for associated detail is less. In one experiment eye fixations were used to assess the amount of attention given to different aspects of a scene with and without a violent incident. Violence tended to increase the amount of attention given to the

*Opposite:
What many victims of violence remember with most clarity are their feelings—fear, anger, helplessness. A few vivid details of the event may be remembered, but incidental features may be very hazy.*

focal incident relative to peripheral features, but even when the amount of viewing time was kept constant by presenting the crucial incident only briefly, there was still a tendency for better recall under violent conditions.

The answer to the San Diego detective's question therefore seems to depend on the details of the situation, and on whether the assailant's face is seen as central or peripheral, or whether the knife is seen as central or peripheral.

There is indeed evidence for the existence of 'weapon focus', whereby the victim may concentrate attention on the weapon itself rather than on the appearance of the assailant. In one simulated study, described by Loftus and carried out at the University of Michigan, a subject was asked to wait outside an experimental laboratory before participating in an experiment. In the 'no weapon' condition the subject was allowed to overhear a harmless conversation about equipment failure in the experimental room, after which someone emerged from the room holding a pen and with grease on his hands, uttered a single statement and left. In the 'weapon' condition a different subject would hear a hostile interchange between two people, ending with breaking bottles, chairs crashing and someone leaving the experimental room holding a letter opener covered with blood; again the person uttered a single line before leaving. Subjects were subsequently given an album containing 50 photographs and asked whether or not the person who had emerged from the room was represented there. In the 'no weapon' case subjects located the correct photograph 49 per cent of the time, but in the 'weapon' case only 33 per cent were correct in their identification.

A single experiment of this sort is rather slender evidence on which to base a firm conclusion, but it does support evidence from other studies which indicates that fear may tend to narrow attention. In other words, fear may put a crucial feature of a situation into sharp focus, but may reduce the reliability of the witness's account of peripheral features.

Leading questions

Eyewitnesses are often asked to recall details of incidents that happen very rapidly and unexpectedly. In such circumstances there is a very real danger that questioning — especially the way in which questions are worded — will distort recall. Loftus has carried out a number of experiments on this point. In one study people watched a film of a car crash and were then asked: 'About how fast were the cars going when they hit each other?' All subjects were asked the same question, except that the word *hit* was replaced with either *smashed, collided, bumped* or *contacted*. Speed estimates were highest (40.8 mph) when the word *smashed* was used, lower with *collided* (39.3 mph), and lower still with *bumped* (38.1 mph), *hit* (34 mph) and *contacted* (31.8 mph). Furthermore, when questioned a week later about whether there had been any broken glass, those who had been tested using the word *smashed* were consistently more likely to report (incorrectly) that glass had been broken.

In another study, again using film of a car accident, subjects were asked either 'Did you see *the* broken headlight?' or 'Did you see *a* broken headlight?' Those who had seen the version of the film with the broken headlight said 'Yes' to both questions with equal frequency, but those who saw the other version of the film were more than twice as likely to falsely recall a breakage when asked about 'the' rather than 'a' broken headlight. Subjects were clearly biased by the wording of the question.

| Original drawings | Reproduced drawings | Reproduced drawings |

These columns of drawings show how easily memory can be distorted by suggestion. The drawings on the left are purposely ambiguous, and were accompanied by one or other of two equally plausible labels. When asked to recall them, people's drawings were distorted in the direction of the labels, as shown in the middle and right-hand columns.

Another series of experiments carried out by Loftus convincingly demonstrated that it is possible to change a witness's recollection of an incident by subtly introducing new information during questioning. In one study subjects were shown a series of slides representing a traffic accident in which a pedestrian was knocked down at a pedestrian crossing. A green car drove past the accident without stopping, a police car arrived, and a passenger from one of the cars in the accident ran for help. Subjects were asked 12 questions about the incident. Question 10 made reference to the *blue* car that drove past the accident. When asked 20 minutes later to recall the color of the car that drove by without stopping, subjects given the false information tended to choose a blue or bluish-green rather than green. In another experiment Loftus managed to persuade her subjects to report a completely non-existent barn that had been 'inserted' into their memory during questioning.

If witnesses' reports of events can be changed, does that mean that what they actually *remember* has changed, or are they simply changing what they say? Are they just 'guessing' differently under social pressure? In order to probe this question Loftus conducted an experiment in which subjects saw a pedestrian accident which involved a car stopping at either a stop sign or a yield sign. Two days later subjects were asked a series of questions about the incident, one of which biased them away from what had actually occurred; if they had seen a stop sign, the biasing question referred to a yield sign, and vice versa. Their memory of the incident was then tested by showing them pairs of slides and asking them which sign they had seen. In the critical pair of slides, one showed a stop sign and the other a yield sign. Loftus argued that if her subjects genuinely remembered the correct version, but simply responded otherwise to please the experimenter, the bias could be overridden if she offered a high enough pay-off for making a correct response. One group of subjects was therefore given no reward, one was promised $1 each if they decided correctly, a third group was offered $5, and a fourth was told that the person in the experiment who scored the highest would receive $25. Despite this, between 70 and 85 per cent of those tested selected the wrong response in accordance with the bias; there was no tendency for higher reward to lead to greater accuracy.

Other experiments showed that subjects reacted just as rapidly and con-fidently when they were responding to the misleading information as they would have done without biasing questions. Finally, Loftus was able to show that the effect was not dependent on subjects' failing to notice the crucial information in the first place. Asked immediately afterwards to give a detailed account of what they had seen, the relevant information was usually mentioned, but subjects who mentioned the crucial feature on immediate test showed the normal process of disruption when asked to respond to misleading questions later.

From this Loftus argues that it is the actual memory trace which is changed by subsequent information. While acknowledging that it is logically impossible ever to prove that a pure and undistorted memory trace still lurks somewhere in the observer's brain, she points out with some justification that all her efforts to get at such a trace have proved unsuccessful. It therefore does appear to be the case that what we remember is an amalgam of what we see and what we subsequently think. In this connection Loftus quotes an intriguing personal reminiscence from the Swiss psychologist Jean Piaget: 'One of my first memories would date, if it were true, from my second year. I can still see, most clearly, the following scene, in which I believed until I was about fifteen. I was sitting in my pram, which my nurse was pushing in the Champs Elysées, when a man tried to kidnap me. I was held in by the strap fastened round me while my nurse bravely tried to stand between me and the thief. She received various scratches, and I can still see vaguely those on her face. Then a crowd gathered, a policeman with a short cloak and a white baton came up, and the man took to his heels. I can still see the whole scene, and can even place it near the tube station. When I was about fifteen, my parents received a letter from my former nurse saying that she had been converted to the Salvation Army. She wanted to confess her past faults, and in particular to return the watch she had been given on this occasion. She had made up the whole story, faking the scratches. I, therefore, must have heard, as a child, the account of this story, which my parents believed, and projected it into the past in the form of a visual memory.'

Loftus' view that the original memory trace is destroyed is not by any means universally accepted. One set of investigators, Bekerian and Bowers, argue that the original trace survives, and can be retrieved, given appropriate cueing methods. They found that the standard Loftus method of asking questions in a relatively unstructured way did indeed produce a biasing effect, but the distortion disappeared when subjects were questioned in a systematic way, beginning with earlier incidents and working chronologically through to later incidents. Other workers, McCloskey and Zaragoza, were unable to obtain the removal of bias by chronological recall, although they did present evidence for the survival of the original memory, providing an alternative interpretation of the effect of leading questions in terms of guessing bias. Misleading information, they suggested, has no effect on people who have successfully remembered an incident, but it does have a distorting effect on the responses of people who have genuinely forgotten, encouraging them to bias their responses in the direction of the misleading information. Loftus remains unconvinced by this argument. It is in fact possible that there may be more than one source of distortion. However, regardless of the theoretical interpretation of such effects, there is no doubt that the testimony of eyewitnesses can be distorted by material introduced during cross-examination. It is clearly essential to bear this in mind when interviewing suspects, and when interpreting evidence obtained under sub-optimal conditions.

Look carefully at the colors and markings of these three butterflies. You may be required to answer questions about them later in this chapter!

What should lawyers learn from these demonstrations of the fallibility of eyewitness testimony? The Denning Commission, which was set up to re-evaluate the role of eyewitness testimony in a wide range of British cases, came to the conclusion that unsupported testimony should never be sufficient to secure a conviction. British police procedures have also accepted the need for the careful monitoring of interviews, which are now routinely recorded. The practice of showing a picture of the suspect to witnesses before attempts at identification, such as apparently occurred in the George Davis case, is clearly something to be avoided.

Extensive psychological research in this area has resulted in attempts to develop improved interview techniques based on psychological principles. A good example of this is the Cognitive Interview schedule devised by Fisher and Geiselman. This is based on four general retrieval principles.

1   Mental reinstatement of the environment and any personal contact experienced during the crime.
2   Encouraging the reporting of every detail, regardless of how peripheral to the main incident.
3   Attempting to describe the incident in several different orders.
4   Attempting to report the incident from different viewpoints, including that of other participants or witnesses.

The first two of these are based on the concept of *encoding specificity* — attempting to provide maximum overlap between the context in which the crime was witnessed and the context in which the recall attempt is made. The third and fourth principles try to capitalize on the idea that material can be retrieved using a number of different routes that may provide information about rather different aspects of the original experience.

An initial test of this interview approach used a police training film of a violent crime, with subjects interviewed 48 hours later using one of three schedules. The first was the New Cognitive Interview, the second was the standard Los Angeles Police Interview, while the third involved hypnotizing subjects and then asked them to recall the incident using the standard procedure. It should perhaps be pointed out that the use of hypnosis is highly controversial; in general, although it tends to increase the amount of information recalled, it increases the subject's suggestibility, and often increases the amount of false information reported. The three methods did not differ in the amount of false information they elicited, although the standard interview provided less information (29.4 items) than either the hypnosis interview (38.0) or the cognitive interview (41.2).

A second study attempted to introduce misleading information during the interview, asking the question 'Was the guy with the green backpack nervous?', and then testing for whether subjects would falsely report that the backpack was green. Those subjects tested using the cognitive interview were less likely to be misled in this way.

Fisher and Geiselman have continued to develop the cognitive interview, using hints obtained from watching 'good' and 'poor' interviewers to develop and introduce modifications. These have included a greater use of open-ended questions rather than short 'Yes' or 'No' questions, and attempting to fit the order of questioning to the witness's order of experience. Using these methods, they found that the level of correct reporting rose from 40 per cent to almost 60 per cent.

In recent years a considerable number of investigators have compared the effectiveness of the cognitive interview with more standard techniques. A total of 27 experiments making this comparison have been reviewed by Bekerian and Dennett, who find an advantage in favor of the cognitive interview for all 27 comparisons. The extent of the advantage varies, but on average about 30 per cent more information is accurately reported. In general, relatively little false information is reported, with a slight tendency for such errors to be less common following the cognitive interview.

Remembering faces

'I never forget a face!' One often hears people making such claims, but how justifiably? Muriel Woodhead was particularly interested in this issue and conducted an experiment in which some 100 Cambridge housewives were shown a series of unfamiliar faces on slides and then asked to recognize them when they were re-presented together with a series of similar but new faces. They were also asked how good they thought their memory for faces was. There were large differences in how well they performed on the recognition test, and considerable variation in how good they thought their memory was. Most interesting of all, there was absolutely no relationship between performance and self-rating. Some

Buildings are easier to recognize upside down than faces. This is because recognition of faces seems to involve different subprocesses. Cover up the rest of this caption and see how many of these buildings you recognize. They are, upside down and left to right, Brighton Pavilion, the cathedral of San Marco in Venice, the Taj Mahal in Agra, and Sacré Coeur in Paris.

women performed extremely well but made very modest claims; some claimed to have a remarkable memory for faces and performed very poorly; some were reasonably accurate in their claims; most were somewhere in between. This may of course have meant that the test was not very realistic — it did not test memory for faces outside the laboratory — or very reliable. Taking advantage of the fact that we had already tested a large number of subjects over a period of two years or more, Muriel Woodhead and I decided to follow up this experiment by investigating whether there were consistent differences between people's memory for faces. We selected people who had performed particularly well or particularly badly in previous experiments and invited them back for further testing. We found that those who had performed well on previous face-memory experiments performed substantially better on retest than those who had performed poorly. We also compared their memory for two other types of material, typewritten words and reproductions of paintings. The purpose of these further tests was to examine whether the enhanced performance of our good recognizers would apply to all memory, to all visual memory, or only to faces. Good face recognizers proved to be better at recognizing paintings, but did not differ from poor recognizers in their verbal memory score. This suggests that there is something special about visual memory which separates it from verbal memory, but it does not indicate a clear distinction within visual memory between remembering faces and remembering pictures of objects and scenes.

In fact it has sometimes been suggested that memory for faces depends on a particular system located in a special part of the brain. One piece of evidence that is sometimes held to support this comes from patients suffering from *proso-pagnosia*, a rare neurological condition in which the person is unable to recognize the faces of previously familiar people, although he or she has no difficulty recognizing objects and no general visual impairment. A second argument in favor of the view that the perception and memory of faces is special stems from the observation that the angle from which a face is viewed is particularly important. An inverted face is much harder to recognize than an inverted building; it is also very difficult to perceive the emotional expression on a face that is inverted.

One neuropsychological study tested the memory of patients with right hemisphere damage for faces and buildings both the right way up and inverted. For upright faces the control patients, with other types of brain damage, made far fewer errors than those with right hemisphere damage. But when

Whose faces are these? Answer: Boris Yeltsin (left), Madonna and Arnold Schwarzenegger. Why is it so difficult to judge expression when a face is upside down?

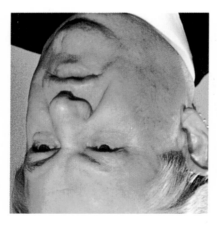  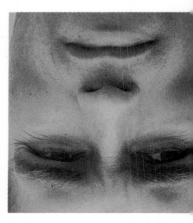

the faces were inverted the reverse was true; those with right hemisphere damage did better than the controls. This pattern did not emerge in the case of pictures of houses, where the controls did slightly better under both conditions. While such results may be peculiar to faces, other evidence suggests that they are not. For example, one patient with right hemisphere damage, who was a very keen birdwatcher, had recognition difficulties which extended beyond faces; he found it very difficult to make the subtle discriminations necessary to tell one species or subspecies of bird from another. Even if face recognition proves not to be a separate function, it does seem that recognizing faces depends on detecting relatively subtle differences in the relationship between their component features.

It is clear from the first section of this chapter that memory for faces is very fallible. Can it be improved? A few years ago Muriel Woodhead, Derek Simmonds and I were invited to evaluate a course specifically aimed at improving ability to recognize and remember faces. It was based on an approach to face perception popularized by Jacques Penry, the inventor of the system called Photo-fit. Photo-fit comprises a box containing sets of features — chins, noses, eyes, types of hair and so on, all taken from actual photographs — which can be put together to construct a face. By combining such features it is possible to produce a very large number of different faces. With a skilled operator, so it is claimed, it is possible to reproduce any given face. Penry believed that in order to perceive and remember a human face one has to abstract the various features and categorize them systematically. He talks of 'reading' a face, noting the nose, for example, and categorizing it in terms of size and shape, then going on to perform similar categorization for all the other features. Such a view is not of course original to Penry. It goes back at least to Leonardo da Vinci, who discusses memory for faces in his treatise on painting, advising the artist to divide the face into four parts — forehead, nose, mouth, chin. He advises the artist to study the possible forms of each of these features and, having learnt the range of categories, apply them to any face he sees. This, claims Leonardo, will enable the artist to memorize a face at a single glance.

What, in your opinion, are the most recognizable features of this face? How good would you be at describing it?

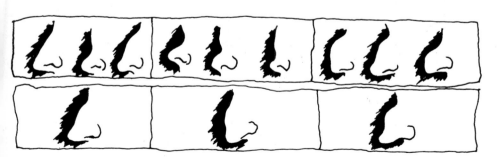

Various categories of nose, as sketched by Leonardo da Vinci.

The course which my colleagues and I evaluated was inspired by Penry's approach and devoted a good deal of attention to his classification system. It was carried out with great enthusiasm and imagination, and involved lectures, film demonstrations, discussions, case histories and field exercises. Then, in order to see how effective the course was, we carried out three experiments. In the first subjects were tested for their ability to commit faces to memory and subsequently recognize them. In the second and third studies subjects were allowed to refer to a set of photographs, just as if they were passport officials at an airport with photographs of wanted men. In all three studies we tested two groups of similar people; one group took the three-day course being evaluated, while the other went about its normal business. The first two studies failed to show up any difference between the two groups. The third did show a small difference: the trainees were actually *worse* than those who had not taken the course.

Opposite:
Four Photo-fit
pictures of the same
man, wearing three
items of disguise
(glasses, beard, wig).
Would you have
recognized any of
them as the man on
page 197?

Why was the course so ineffective? One possibility is that since we spend our whole lives recognizing faces, a two- or three-day course is unlikely to make much impression on the way we experience faces. Another possibility is that the training course was based on inappropriate principles. The Penry approach is very much concerned with analyzing a face into its component features. It could be argued that perception of a face depends on processing the *pattern* of features, paying attention to the way in which each feature is related to another, rather than isolating individual features. Expert chess players are very good at perceiving and remembering chess positions because the *pattern* of pieces is meaningful to them, not because they concentrate on the location or appearance of particular pieces. Such a view would be consistent with the 'levels of process-ing' approach to memory discussed in Chapter 9. This theory claims that 'shallow' processing (reading the superficial features of a stimulus) gives rise to poor memory, whereas 'deep' processing (probing the meaning of the stimulus) leads to much better memory.

Karalyn Patterson and I decided to test this view by doing an experiment in which subjects were required to categorize photographs of unfamiliar people either on the basis of some of the physical dimensions advocated by Penry or on the basis of several 'deeper' dimensions, such as honesty, intelligence, or live-liness. We also included another factor, namely disguise. We reasoned that although it might be easier to remember a face for its honesty or intelligence than for its nose or ears, it might well be the case that a broad judgement of character would be much more easily misled by disguise. It may be much easier to make a person look more friendly or less intelligent than to change the shape of his face or size of his nose.

As recognition material we used photographs of amateur actors and of colleagues, all of whom were photographed either undisguised or wearing a beard, wig, spectacles, or any combination of these. The photographs were taken either full face or profile; a colleague, suitably disguised, agreed to pose for them. Our subjects were familiarized with one photograph of each person in any one combination of disguised features. This was repeatedly presented until it was consistently recognized and the person's name given correctly. Our subjects were then presented with a set of photographs comprising the target people in all

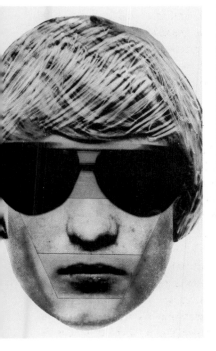

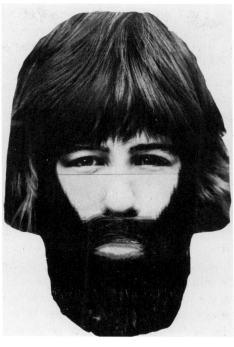

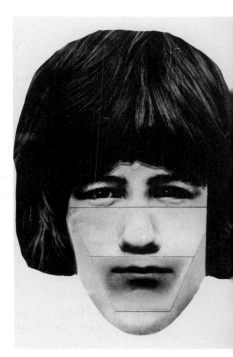

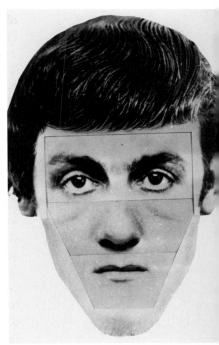

possible combinations of disguise, either in full frontal view or in profile, together with a number of similarly disguised but unfamiliar people. Their job was to detect and name the targets.

Our results had two interesting features. First, we found that under all conditions subjects were somewhat better at recognizing the faces they had categorized using the 'deep' dimensions of intelligence, liveliness, and so forth. This effect was not particularly great, but there was no evidence to suggest that analyzing a face into its component features was helpful either with disguised or undisguised faces. Second, we found that the effect of disguise was very dramatic. Every time an item of disguise was added or removed the probability of recognition went down. Performance ranged from extremely good when the face was presented in its originally learnt form to virtual guesswork when the maximum number of disguised features was changed.

There is no doubt that disguise can be very effective. Consider the case of the Cambridge Rapist. A few years ago great consternation was caused in the British university city of Cambridge by the activities of a rapist. He was clearly someone with considerable local knowledge, and therefore someone who probably lived locally. A number of his victims had had the opportunity of seeing him, but their descriptions were somewhat variable since he sometimes wore a wig, or even on one occasion a mask with 'RAPIST' written across it. Although by some standards he was probably rather insignificant, for Cambridge he was a major threat. Various precautionary

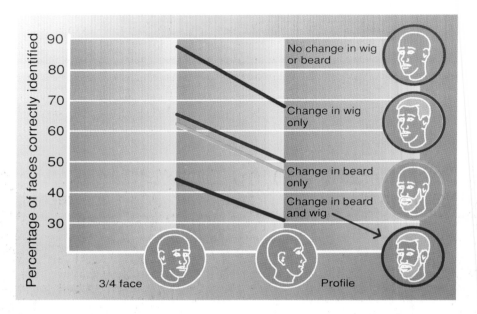

With a wig and beard, you halve your chances of being recognized as the guilty party. Faces seen in three-quarters view are much more recognizable than faces seen in profile.

measures were taken, including the kind offer of a number of male students to sleep in girls' bedrooms! Not to be outdone, Oxford produced its own rapist, although he never achieved the press coverage of his Cambridge counterpart.

The main ways of conveying information about a wanted person are by verbal description, Photo-fit, or artist's drawing. Even when accurate, a verbal description is clearly a very unsatisfactory way of communicating someone's appearance. Try describing your own face. Do you think that you could be recognized from the description, even by your own mother? In consequence Photo-fit and similar systems, such as Identikit, have been widely used by the police, in conjunction with drawings by police artists. How good are these systems at conveying a witness's recollection of a face? This question has been extensively explored by Graham Davis, Hadyn Ellis and John Shepherd (a group of psychologists at the University of Aberdeen) with, on the whole, disappointing results. The average person has great difficulty in producing a likeness of a face even when the face is actually in front of him. When the Aberdeen group tested their subjects by asking them to match up a Photo-fit picture with the appropriate original face, performance was above chance but not decisively so. What evidence we have seems to suggest that the efforts of police artists are not much better. Why? Perhaps because the only way to draw or construct a Photo-fit face is in terms of individual features, whereas, as suggested earlier, we actually perceive faces in terms of meaningful patterns rather than features. No doubt the police will continue to use methods of this kind, simply because it is so desirable to be able to circulate pictures of wanted individuals, but it is essential to recognize the limitations of the material that witnesses are likely to produce.

Consider the case of David Webb, who was sentenced to up to 50 years in prison in 1976 following a rape and an attempted rape and robbery carried out in two grocery stores in Everett, Washington, USA. Webb was identified on the basis of a composite picture built up by witnesses, who also identified him at the trial. He was convicted despite inconsistencies in the testimony of the prosecution witnesses and evidence from defense witnesses that he was elsewhere at the time of the crime. Several months later another man confessed to the crimes for which Webb had been sentenced. The confession was investigated and in 1978 Webb was released. Without the confession, he would probably still be in jail and likely to stay there.

Identity parades and line-ups

Clearly we are much better at recognizing faces than we are at recalling and representing our recall either by Photo-fit or description. For this reason the identity parade or line-up procedure is an important element in the detective process. The suspect is presented together with a number of non-suspects of broadly similar characteristics and the witness is asked if he or she recognizes any member of the line-up as the criminal. It is of course essential that the suspect is not obviously different from the other members of the line-up (the 'distractors') if the evidence is to be at all valid. Loftus describes simple techniques for ensuring that a given line-up is not biased. There have, however, been cases where bias has been extreme: imagine placing one black-haired person in a group of fair-haired people, or a youth suspected of a crime known to have been committed by a young man in a line-up of men over 40. In one extreme case, where the suspect was known to be an Oriental, the line-up included only one Oriental!

Such instances are of course very rare and in any case should be picked up by the defendant's solicitor at the time of the line-up. But other more subtle influences can come into play. For example, if a witness describes a criminal as good-looking, then it would be important to ensure that the line-up consisted of people who are reasonably good-looking. Another source of bias is that which occurred in the case of George Davis, where a photograph of the accused was shown to the witness *before* the line-up. Under such circumstances the witness may be tempted to pick out the most familiar face in the line-up, the familiarity having come entirely from the photograph just seen.

Which one of these butterflies appeared on page 193? Actually, two of these butterflies appeared on page 193. The question was intentionally misleading. Small details become very important when liberty and reputation are at stake.

Many biasing factors come into play when an eyewitness is confronted with a line-up of suspects. They can, however, be substantially reduced by applying our knowledge of human memory.

One particularly powerful source of bias in recognition is clothing. This issue has been extensively explored in Australia by Donald Thomson, who became interested in the question following a legal case in which the clothing worn by a criminal was a very important factor in causing someone else wearing similar garb to be identified as the perpetrator of the crime. Thomson was able to show that context, in terms of the location of the crime or the clothing of the criminal, has an extremely powerful effect on whether a person is recognized or not. He went on to show that this effect is still present even with highly sophisticated subjects who are alert to the possibility of bias.

Thomson became actively involved in presenting the case for the unreliability of eyewitness evidence, and on one occasion took part in a television discussion on the topic. Some time later he was picked up by the police, who refused to explain why they were arresting him. He assumed he was being unofficially harassed because of his strong views on eyewitness reliability. At the police station he was placed in a line-up; a woman, clearly very distraught, identified him, and he was then told he was being charged with rape. When he asked for details, it became clear that the rape had been committed at the same time as he had been taking part in the television discussion. He said he had a perfectly good alibi and a large number of witnesses, including an official of the Australian Civil Rights Committee and an Assistant Commissioner of Police. To this the policeman taking his statement replied: 'Yes, and I suppose you've got Jesus Christ and the Queen of England too!' It transpired that the woman had been raped while watching the program. Thomson was a victim of what is often termed *unconscious transference*, whereby a witness correctly recognizes a face as being that of someone seen before but incorrectly assigns that face to the crime.

Thomson also drew attention to another important aspect of identification, namely the role of knowledge other than memory for the target event. He cites a case in which an accused person, having been identified in a line-up, swapped identities with another man in the remand cell. The accused thoroughly briefed his substitute, and it was the substitute who was interviewed by the defense lawyer. In court all the witnesses identified the substitute as the offender! After all, he was the person in the dock, wasn't he? When the ruse was revealed, the accused was acquitted. The witnesses unquestioningly believed that the man produced in court by the police was the man picked out from the line-up.

As in the case of interview procedures, the problems of line-ups have encouraged some psychologists to try to develop better methods. This is particularly important in the case of child witnesses, who may well be intimidated by having to confront a line of adults all resembling the stranger who may have attacked them. One way out of this problem is to use video line-ups, a procedure that also has the advantage of obviating the need to assemble a plausible array of characters whenever a new witness is interviewed.

One source of bias in line-ups can be the assumption, sometimes implicit, but on occasion even explicit, that the line-up includes the criminal. Since this may well not be the case, there is clearly a danger that false identifications will be encouraged. Even when it is not explicitly stated that the line-up contains the criminal, witnesses tend to assume that this is the case, and feel obliged to come up with a positive identification. One way of avoiding this is to present the people in the line-up one at a time, without telling the witness how many will be presented. This approach was used by Lindsay and his colleagues in Canada, who carried out a series of experiments in which subjects saw a staged crime — someone stealing a radio from the room in which the subjects were waiting, for example — and were then asked to identify the culprit from an array of photographs. The photographs were presented simultaneously or one after the other, and either included or did not include the culprit's photograph. There was no difference in the likelihood of correctly identifying the 'thief', but the sequential method (showing the photographs one after the other) did reduce the occasions on which subjects identified an innocent person.

11 Amnesia

A mnesia is a general term meaning temporary or permanent impairment of some part of the memory system. In Chapter 5 we discussed hysterical amnesia, which may involve forgetting an intensely stressful experience or even forgetting who one is (fugue). As we saw, hysterical amnesia is almost always associated with a need, conscious or unconscious, to escape from intolerable anxiety, and it is usually temporary — in due course there is a return to a normal state of memory. Sadly this is not the case with most other types of amnesia, where the memory defect is the result of some kind of brain damage.

The causes of such amnesia are various, ranging from a blow on the head, through brain damage due to alcohol or infection, to the effects of aging. In all cases loss of memory is more specific than occurs in hysterical amnesia: the person rarely loses his or her sense of identity or awareness of the past, but usually has great difficulty in acquiring new information, a memory defect which can be extremely incapacitating.

What is it like to be amnesic?

We described in Chapter 1 the terrible plight of Clive Wearing, who is so densely amnesic that he perpetually believes that he has just woken up from a long period of unconsciousness. Fortunately memory deficits are very rarely as dense as this, but even a relatively mild memory problem can be quite disabling. Some idea of the experience of being moderately memory impaired is given by a clinical psychologist, Malcolm Meltzer, who suffered brain damage as a result of anoxia following a heart attack. Fortunately he recovered sufficiently to return to work and write about his experience.

Meltzer suffered his heart attack at the age of 44 and emerged from a six-week coma with memory problems, although not dense amnesia. He recognized his family, although not all of his friends, He knew who he was, and what his job was. Initially he thought that he had two children, although he had only one, and believed that his age was 33, rather than 44. When he returned home the route seemed unfamiliar, but his house was familiar. However he could not remember where things were kept, and had to relearn skills such as how to play the stereo, change a razor blade and set the alarm clock, and the relearning process was relatively slow. He seemed to have lost access to the 'scripts' for everyday activities. He reports: 'The feeling engendered by this inability to do things done in the past was that of incompetency. When should bills be paid? What is used to fix a broken chair? When should oil be changed in the car? . . . Which are good places to go for a vacation? How

Is it possible to have an identity if you do not have a memory?

do you get there? Where do you stay? What have you enjoyed and not enjoyed in previous vacations?' He also suffered from more general cognitive processing problems: 'Organisation of thinking was hampered . . . I had trouble keeping the facts in mind, which made it difficult to organise them . . . Comparing things along a number of variables is difficult to do when you cannot retain the variables or retain the comparison after you have made it.'

Spatial memory was also disturbed: 'Even inside a building, getting lost was commonplace, and sometimes it took days for me to figure out and remember how to get out of the building. In taking walks, even in the familiar neighbourhood I could get lost.'

Such problems clearly interfered with his life. Interpersonal relationships were also hampered by his memory deficit: 'Having conversations could become a trial. Often in talking with people I was acquainted with, I had trouble remembering their names or whether they were married or what our relationship had been in the past. I worried about asking where someone's wife is and finding out that I had been at her funeral two years ago . . . Often if I didn't have a chance to say immediately what came to mind, it would be forgotten and the conversation would move to another topic. Then there was little for me to talk about. I couldn't remember much about current events or things I read in the paper or saw on TV. Even juicy titbits of gossip might be forgotten. So in order to have something to say, I tended to talk about myself and my "condition". My conversation became rather boring.'

Even recreation became difficult: 'Movies and TV-watching became work. If it is a story, the trouble is remembering the beginning of the story or who the characters are . . . In terms of sports on TV there is trouble remembering which team is which, which team is ahead, which players did the scoring, and how it all relates to their past performance.'

Despite these handicaps Meltzer persevered and with help was able to improve sufficiently to return to work and produce at least one paper, which provides valuable insight into the problems of coping with even relatively mild amnesia.

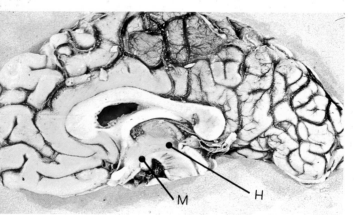

A section through the brain, showing the location of the mamillary body (M) and hippocampus (H), two areas vital for memory functions. While the capacity to remember may be more or less destroyed in amnesia, the capacity to acquire new skills is usually preserved.

M   H

Causes of amnesia

Almost anything that damages the brain will tend to slow down the rate of acquiring new information and the speed of retrieving existing knowledge. There are, however, certain areas of the brain which appear to be particularly crucial for memory, and where damage can produce the much more dense impairment in memory that is termed amnesia. The areas in question tend to involve a circuit linking the temporal lobes of the brain with the frontal lobes and the so-called limbic system, comprising a number of structures such as the hippocampus and the mamillary bodies. Damage to these areas can come from a number of sources, including encephalitis resulting from brain infection, anoxia, as in Meltzer's case, stroke, or Korsakoff's syndrome. The most common cause of the latter is alcoholism — prolonged, excessive drinking and poor diet eventually lead to a dificiency of vitamin B_1 (thiamine), which results in a catastrophic breakdown of cognitive function. During this phase the person is typically confused and disoriented. Treatment with thiamine leads to an alleviation of the confusional state, but by this time damage is likely to have occurred to the parts of the brain crucial for memory, resulting in permanent amnesia. This can be relatively pure, but more commonly is associated with other intellectual deficits. Frontal lobe damage in particular can often produce deficits in the operation of the central executive component of working memory.

Many accident victims never manage to remember the last few moments before their accident. Once they regain consciousness, they may appear to act normally, but it may take weeks or months before they are able to reconstruct events in their recent past.

Probably the most common source of memory deficits in younger patients however is *traumatic amnesia* resulting from the effects of closed head injury (brain damage that occurs in the absence of penetration of the skull by a missile or other object). Road traffic accidents are the most frequent cause of closed head injury. A sudden acceleration or deceleration of the head may cause twisting and shearing of the meninges that cover the brain, together with temporal lobe damage as the brain is forced past or against the bony eminences that occur on the inner surfaces of the cranial bones.

Traumatic amnesia

Four days before writing this I was sitting in my car in a line of traffic, waiting to cross a busy seaside road. In front of me was a car, and in front of that a tractor and cart. Quite suddenly the body of a man wearing a blue crash-helmet sailed high in the air across the front of the tractor, landed in the road, and lay motionless. It was a motorcyclist whose bike had apparently struck a car turning into our side road. A woman passenger in the car in front got out and began to weep hysterically, crying that it was someone's son, while a swarm of helpers gathered to render what first aid they could, call the ambulance and generally control the traffic. It was yet another head injury. What were the chances of survival for this young man? If he survived, what was his likely quality of life?

There are an estimated 7,500 serious head injury cases in Britain every year, with young men being the most likely victims. About 97 per cent of those who reach hospital survive, with varying degrees of disability. An unfortunate few are so intellectually impaired as to be virtually vegetables, but most make an almost complete recovery. However, even if an accident victim is fortunate enough to recover completely, he will have difficult months ahead. A severe blow to the head is likely to lead to loss of consciousness for a period lasting from a few seconds up to several months and, in the extreme, to failure ever to recover consciousness. The process of recovery is gradual, and depends on careful nursing and monitoring.

On emerging from coma the patient is likely to go through a confused state known as *post-traumatic amnesia*. He will appear to be conscious and may often be able to converse relatively fluently. However, he is likely to be disoriented, not knowing where he is and not remembering when told. He may fail to recognize familiar objects and people, and may be incapable of building up a consistent, coherent picture of himself or his plight. This confused state may last from a few minutes to a matter of months, but it almost invariably passes. The state that follows is one in which the patient is likely to be able to build up an increasingly coherent picture of himself and his surroundings, but he is still likely to have no memory of the accident, and indeed may have an amnesia extending back for several years. This state is known as *retrograde amnesia*. As the case history below illustrates, this form of amnesia may gradually recede.

Retrograde amnesia

A greenkeeper, aged 22, was thrown from his motorcycle in August 1933. There was a bruise in the left frontal region and slight bleeding from the left ear, but no fracture was seen on X-ray examination. A week after the accident he was able to converse sensibly, and the nursing staff considered that he had fully recovered consciousness. When questioned, however, he said that the date was February 1922 and that he was a schoolboy. He had no recollection of five years spent in Australia or two years in Britain working on a golf course. Two weeks after the injury he remembered the five years spent in Australia and the fact that he had returned to Britain, but the past two years were a complete blank. Three weeks after the injury he returned to the village where he had worked for two years. Everything looked strange — he had no recollection of ever having been there before. He lost his way on more than one occasion. Still feeling a stranger to the district, he returned to work; he was able to do his work satisfactorily, but had difficulty remembering what he had actually done during the day. About ten weeks after the accident the events of the past two years were gradually recollected and finally he was able to remember everything up to within a few minutes of the accident.

The consistent tendency for the period blanked out by retrograde amnesia to shrink over time is very characteristic, as is the failure ever to recover the last few seconds before the accident. Why is this? Could it be that the accident victim represses the event, refusing to recall it because it is emotionally painful? This is not really a plausible explanation since head injuries resulting from penetrating or crushing wounds which do not result in loss of consciousness do not produce this totally amnesic period, despite the fact that such events are clearly emotionally significant and

very unpleasant. Could it be that the person simply fails to take in the necessary information over the last few moments? This view is refuted by studies carried out by Yarnell and Lynch on American football players who had been 'dinged' (concussed). Immediately they regained consciousness the players were asked the name of the particular play that had preceded the incident (for example, 32 pop). Immediately after the concussion they were able to answer the question, indicating that the information had certainly been registered. When asked again some 3 to 20 minutes later, however, they were quite unable to recall any of the relevant information. A subsequent study of the memory of football players taken off the field with other types of injury indicated that this very rapid forgetting was not simply a characteristic of the memory capacity of the average American football player! It appears that a memory trace requires a certain amount of time to consolidate. A blow on the head, or possibly, as we shall see later, an electric current passed through the brain, probably prevents the physiological process of consolidation, and hence no permanent record is left.

A few seconds of total amnesia is a small price to pay for recovery from a head injury, but is it the only price? Unfortunately not, since the process of

Having one's head punched regularly, as boxers do, entails significant risk of brain injury. Although the memory problems that result from concussion may be temporary, there may be longer-term and more distressing consequences, such as violent changes of mood, 'out-of-character' behavior and concentration difficulties.

recovery is typically a very gradual one often accompanied by cognitive and emotional problems. Most patients complain of difficulty in concentrating, of becoming tired very easily, and of memory difficulties. They may also experience irritability and sudden rages, or periods of uninhibited and childlike behavior which in more severe cases may reflect an apparently altered personality. It is these changes, rather than any physical disability, that the person's family is likely to find most difficult to accept. It is very hard to come to terms with the feeling that someone is not only handicapped but has become a different person.

Retrograde amnesia is by no means limited to traumatic amnesic patients. Indeed most patients who have problems with new learning (anterograde amnesia), will also suffer from retrograde amnesia, although the extent of the two types of amnesia may not be correlated. Typically, retrograde amnesia will extend across the whole lifespan, but may show a gradient, most commonly being densest for recent events and less so for facts and events from the patient's early life.

Pure amnesia

In all the cases we have discussed so far memory problems have been only one of several symptoms of intellectual impairment. Often it is difficult to know to what extent a memory problem is primary, reflecting a basic inadequacy of the memory system, and to what extent it is a consequence of other problems. In someone who has suffered a head injury the memory problem is often compounded by difficulty in concentrating, and may be complicated by the presence of additional brain damage, possibly producing problems of perception, language comprehension, or personality difficulties.

There are, however, a few patients who suffer from a truly dense amnesia and yet show no general intellectual impairment. Although comparatively rare, such patients are of considerable interest because of the light they cast on our understanding of the normal and the amnesic memory.

The most celebrated case of a relatively pure amnesia is provided by a patient, HM, who became amnesic after being treated surgically to alleviate incapacitating attacks of epilepsy. One source of epilepsy is scar tissue in the brain, and in some cases removal of this tissue can substantially reduce the number of seizures. Today, if such an operation were performed, it would be limited to one side of the brain, since most brain functions have some representation in both hemispheres. In HM's case, however, brain tissue was removed from both sides of the brain, with the drastic result that he became grossly amnesic. He was still able to talk quite normally and to remember his early life, but seemed unable to commit new material to memory. He was dismally bad at memorizing lists of words, or indeed at becoming familiar with the faces of the people around him. He could still perform old skills such as mowing the lawn, but could not remember where the lawnmower was kept. His amnesia did have some minor advantages — he could go on reading the same magazines repeatedly without apparently getting bored — but it also had some bizarre costs. While he was in hospital a favorite uncle had died. When he asked about the old man he was told of his death and exhibited considerable distress. On numerous occasions afterwards he would ask about his uncle and each time he appeared to show the distress appropriate to hearing the news for the first time. His memory problem was so crippling that he was quite unable to cope with his normal job.

Needless to say, neurosurgeons learnt from the case of HM that it was essential not to remove equivalent tissue from both sides of the brain, so there have been no subsequent similar cases. There are, however, a number of conditions that produce somewhat similar results. Infections can cause damage to those areas of the brain which appear to be essential to long-term memory. Stroke victims can sustain damage to both sides of the brain in areas that appear to mediate memory. Poisoning by coal gas can produce a relatively pure amnesia. Perhaps the commonest cause of gross and relatively specific amnesia is alcoholic Korsakoff's syndrome.

In pure amnesia both sides of the brain appear to be affected; the temporal lobes are involved and/or the hippocampus (a subcortical structure) and/or the mamillary bodies (small but comparatively important structures deep inside the brain). There is a good deal of controversy over whether damage to these different sites causes a single pattern of amnesia. Also it is comparatively rare to find an amnesia which is not associated with other aspects of intellectual impairment, and even rarer to be able to investigate cases in which one knows both the detailed psychological nature of the impairment and the anatomical nature of the brain damage. Nevertheless 'pure' amnesic patients seem to present a broadly consistent picture.

Happy memories can be an important solace in old age. In some amnesic patients social and conversational skills learnt over a lifetime may mask a very real inability to remember current or even distant events.

Pure amnesic patients are quite likely to appear entirely normal on first meeting. Speech and social manner are quite unimpaired. Usually they can talk about their early lives with apparent ease. They may or may not be aware of a memory problem; if they are, they may have developed strategies for hiding it. A Korsakoff patient I know is an absolute master at this, with a large repertoire of socially acceptable responses which keep the conversation going without actually revealing the fact that he can remember nothing about the topic in question. Asked what he thinks about the

To function effectively — to behave autonomously, set goals and work towards them — one has to have a firm grasp on the present and understand how it relates to the past. For many amnesics the present is dreamlike, far less real than the past, hence the need for a sheltered environment.

government's economic policy, he is likely to say something like 'Well of course politicians are all alike, aren't they?' Asked who is likely to win a sports contest like the FA Cup, he is likely to come up with some comment such as 'They're both good sides so it should be a close game.' He once ran a pub.

In contrast with this apparent fluency, an amnesic patient is likely to be quite lost for an answer if one asks him what he had for breakfast or what day of the week it is, or indeed even the month or year. When asked the name of the current Prime Minister, one patient came up with 'Winston Churchill', who died in 1965. When told that his answer was not correct, he suggested 'Mr Attlee' (who died in 1967), and then said he simply was not very interested in politics. One can spend a whole morning with such a patient and in the afternoon he will completely fail to recognize you. For a patient who is intellectually otherwise intact, and who recognizes his problem, the situation is a very alarming one. It is sometimes described as like living in a dream, with no feeling of continuity or ability to reach out of the dream or plan for the future. Such a person, although perhaps physically fit and above average in intelligence, will not be able to cope with life in any other than a sheltered and carefully protected environment.

Pure but dense amnesia is rare, but because of its theoretical interest such patients have been studied extensively. What then are the characteristics of this type of amnesia? Short-term memory may be quite normal, hence a typical amnesic patient will have a normal digit span and can therefore repeat back a telephone number just as well as a person with normal memory. Performance may also be unimpaired on the Peterson Short-Term Forgetting Task (see page 32–33), which involves holding a small amount of information in memory for 20 seconds or so, while counting backwards to prevent rehearsal. Some amnesic patients do appear to be impaired on this task, but it is probable that this stems from a rather more general intellectual impairment than from a short-term memory deficit. Given a string of words to remember, amnesics will show the normal tendency for the last few words to be very well recalled, but will do poorly on the earlier items, retention of which is normally assumed to depend on long-term memory.

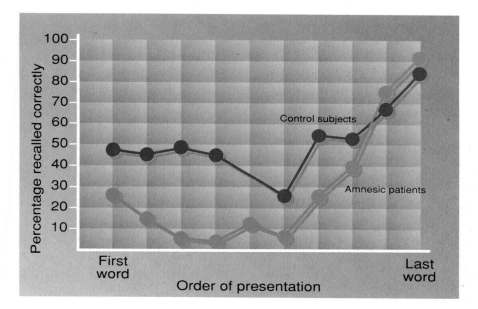

The recency effect is well maintained in amnesic patients. The last words in a series of words are well remembered. Performance on early words, however, is poor when compared with that of subjects without memory problems. (Baddeley and Warrington, 1970)

Amnesic subjects also exhibit gross impairment on a very wide range of long-term memory tests. While their ability to repeat back a string of digits is normal, once one exceeds the amount that can be recalled in one trial, performance declines catastrophically. Learning of pairs of words is also very poor. The ability to repeat back a simple story after a brief delay is disastrous. Lists of unrelated words are very poorly learnt, whether the testing is carried out by recall or recognition. Ability to remember faces is poor, and so is capacity for memorizing complex visual patterns, indicating that the deficit is not purely verbal.

Amnesia and everyday memory

Until quite recently most clinical measures of memory were based on standard laboratory tasks such as learning lists of unrelated words. Amnesic patients who are tested with such material sometimes object, with some justification, that their problem does not reside in their failure to learn to associate pairs of words or recognize unfamiliar geometric designs, but in their inability to cope with everyday life. I therefore set out, in collaboration with two colleagues, Alan Sunderland and John Harris, to discover to what extent standardized clinical measures of memory are useful predictors of everyday memory failures.

Our subjects were a number of head-injured patients, all of whom had sustained moderate to severe injury leading to a period of post-traumatic amnesia of at least 24 hours. We gave them a range of standard memory tests known to be sensitive to the effects of head injury. These included paired-associate learning, recognition of words, faces, and designs, and recall of a brief news story. The second aspect of our study was more challenging: How were we going to measure everday memory? We could not follow our patients' every move for weeks and weeks, and even if we could, how would we know when they made a memory lapse? We eventually settled on two methods, a questionnaire about the frequency of everyday memory lapses and a diary to be filled in every evening. We also asked a close relative, usually a wife or mother, to complete the questionnaire and to keep a diary as well.

The trouble with asking amnesic patients to keep a record of their memory lapses is that they frequently forget that they forgot! Forgetting to bring the milk in or feed the cat is more likely to be spotted by carers and relatives.

What happened? We found that asking patients about their memory lapses was not a very reliable way of obtaining information; they simply forgot that

they had forgotten! Questionnaires and diaries completed by relatives were somewhat more reliable; they allowed us to study the correlation between performance on the objective tests and the frequency of lapses of everyday memory. We found that the correlation with everyday memory tended to be extremely low for most of our objective test measures, despite the fact that the measures themselves were clearly sensitive to the effects of head injury. On their own these tests did not provide a good measure of everyday memory.

At about the time that we were carrying out this work a clinical psychologist in Oxford, Dr Barbara Wilson, was attempting to tackle the same problem. Noting our lack of success in using questionnaire methods, she devised a novel approach. This involved first of all noting the types of memory lapse reported most frequently by patients, and then attempting to design simple tests to measure each kind of lapse. The end result was the *Rivermead Behavioral Memory Test* (RBMT).

The various components of the RBMT are listed opposite. Subtests include showing the patient a portrait of a person and requiring them to remember the name, and two measures of prospective memory (remembering to do things). One of these involves asking the patient for a belonging such as a comb, which is then secreted in a specified place, with the instruction to ask for it at the end of the test. A second prospective memory test involves setting a timer which rings

20 minutes later, at which point the patient is instructed to ask when the next test session is. Other subtests involve recognizing drawings of 20 objects and photographs of faces of five unfamiliar people. Spatial memory is tested by asking the patient to imitate the tester following a simple route around the room and leaving an item at a specified location. The patient is also asked to remember a short news story both immediately and after a brief delay. Orientation in time and space is tested by asking questions about when and where the test is taking place. The whole test takes about 30 minutes and is typically enjoyed, even by patients with memory problems. But does it work?

The effectiveness of the RBMT was first assessed by asking the occupational therapists working at Rivermead Rehabilitation Centre to categorize their patients as having/not having memory problems severe enough to interfere with therapy. The test was reasonably effective in separating patients with and without significant memory problems. However, a more detailed assessment was made by asking the therapists to keep a diary of memory lapses over many hours of treatment, and then correlating performance on the RMBT with the observed frequency of memory lapses. The relationship was a strong one.

Rivermead Behavioral Memory Test

1   Remembering a new name — first name
2   Remembering a new name — second name
3   Remembering a belonging
4   Remembering an appointment
5   Picture recognition
6   Newspaper story — immediate and delayed recall
7   Face recognition
8   Remembering a new route — immediate recall
9   Remembering a new route — delayed recall
10 Remembering to deliver a message
11 Orientation
12 Date

However, both of these measures were based on performance within the clinic. What of performance in the world outside? Information on this was provided by a follow-up study in which Wilson retested 28 patients she had seen at Rivermead between five and ten years earlier. In addition to many more detailed measures, she categorized each patient in terms of his or her ability/inability to function independently (defined as having a full-time job and/or living independently). There was a clear relationship between score on the RBMT and independence, a relationship that was not found using other more conventional memory tests. This does not mean that standard tests are not useful, merely that their function is to probe specific aspects of memory rather than predict the likelihood of memory problems in everyday life.

The RMBT has now been translated into many different languages, and modified versions have been produced for testing children and for use with the elderly. In its present form, however, the test is not suitable for subjects with comparatively normal memory; it is simply too easy. We are currently developing a more difficult version that appears to offer considerable promise in this respect. It could, for example, be used to predict whether a particular drug is likely to influence the everyday memory performance of normal people.

Amnesic patients can still learn

A theme running through the preceding chapters has been the claim that memory does not represent a single system, but rather an alliance of subsystems. Are all of these impaired in amnesia? Certainly not. Short-term memory in amnesics is typically normal, whether measured in terms of digit span or recency effect in free recall. Semantic memory may also be well preserved, whether measured by vocabulary tests or speed of sentence verification. Gross impairment only becomes obvious when amnesic subjects try to add new material to semantic memory. They have great difficulty in updating their knowledge of current affairs or learning the names of people they meet regularly. The same difficulty applies to developing professional expertise. One amnesic patient, for example, was an expert on lasers. Some time after the onset of his illness he was given an article on recent developments in laser technology, which he was able to understand and explain to the psychologist. When questioned later, however, he showed no evidence of having absorbed the new material, presumably because semantic memory depends upon explicit or episodic memory for the acquisition of new material.

The sort of long-term learning we have discussed so far has all been concerned with declarative memory, with explicitly learning new facts or recollecting particular experiences. In contrast to the universal disruption of such learning, non-declarative or implicit learning is typically preserved in amnesic patients. This is true of each of the four sub-types proposed by Squire.

Skills Amnesic patient HM satisfactorily learnt basic motor skills. Two teenagers who had become amnesic as children showed normal rates of learning a pursuit rotor task.

Priming It will be recalled that this refers to enhanced performance on items previously presented. Verbal priming can be detected in a number of different ways. One is by presenting a fragmented version of the original word and asking the subject to identify the word. For example, if you have recently read the word *crocodile,* you are likely to be able to fit a word to the pattern c—o—o—i—e much more quickly than if you had seen a word such as *alligator*, or indeed a picture of a crocodile. Amnesic patients show this effect very clearly.

Another version of priming comes from the task of stem completion, in which a subject is first shown a word (e.g. *single*) and subsequently cued with the stem (*sin . . .*). When asked to provide a word that will fit that particular pattern, both amnesic and normal subjects tend to provide the previously primed word rather than some alternative response, such as *sinful*. On the other hand, when asked to recognize the word *single* as one that has recently been presented, amnesics perform very badly.

Classical conditioning One of the earliest observations of preserved learning comes from an effect that is probably based on classical conditioning. The Swiss psychiatrist Claparède described secreting a pin in his hand before shaking hands with an amnesic patient on his morning round. The following day the patient showed no evidence of remembering this, but was nevertheless reluctant to shake hands. More conventional experiments have confirmed that conditioned responses are indeed preserved in amnesic patients.

Non-associative learning A good example of this is the Korean melody task described on page 91. On first hearing, subjects tend to rate unfamiliar melodies in unfamiliar styles as not very pleasant. With repeated hearing, however, pleasantness increases. The same effect is found in amnesics, even though they deny having heard the music before.

What are the implications of these results for understanding amnesia? First of all, they seem to be consistent with the generalization that amnesic patients perform badly on tasks that require them to recollect or re-experience earlier events. The ability to do this seems to depend on the operation of the brain circuit that

Although amnesic patients may not remember acquiring a new skill, their capacity to learn and perform new skills may be unimpaired by deficits in other areas of memory.

involves the temporal lobes, hippocampus and frontal lobes; damage to this circuit seems to lead to impaired capacity to recollect the past. On the other hand, the implicit or non-declarative learning measures that are preserved in amnesic patients all have in common the fact that they can be performed without needing to recollect the earlier learning experience. Learning is demonstrated through performance, not through recollection.

The evidence of preserved implicit learning in amnesic patients raises the further question of whether implicit memory is *ever* impaired. It certainly appears to be remarkably robust, even in other conditions that affect explicit learning, such as schizophrenia. However, evidence is beginning to emerge that specific subtypes of non-declarative learning may be impaired differentially. In Alzheimer's disease, for example, verbal priming may be disrupted although skill learning may be preserved. The converse pattern is found in patients suffering from Huntington's disease, another form of dementia, where skill acquisition seems to be impaired although verbal priming is normal.

Managing memory problems

To what extent can amnesic patients be helped? Is it possible to replace a defective memory? At present the answer is 'No', although there is currently a great deal of excitement about the possibility of treating cognitive deficits by implantation of new brain tissue. Work using rats has shown that brain damage that impairs learning can to some extent be replaced by grafting in brain cells from fetal rats. Using fetal cells overcomes the problem of rejection. The need for fetal tissue is not necessarily a major long-term limitation, since it seems likely that in the not too distant future biotechnological methods will be found for manufacturing such material.

This approach clearly has promise. Tissue implantation in humans is already being explored in patients suffering from Parkinson's disease. However, there are still many technical questions to be solved before this is likely to become standard treatment for Parkinson's, and even longer before it will be possible to estimate what help, if any, implantation can offer to amnesic patients.

In the meantime, patients can be helped, although in a rather less spectacular way. Three approaches show promise; all of them involve carefully analyzing the patient's problems and selecting for treatment a problem that is both tractable and important to the patient. The most successful methods so far typically rely upon providing external aids, such as diaries and reminders. These will be discussed further in Chapter 14.

A second approach capitalizes on any remaining declarative memory, and utilizes mnemonic techniques known to be helpful to normal subjects. One example of this is shown in the graph below, which displays the results of a study in which four amnesic patients were taught names using visual imagery. For example, if the occupational therapist's name is Stephanie, the patient might be encouraged to remember it by creating an image of a step and a knee, and linking this up with some feature of the therapist, perhaps her knees! In the absence of a mnemonic, all four patients continued to perform at the baseline level, zero. Once a mnemonic was introduced on a different day for each patient, performance improved markedly.

A third approach to treatment involves building on preserved implicit learning. This strategy is considerably more dif-

These four graphs show how four amnesic patients' memory for names began to improve once a visual mnemonic was introduced. Even if your memory is quite normal, visual imagery is a good way of remembering people's names. (Wilson, 1986)

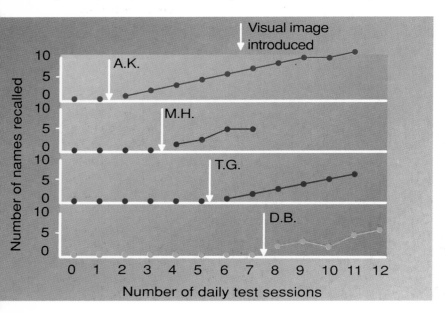

ficult than one might imagine, since explicit memory seems to be used even in acquiring new skills, if only to remember instructions and correct earlier mistakes. However, by carefully utilizing the stem completion or 'vanishing cues' procedure, Glisky, Schacter and Tulving in Toronto were able to teach their patients the elements of computing. Consider, for example, teaching the meaning of the term *loop*. This was done by presenting the definition of the term ('A repeated portion of a program — LOOP') and then testing recall by presenting the definition again but omitting the last letter of the target word. Each time subjects successfully completed the word a further letter was dropped, until finally they could produce the whole word, given the definition. Subjects attended sessions twice a week and, using the method outlined above, moved from acquiring terminology to learning simple computing skills. Initially the training program was very supportive, with support gradually diminishing unless performance level dropped. The end result was a rather rigid and inflexible type of learning, but at least it allowed the patients to gradually acquire a new skill. This aproach offers a possible line for the development of new therapies, although our understanding of how to train, in the absence of explicit memory, is still at an early stage of development.

Using the 'vanishing cues' procedure, amnesic patients can learn basic computer skills. Success depends on using preserved implicit learning capacity.

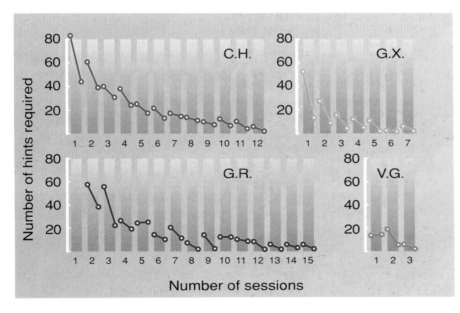

These four graphs show the different speeds at which four amnesic patients learnt computer-related vocabulary. Briefer and briefer memory prompts were required with each successive session. (Glisky, Schacter and Tulving, 1986)

12 Memory in childhood

A great deal of learning, and presumably memorizing, takes place before the age of three, yet memories of specific experiences at this age are scarce. There may be neurological, linguistic or emotional reasons for this.

What is your earliest memory? What else can you remember from that period? Perhaps you remember only a single isolated incident. Few people remember very much of what occurred before the age of two or three. Systematic studies of auto-biographical memory suggest a paucity of memories before the age of about five years, a phenomenon known as *infantile amnesia*.

While infantile amnesia has been known about for many years, it is not easy to investigate. One problem is identifying events that are of importance to a child, events that can be precisely dated and verified by a third party. The birth of a brother or sister falls into this category, and has been investigated in a number of studies. In one experiment college students and children aged four, six, eight and twelve were asked to recall the birth of a brother or sister when they were between three and eleven years old. They were asked questions such as 'Who took care of you while your mother was in hospital?' 'Did the baby receive presents?' 'Did you receive presents?' and so on. The mothers were asked

When college students were asked to recall the birth of a sibling, they remembered virtually nothing if the event had occurred before they were three years old, an example of the phenomenon known as 'infantile amnesia'. (Sheingold and Tenney, 1982)

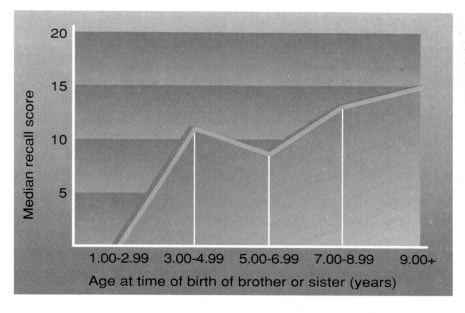

the same questions. The study found surprisingly little forgetting regardless of time since the event, but there was a clear age effect. Children under three at the time remembered virtually nothing, while three- to five-year-olds recalled almost as much as older children. In short, the phenomenon of infantile amnesia was confirmed.

Infantile amnesia

Why do we remember so little from the first few years of our lives? A number of interpretations have been proposed, with perhaps the most dramatic being Freud's suggestion that infantile amnesia occurs because children repress sexual feelings towards their parents. Coming to terms with such repressed feelings is an important step in classical psychoanalysis.

A second interpretation is that in the first few years of life the brain, or more specifically the hippocampus, is simply not mature enough to lay down explicit memories. Young children are assumed to depend upon implicit learning, which does not provide a basis for experiences to be recollected .

A third interpretation has to do with the fact that language in a young child is still developing. As language develops, does the structure of a child's mind change in a way that makes very early experiences inaccessible? This view is in fact a particular version of a more general retrieval hypothesis, which argues that children are capable of laying down episodic memories, but have difficulty in retrieving them. Adequate retrieval depends upon events being logged into a sufficiently structured schema or framework. Perhaps such schemata have not yet developed in the infant. To return to the library analogy, it is as if early books are hard to find because they were acquired before the cataloging system was developed.

Asking questions about the episodic memory of prelingual children poses particular problems. However, in recent years a number of ingenious techniques have been developed to investigate the extent to which infants appear to remember experiences. One particular series of

In the half-century or more that psychologists have been studying memory in children, no good evidence has emerged that infantile amnesia is due to repressed sexual feelings towards the parent of the opposite sex.

studies developed from an interest in the auditory capacities of young infants. The test situation involved encouraging babies to reach out for a sounding object (a rattle), with testing taking place in the light and the dark. Infants tested between the age of six and 40 weeks were retested two years later and proved much more likely to reach for the rattle than children who had not been tested earlier, suggesting some kind of retention from a very early age. This first study used multiple test sessions, but a later experiment studied infants who had had only a single experience at the age of six months and were then retested one or two years later. Those who had previous experience were more likely to respond to the sound and less likely to be alarmed when the room was darkened. The performance of the 'experienced' babies was also enhanced by presenting them with a 'reminder' (a single exposure to the rattle) before the test session began.

Research like this indicates that learning certainly can occur during the first few months of life, while the 'reminder' effect suggests that retrieval may be an important factor in performance. However, the task outlined above could be interpreted as testing implicit learning rather than explicit declarative memory. Obviously we need to explore the nature of early learning in more detail.

Do babies have episodic memory?

Probably the most extensive investigation of infant memory has been carried out by Carolyn Rovee-Collier and her colleagues. She argues that to assess learning in babies it is important to produce a situation which interests and motivates them. This she achieves by suspending a mobile over the baby's crib and also attaching it to the baby's foot. When he or she kicks, the mobile moves. Young babies seem to enjoy this, since they rapidly learn to kick when the mobile is present.

The graph below shows what happens when the mobile is reintroduced after a delay ranging from one to fourteen days. Both two- and three-month-old babies show retention, although the level of performance in two-month-olds drops to a level comparable with the initial baseline of kicking after two days, whereas the three-month-olds still show a reliable effect after a week. As in the sound localization studies just described, a reminder (in this case a moving mobile, presented before the test begins) results in memory returning to virtually its initial level even when tested after a delay of two weeks; even after a month, the reminder is sufficient to reactivate a significant amount of kicking.

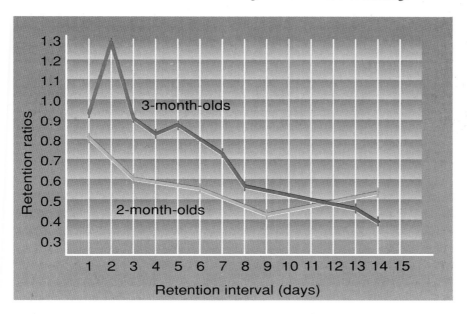

Even two-month-old babies show evidence of 'remembering' the experience of finding a mobile moves when they kick. In three-month-olds the effect is very clear. (Rovee-Collier, 1989)

The learning that takes place in these circumstances appears to be quite specific. Babies trained on a mobile consisting of yellow blocks, for example, will not respond to a mobile comprising metal butterflies. On the other hand, if infants are trained on a range of different mobiles, then generalization does seem to occur, with the result that a novel mobile will readily evoke kicking. In short, babies do appear to be able to acquire something analogous to a concept. Another feature of learning is that it appears to be context-sensitive. Hence if a baby is tested in the bedroom or the kitchen rather than the test crib, then no kicking response occurs. Similarly, if the decor of the crib is changed, the response is reduced.

Taken together, these experiments demonstrate that infants can learn to respond to specific stimuli, and can retain their learning at least over a period of weeks. Their learning is relatively specific and also context-dependent, but given appropriate conditions they do appear to generalize what they have learnt. This looks more like explicit declarative learning than implicit memory. It would be very interesting to test the extent to which amnesic adults are able to learn equivalent associations given an adult activity equivalent to mobile kicking.

Autobiographical memory in infants

Probably the strongest evidence for the explicit nature of learning in children comes from autobiographical memories elicited from infants at an age when they are able to use language. Katherine Nelson describes a number of investigations of this type. In one study involving children aged between 21 and 27 months, mothers were encouraged to keep diaries of their children's memory behavior. In the youngest children this mostly took the form of remembering where particular objects were located (where in grandma's house the cookie tin was kept, for example). The older children, however, were able to recall particular events (an occasion when another child had broken a toy at a party, for example).

Memory for location is of course something that can be tested experimentally. Two-year-olds are quite capable of remembering 24 hours later where a favorite toy has been hidden. But then some birds, the marsh tit for example, can remember over 100 locations in which they have hidden food and refrain from revisiting them once the food has been removed, an impressive feat, although not necessarily evidence of autobiographical memory. The nature of memory in animals remains controversial and is certainly beyond the scope of this book.

Since the interpretation of purely behavioral evidence remains problematical, let us return to verbal recall in children who have just learned to talk. Nelson describes the intriguing single case of Emily, a child who developed the rather convenient habit of soliloquizing in her cot before she went to sleep. From the age of 21 months, and until she was 36 months, her nightly monolog was recorded and analyzed. At 21 months she was already recalling events from two months before, such as the family car breaking down. Her monolog tended to be very unstructured, and typically did not comprise particularly salient or important events such as Christmas or the birth of a baby brother. She was much more likely to talk about more mundane things, such as being picked up at the babysitter's or other children at playgroup quarrelling.

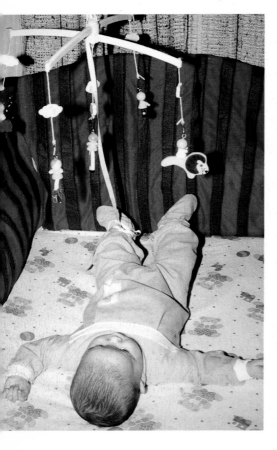

Even very young babies rapidly learn that kicking can cause a mobile to jiggle around. They also notice when the objects on the mobile are changed. If they are trained with five objects and then tested with four of them plus one new one, their kicking performance goes down.

While many of Emily's reminiscences were from the previous day, some went back as far as six months. At about 24 months she began to formulate explicit rules and generalizations ('You can't go down the basement with 'jamas on' or 'When Emily go mormor (grandma) in the daytime . . . that's what Amy do sometime') or speculations about the future ('Maybe the doctor take my 'jamas off'). At about age 36 months Emily stopped soliloquizing and the study ended. The insight it gives into the development of episodic memory is intriguing. In this

particular and perhaps rather precocious two-year-old, recollection of specific events, episodic memory, certainly did occur. The study also threw some light on the development of world knowledge, or semantic memory.

It seems likely that semantic and episodic memory develop interactively. Some evidence of this comes from a study of kindergarten children who attended up to four creative workshops and were then tested for recall a month later. In general, the older children remembered more, and those who had attended four workshops were better at judging which events had occurred during the last workshop and which had occurred earlier. In other words, older children are better at separating specific episodes from a developing generic or semantic memory.

What is the role of the parents in the development of memory in children? There is some evidence that different styles of interaction lead to somewhat different early develop-

ment. One way of encouraging memory is through mutual reminiscence: 'Remember when we went to Vermont and saw cousin Bill?' Another way is more 'practical'; for example, one might encourage a child to use memory to solve a problem such as a jigsaw puzzle: 'Where does this piece go? You remember we did that one yesterday.'

In one study mothers and children were recorded while wandering around a museum. Modes of interaction were categorized as either freely interacting, analogous to the reminiscing style, or as more practical. When tested for memory of the experience a week later, the mothers and children who had interacted in the more free-wheeling reminiscing style were able to answer an average of 13 out of 30 questions, while the more practical group could only answer five. Naturalistic data of this type should not be overinterpreted, but they do suggest that the way in which parents interact with their children might prove to be a fruitful area of study, and one with long-term educational implications.

So are infants amnesic? And if so, why? It certainly seems that adults are

For the fond parents this may have been 'a day to remember', little Enid's first birthday or the day they moved into a new house. But young children seem to have a better memory for more humdrum and trivial occurrences.

It seems that children remember more about outings and visits if the experience is shared with adults rather than orchestrated by them. The pupil-teacher relationship can be a restricting one for both children and adults.

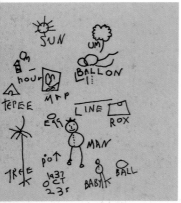

Drawings done at the age of six (top) and drawings by the same person 'regressed' under hypnosis. (Orne, 1951)

amnesic for most of the events that happened during the first few years of their lives. However, Rovee-Collier's experiments suggest that children as young as two to three months can learn quite complex associations, while children who are just beginning to talk show evidence of a capacity to recall specific events from well before that time. Infants do appear to learn and remember. On the other hand, the rate of forgetting was very rapid for Rovee-Collier's two-month-old infants, and quite rapid at three months. The fact that reminders worked effectively, though, suggests that the problem is not failure to store information, but failure to retrieve it. Could adults retrieve information from the first year of life if the right retrieval cues were given? One approach to this is to use hypnosis and 'age regression'. As always with hypnosis, there is a problem in interpreting the results. Are they genuine memories, or is a subject in a heightened state of suggestibility simply being encouraged to confabulate? The lower group of drawings on the left was done under hypnotic regression; the top group was done by the same person at the age of six. The drawings done in the hypnotic state strongly suggest confabulation rather than genuine age regression.

To return to infantile amnesia, however, how do the three interpretations offered on page 222 fare? The Freudian interpretation does not account for the rapid forgetting seen during infancy; it seems somewhat unlikely that the three-month-old infants studied by Rovee-Collier forgot about the mobile because of the need to repress memories of lusting after their parents. In general, I know of no objective evidence supporting the Freudian view of infantile amnesia, and regard it as having historic interest only.

The view that an infant's brain is not mature enough to lay down episodic memories does not square with the Rovee-Collier results either. One could argue that implicit memory systems do not require the brain structures that underpin explicit memory, although the sensitivity to context makes this seem unlikely. The Emily case study certainly seems to suggest the occurrence of episodic memories at 21 months, some of them reaching back to a younger age. In short, it seems that babies do show evidence of learning and remembering, but have substantial problems of retrieval. In infancy we are in the process of constructing our internal view of the world; in time it is this which provides a framework for the explicit retrieval of experienced events.

Children as witnesses

Given that young children can remember specific events, how good is their memory and how reliable is it? A number of studies have investigated the recall of specific events by young children. For example, one study investigated memories of a visit to the Jewish Museum in New York by a number of five-year-olds; the visit included an explanation about archeological methods and the opportunity to dig in a sandbox to find artefacts. Recall of the event showed considerable forgetting. However, given appropriate cues, six years later

A young Jamaican boy helps the author to develop tests of learning and memory that will be used to evaluate the effects of malnutrition and parasitic infections on Third World children.

the children managed to recall no less than 87 per cent of the original information. There is evidence from other sources to suggest that cueing may be particularly important for children. During development of a children's version of the Rivermead Behavioral Memory Test children were asked to recall a brief story; this was followed by probe questions regarding features that had been omitted. The questions proved particularly helpful for the five- and six-year-olds, but added relatively little to the performance of older children. Unfortunately, of course, unless phrased very carefully, such questions can also distort memory, as we saw in Chapter 10, raising the issue as to whether child witnesses are particularly susceptible to suggestion.

The importance of children as witnesses has increased in recent years as the extent of child abuse has become more fully realized. Inevitably in such cases, the evidence is likely to depend upon the testimony of a child or children. In 1983 a 36-year-old woman who ran a nursery school was convicted of murder and of 12 counts of child abuse principally on eyewitness testimony from 29 children who had attended the school. The U.S. legal system tends to be extremely nervous about relying on child witnesses, possibly hearing the echo of the notorious Salem witch trials of 1682, when nearly 20 people were hanged following the accusations of a group of girls aged between five and twelve who reported seeing the accused change themselves into cats and dogs and fly off on broomsticks.

How suggestible are children? Some studies show that they are more susceptible than adults to misleading questions, but others indicate that they are not. A possible answer has been proposed by Stephen Ceci and his colleagues, who found enhanced susceptibility to suggestion in three- to four-year-olds, reducing as children get older, with ten- to twelve-year-olds being no more suggestible than adults. They used a method in which groups of children were read a story about a little girl called Lauren on her first day at school. Lauren eats eggs for breakfast, then has a tummy ache, which she forgets about when allowed to play with another child's toy. Misleading information was introduced by asking the question 'Do you remember the story about Lauren, who had a headache because she ate her cereal too fast? Then she felt better when she got to play with her friend's game'. The children were tested individually for their understanding of the story and then the experimenter left. Two days later the children were again tested individually, and required to choose between pairs of pictures; one picture depicted Lauren eating eggs and the other cereal; another pair portrayed Lauren with a stomach ache or a headache. The results of this experiment are shown in the graph below.

Ceci and his colleagues went on to show that misleading information was more influential when presented by an adult than by another child. Further evidence suggested bias in the guessing of children who had actually forgotten (as

This graph shows the effect of misleading information on the memory of children of different ages. When no misleading information is given, recall is more or less equally high across the age range, but under biased conditions younger children are more easily misled. (Ceci, 1988)

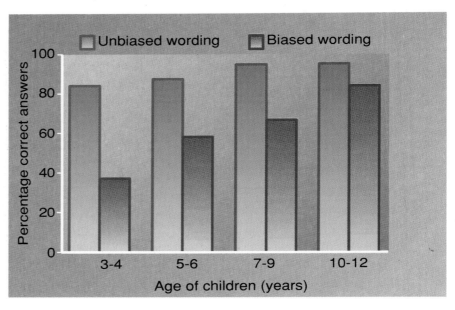

McCloskey and Zaragoza would have predicted) and also disruption of earlier learning (as Loftus would predict). Ceci and his colleagues concluded that young children are somewhat more susceptible to bias, although this seems to be less of a problem for children of five and above. They also make the point that their experiments were based on neutral material. A child who is reporting a terrifying experience may not behave in the same way.

Do children forget faster than adults?

There appears to be a belief in the legal profession that children are unreliable witnesses because they forget faster. This has recently been investigated by Flin and her colleagues in Scotland, comparing six- and nine-year-old children with adults. For the purposes of experiment the incident to be remembered was staged: a nurse is giving a lecture on foot hygiene and is interrupted when a projector and tray of slides are overturned by two helpers, who then start arguing about whose fault it was, before being banished by the nurse who continues the lectures without her slides. As the graph below shows, the amount of information recalled by the three groups was very similar when tested the next day. When retested after five months, however, the adults showed very little forgetting, the nine-year-olds showed some, while the six-year-olds showed quite marked forgetting. There was relatively little evidence of suggestibility, as indicated by the importation of erroneous facts mentioned during the interview, but such importations as did occur were limited to the children and seemed more likely after the five-month delay. These findings support the view that children can be relatively good witnesses, but also vindicate legal practice in Britain, which is to take videotaped evidence from children as soon as possible after the event in question.

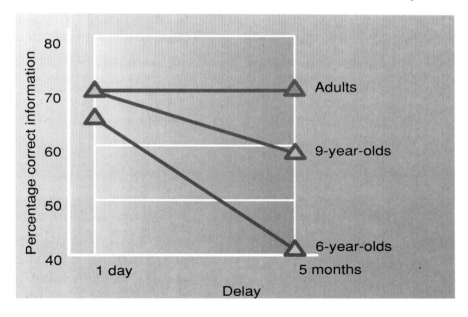

Children do appear to forget information faster than adults, but their testimony is not necessarily unreliable. The results of this study support the view that evidence should be obtained as soon after the event as possible. (Flin, 1992)

What develops in cognitive development?

Developmental psychology is concerned with understanding the processes underlying the maturation of the individual from infancy to adulthood. During the middle years of this century the field was dominated by the ideas of the Swiss psychologist Jean Piaget, who argued that the cognitive development of children

Children love stories whether traditional, as in this Punch and Judy show, or modern, as in television serials. Familiar stories become more enjoyable with each retelling, perhaps because more attention can be devoted to nuances and detail.

proceeds through a series of distinct stages. Piaget supported his views with a number of ingenious and often counterintuitive demonstrations of apparent illogicality in young children. Subsequent research, however, has suggested that the child's problem is frequently not one of absence of logical capacity, but rather the result of a range of other factors, including failure to understand the linguistic form of questions, susceptibility to the social rather than logical demands of the situation, and limitations in memory capacity. As a result of the rejection of Piaget's theories, a number of other approaches have begun to develop, many of them concerned with producing a more detailed account of specific tasks using one or other information processing approach, often derived from theories in adult cognitive psychology.

One influential theory in this area is that of Case, who explains improved cognitive performance as children develop in terms of a working memory model.

This assumes a limited-capacity system that is responsible both for temporary storage of information and for information processing. The greater the storage load, the less capacity is left over for processing, and vice versa. Case suggests that the total capacity of this working memory system remains constant, but that as children get older they become better at chunking information, and also develop the capacity to process information more rapidly, hence using their available working memory capacity more efficiently. Note that this view is similar but not identical to the Baddeley and Hitch account of working memory. It echoes our initial concept of a central executive, which was assumed to have both storage and processing capacity. Later of course we moved away from the idea that the executive itself stored information, and towards the view that it comprised an attentional scheduler that depended for storage on the slave systems, and on long-term memory. Case does not have any direct equivalent of the phonological loop and sketch pad systems of the Baddeley and Hitch model, and while his approach has been successfully adapted to investigate individual differences in working memory (by Daneman and Carpenter, for example), it has not, to the best of my knowledge, attempted to account for neuropsychological evidence.

One of the most striking features of child development is the way digit span increases with age. Case argues that this occurs because young children are less skilled at identifying digits, with the result that identification takes up a greater proportion of the processing capacity of working memory, leaving less capacity for storage; as children get older, ease of identification increases, the amount of working memory capacity taken up reduces, and more digits can be stored. He tested this in a range of studies; in one of them three- to six-year-old children were tested for their memory span for words, and for the speed with which they could identify and repeat a spoken word. The two measures were highly correlated. Another experiment attempted to reduce the repetition speed of adults to that of children; this was achieved by using unfamiliar nonsense syllables in place of digits. This had the desired effect of reducing speed of identification and making it equivalent to the speed with which six-year-olds identify digits. As predicted, memory span for such material was equivalent to the digit span of six-year-olds.

An alternative interpretation of the development of span in terms of Baddeley and Hitch's phonological loop was suggested by Nicolson, who proposed that the crucial factor was speed of articulatory rehearsal rather than identification time. He studied the word-length effect across a range of ages and was able to show that the results both in children and adults fell along the same straight line, suggesting that older children simply rehearse more rapidly, allowing more items to be maintained within the phonological loop. This result has since been replicated on a number of occasions. Hitch and colleagues went on to compare the identification time and rehearsal rate explanations in a study in which eight- and eleven-year-old children named, repeated and remembered words comprising one, two or three syllables. The results were consistent with the view that articulation rate is crucial, rather than identification time, supporting the phonological loop interpretation. At the very least, this suggests that Case's model needs to be elaborated so as to produce something equivalent to the phonological loop.

However, it seems unlikely that speed of articulation is the only variable which develops as a child grows up. Even memory span is probably influenced by factors other than simple rote rehearsal. One such factor is the selection of strategies. There has been considerable interest in recent years in the strategies that children adopt in memory situations. For present purposes, however, I will limit discussion to the simple task of a child attempting to remember a sequence of pictures or words.

When adults are shown unrelated pictures, they spontaneously tend to encode them as words and rehearse them subvocally. It has been known since at least the 1960s that children aged six and younger tend not to use spontaneous verbal rehearsal when remembering pictures or objects. On the other hand, the word-length effect, which is assumed to reflect articulatory rehearsal, has been found in children as young as four. The crucial factor turns out to be the way in which material is presented; if presented auditorily, even very young children appear to use something analogous to subvocal rehearsal; if presented as pictures or objects, a reliable strategy of recoding them into words does not emerge until children reach the age of six to eight years. This was demonstrated quite neatly in a study in which Hitch and his colleagues asked six- and ten-year-old children to remember sequences of items having names with one, two or three syllables, presented either as pictures or words. The six-year-olds showed a clear effect of word length when presentation was spoken, but not with picture presentation, whereas ten-year-olds showed a word-length effect for spoken words and pictures.

Another way of finding out how the children encode material is to manipulate similarity, presenting sequences of items that either have names that are similar in sound *(hat, rat, cat)* or are visually similar *(pen, fork)*. Or one can compare the encoding of long names *(kangaroo, umbrella)* and short names *(pig, cake)*. In two studies in which the performance of five-year-olds was contrasted with that of ten- or eleven-year-olds the children were shown pictures and then asked to point to them in the order in which they had been presented. The five-year-olds appeared to have problems with the visually similar pictures, suggesting that they were using the visuo-spatial sketch pad, but they showed no evidence of storage using the articulatory loop, since neither phonological similarity nor name length were important factors. The ten- to eleven-year-olds showed exactly the opposite pattern, indicating that they were relying mainly on verbal coding and using subvocal rehearsal.

Why does it matter how children remember sequences of pictures or words? One reason is that the method of encoding will influence long-term learning. Since children spend a great deal of time learning in both formal and informal situations, the more we know of the underlying processes the better. There is, for example, a great deal of evidence to suggest that children who have problems in learning to read also have reduced digit spans. This does not necessarily imply a causal link. It might be, for example, that both depend upon a common third factor. This third factor may be something called 'phonological awareness', the extent to which a child can analyze language into its subcomponents. It has been suggested that learning to read a language like English involves 'cracking the alphabetic code', that is appreciating that a spoken word can be split up into subcomponents, which can then be mapped onto individual letters. Phonological awareness may develop as a result of exposure to nursery rhymes and word games.

Preschool children may benefit from exercises aimed at this awareness. This is an area of considerable current activity, with the outcome still far from clear. Reading is a complex skill that calls on a range of subprocesses, which include both phonological awareness and phonological memory. Different methods of teaching reading tend to stress the application of different cognitive subsystems and have a mixture of strengths and weaknesses. We are gradually beginning to understand what these are, giving hope that one day the teaching of reading will be based on good scientific understanding rather than vociferously held, but largely unsupported, educational opinion.

There is a great need for more thorough investigation of the memory subprocesses involved in learning to read. Making the link between visual and auditory information is crucial.

13 Memory and aging

I can remember when I still had a good memory. I was in my mid-30s. I remember that time because I was spending a sabbatical year abroad. I was beginning to write a memory text and had no difficulty remembering appropriate experiments, readily coming up with names of authors, and dates and places of publication. My host, who was about ten years older, warned me that it would not be too long before all that started to change, He was right. A few years later I would confidently reach for the name of an investigator I knew well and find nothing there, although I could happily tell you where he worked and all about him. The first signs of aging? Well, not quite the first. As an enthusiastic but untalented rugby player I was already past the age at which most of my more talented colleagues had hung up their boots. However, I continued to play for a good few years, compensating for declining speed by an increase in low cunning. By trundling towards the point at which I anticipated play would break down, I often managed to arrive at the same time as my fitter, younger colleagues, who no doubt got used to my occasional sallies in the wrong direction when I made a wrong guess.

These autobiographical ramblings aim to make two points about aging. The first is that aging is not a phenomenon that starts on a specific date — when one retires or reaches three score years and ten, for example — but a continuous process of change. Different activities reach their natural peak at different times. Female gymnasts appear to be over the hill by the time they reach puberty; mathematicians are said to do their most original work before they reach their 30s; great conductors seem to go on until they virtually fall off the rostrum. I assume, however, that aging gymnasts find other sources of fulfilment, just as aging rugby players find less robust ways of spending Saturday afternoons.

My second point is that dealing with aging is a question of optimization. In rugby that means using your head to save your legs. In memory it means finding ways to ensure that increasing fallibility does not mean a decrease in overall effectiveness. So, for each aspect of memory I describe, I will be providing the bad news and the good news. The bad news is that memory gets worse with age, and the good news is that there are ways of coping. In giving the so-called good news I do not wish to deny that memory on the whole gets worse, and shows its first signs of deterioration at a depressingly early age, but I am not of the persuasion that all handicaps are blessings in disguise. I shall not be using the newly-invented acronym AAMI (age-associated memory impairment), which smacks too much of creating a new disease which can then be expensively treated. Old age has enough genuine diseases without the need to invent new ones.

'That Harry was a funny one. I remember him when he was a nipper . . .'. Age brings with it a change of emphasis in the things we like to remember. When we are young we tend to concentrate on current events and recent experiences; when we are old we prefer to remember people and the past.

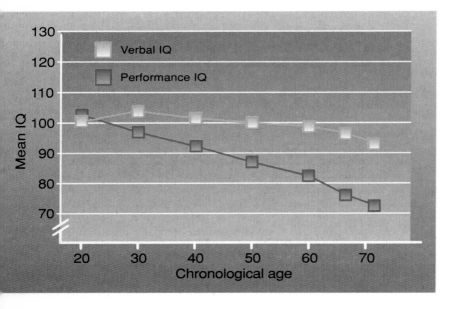

Age and cognitive processing

While memory may be the most obvious faculty to deteriorate with age, it is certainly not the only one. In interpreting age-associated memory deficits it is important to bear in mind that aging is associated with general cognitive slowing. American gerontologist Warner Schaie, who has tested the cognitive abilities of a sample of Seattle, Washington, citizens over a period of years — the tests included measures of reasoning, and of spatial and verbal ability — has shown that there is a gradual

Mean IQ levels, whether measured by means of verbal or performance intelligence tests, show a gentle but steady decline with age. (Salthouse, 1992)

decline beginning in the sixth decade of life. The deterioration does not accelerate until the eighth decade. Shaie's data of course reflect average performance rather than individual performance. There have been a number of attempts to explain age-related cognitive decline in terms of a single variable. Two variables that have been explored in some detail are *fluid intelligence* and *speed of processing*. Fluid intelligence is the term applied to performance on intelligence tests in which high scores correlate with current processing rather than prior knowledge. Fluid intelligence declines with age, in contrast to *crystallized intelligence*, which is measured using tests of accumulated knowledge, such as vocabulary. Crystallized

Not everything gets worse as we get older. Vocabulary, as measured by the ability to distinguish between real words and nonwords, improves with age. (Baddeley, Emslie and Nimmo-Smith, 1993)

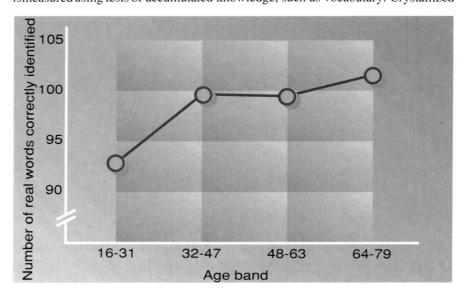

intelligence is maintained, and may continue to increase with age. As for speed of processing, the argument is that as we age the rate at which the nervous system can receive and transmit information becomes slower. However, there is a third possibility, and this concerns working memory.

Working memory and aging

Working memory, the system that allows us to simultaneously hold and manipulate information, has been implicated in aging decrements at least since the 1960s. The graph below shows the effect of aging on two measures of working memory, one linguistic and the other based on arithmetical calculations; in this case the data come from one of a range of American studies carried out by Timothy Salthouse. While there does seem to be evidence for executive deficits in aging, the exact nature of these is not yet entirely clear. For instance, requiring subjects to perform two tasks at once — verifying sentences at the same time as remembering digits, for example — is no more problematic for the elderly than for the young. However, increasing the complexity of one of the tasks (more complex sentences, for example) *does* seem to penalize the elderly more than the young.

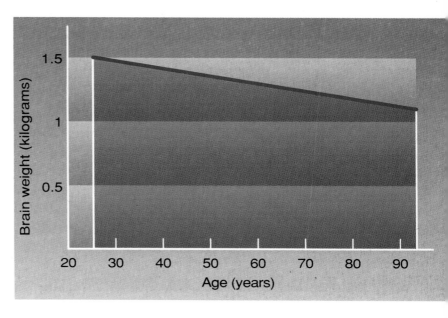

The weight of the human brain declines with age.

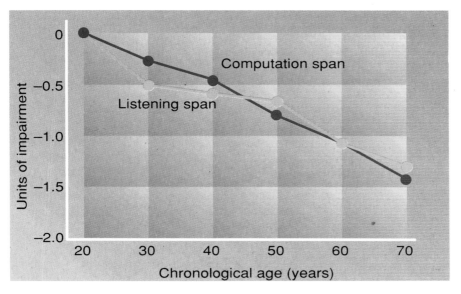

This graph shows the effect of age on working memory. The zero line represents the level of performance of young subjects. As we get older we become less efficient at processing both numbers (computation span) and words (listening span). (Salthouse, 1992)

We shall return to the issue of grammatical complexity later.

The bad news then is that as we get older we seem to respond more slowly. If the rate of flow of information is not under our control, we are likely to make more errors than the young. On the other hand, if we are in control, then slowing things down will keep our error rate down. In the case of driving, this may be at the expense of increasing the frustration level of younger drivers behind!

Is there any good news on the working memory front? Yes. The elderly certainly take advantage of their lengthier experience. In a study comparing young and middle-aged typists Salthouse found that the two groups differed markedly in their basic reaction time and in their speed of information processing as measured by a number of laboratory tasks, but they did not differ in typing speed. This was because the older typists looked further ahead in the text and were able to do more pre-planning. The laboratory situation, in which randomly selected stimuli appear for immediate response, is of course not typical of most real-life situations, which are structured and to a considerable degree predictable. Older people can learn to take better advantage of this predictability.

Mrs Jones may not be as quick on the uptake as her younger colleagues, but she mends clothes just as fast. What she lacks in speed she makes up for in method.

What of the slave systems of working memory? The good news is that on the whole, as measured by digit span at least, the phonological loop system holds up reasonably well, although, as we shall see in discussing language production, its operation in association with the central executive seems to decline. The visuo-spatial sketch pad seems to show a more obvious degree of impairment, whether this is measured in terms of ability to manipulate spatial images, as in the paper-folding test shown on page 240, or in terms of more naturalistic tasks. For example, when Rabbitt tested elderly and younger inhabitants of Oxford who had lived in the city for 30 years, asking them to take a mental 'walk' along a particular street and describe the shops located there, the older subjects performed significantly worse. Nevertheless when asked specific questions such as 'Is there a cake shop there?' or 'Is there a dry cleaners?' they were perfectly capable of giving the correct answer. However, when the equivalent experiment was run in Newcastle, using a larger and more complex street, the older subjects performed more poorly on both tasks. In an American study which examined the capacity of young and old people to find things in a supermarket younger people did better if the supermarket was unfamiliar, but there was no difference between the two groups when it came to finding things in their regular supermarket. Although Rabbitt's study convincingly demonstrated the effects of aging on visuo-spatial memory, it is unlikely that his subjects were experiencing major problems with their weekly shopping.

What of tasks involving the central executive component of working memory? One such task is chess. It seems that chess skill, as measured by a standardized rating system (Elo rating), steadily declines from the fourth decade onwards, at least in those Grand Masters who continue to play, who may of course be those who are least affected by advancing years. Charness has compared young and older players of equivalent Elo ratings, and finds that whereas young players consider a wider range of potential moves, older players appear to analyze situations more deeply. Rabbitt, using a procedure in which players were required to think aloud,

Shoppers browse in Newcastle's Central Arcade. See if you can list the shops along one of your regular routes.

The capacity to manipulate and inspect mental images seems to decline with age. When asked to remember the location of shops along a familiar street, elderly subjects did consistently less well than middle-aged, but they had less difficulty answering questions about shops and locations. (Rabbitt, 1989)

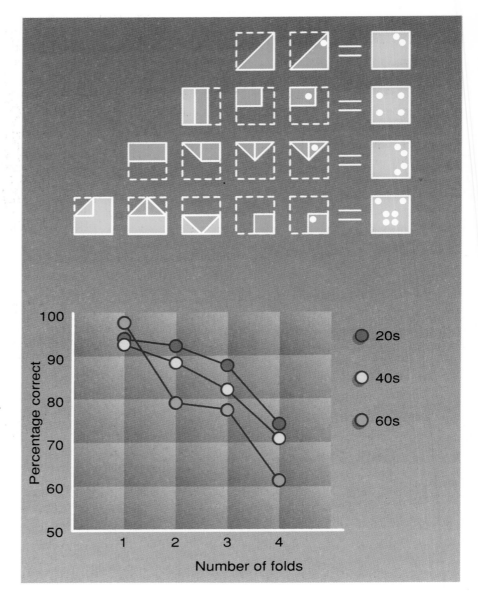

This is the paper-folding test, designed to test capacity for visualization. The greater the number of paper folds required to produce the dot patterns shown on the right, the more performance declines in all age groups, with decline being steepest in the oldest age group. (Salthouse, 1992)

noted that older players were more likely to reconsider a move they had already rejected, forgetting their earlier analysis and unwisely selecting that move.

One executive task that we all indulge in is that of producing language. Susan Kemper of the University of Kansas has carried out a number of intriguing studies on the effects of age on language production. One study analyzed in detail a number of diaries written by early Kansas settlers. Comparing texts produced at different periods in writers' lives, Kemper was able to carry out a 70-year longitudinal study of language use. Her initial investigation concentrated on grammar, in particular on certain forms of syntax that place particularly heavy demands on working memory. One such form is the substitution of pronouns for previously mentioned nouns. Here is an example: '*My Uncle John* was a collier who worked in the northern coalfields. *He* took early retirement after an accident under-ground.' The graph below shows the frequency of pronoun-noun substitution across the years, together with the probability of producing an ambiguous referent: for example, '*Uncle Archie and Uncle George* emigrated to America. *He* worked in the car industry in Detroit.' As the graph shows, as the diarists got older they used pronoun-noun substitution less frequently, but with more ambiguity. The topics typically discussed also changed over time; in their younger days the diarists talked mainly about current events and the activities of the day; as they got older they wrote principally about people and about the past.

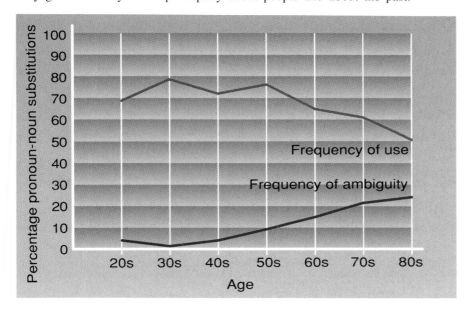

Older chess players seem to be less efficient than younger players at rejecting unwise moves.

Age affects use of certain grammatical devices. The diarists in Kemper's study showed less inclination to use pronouns to refer back to nouns as they got older and when they did the reference was more likely to be ambiguous. (Kemper, 1990)

Kemper went on to collect additional data from contemporary subjects, who were asked to write about various topics and also given a range of cognitive tests. She broadly replicated the diary results, in particular finding a reduced use of so-called left-branching sentences in the elderly. A left-branching sentence is one in which initial information does not become intelligible until the arrival of later information. Comprehension depends on holding the initial information until the rest arrives. 'A roof over his head is the right of every man' is a left-branching sentence; its right-branching equivalent would be 'Every man has a right to a roof over his head.' Kemper demonstrated that the tendency to use

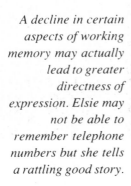

A decline in certain aspects of working memory may actually lead to greater directness of expression. Elsie may not be able to remember telephone numbers but she tells a rattling good story.

left-branching sentences was significantly correlated with both forward and backward digit span, firmly linking the phenomenon with the phonological loop and executive components of working memory.

Kemper's work elegantly demonstrates that a well-practised skill such as writing reflects the gradual diminution of working memory capacity with age. However, when she asked a group of experienced teachers of composition to asses the literary merit of both the early and contemporary material she had collected, the consensus was that the productions of the older writers had greater stylistic merit and interest value. More good news!

Long-term memory

Hazel Emslie, Ian Nimmo-Smith and myself have recently developed a test of visual and verbal long-term recognition and recall. As our visual material we selected pictures of doors, which have the advantage of being meaningful, but not usefully nameable — for example, a stable door can be tested by recognition from a set of four broadly similar stable doors. As the verbal equivalent we selected personal names; personal names can have meanings, but we seem to have had many years, if not centuries, of ignoring the original meaning of names such as Rex, Virginia, Potter, Fletcher, Smith and so on.

The graph on page 243 shows overall performance on our original Doors and Names tests, which comprised two sets of twelve doors and two sets of twelve names, one set being easier to recognize than the other, for use with patients with impaired memory. As you can see, performance declines gradually with age. The graph on page 244 shows the results of two recall tests. Visual recall involved learning four different versions of a cross, with subjects initially copying each version to demonstrate that they were capable of the necessary manual skill and then drawing the four crosses from memory. Subjects were given up to three trials

to learn the crosses, followed by delayed recall after 20 minutes. The verbal recall involved learning and recalling the names of four pictured individuals, a doctor, a newspaper boy, a postman and a vicar. Although all four tests, two of recognition and two of recall, showed a gradual decline, recall appears to be more influenced by age than recognition. This is a frequent observation, and probably indicates that retrieval processes are particularly vulnerable to the aging process. However, the fact that recognition memory is also impaired indicates that the problem is unlikely to be entirely one of retrieval.

A contributing factor to the poorer long-term learning of older people is that they tend not to encode material as richly and elaborately as the young. This was well demonstrated in a study in which older and younger subjects were presented with lists of words; in one condition they were simply asked to commit

Four of the doors used in the visual recognition part of the Doors and Names test, a useful measure of long-term memory.

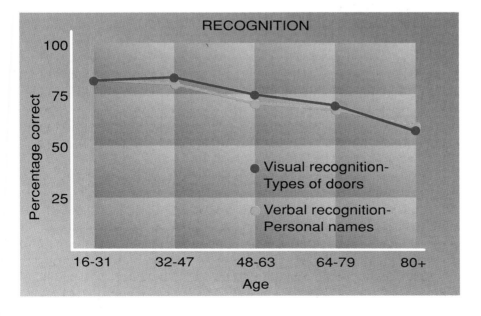

RECOGNITION

In the Doors and Names test we found that both visual and verbal recognition declined with age. (Baddeley, Emslie and Nimmo-Smith, in preparation)

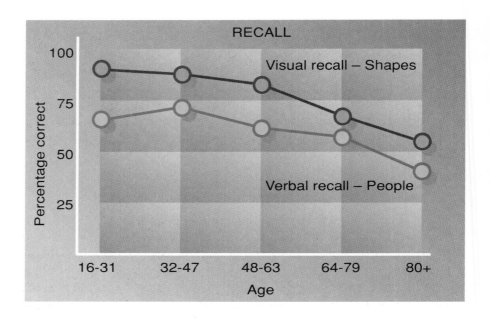

In the Shapes and People test, which tested recall rather than recognition, performance declined more steeply with age. Our ability to recognize things seems to last longer than our ability to actively recall them; this is one of the characteristic features of aging. (Baddeley, Emslie and Nimmo-Smith, in preparation)

the words to memory, leaving them free to process them in any way they wished; in the other condition depth of encoding was controlled by asking them to make semantic judgements about each word, not specifically to commit the words to memory. The younger subjects did significantly better than the older when they were given the general learning instruction, but their superiority was a great deal less obvious when it came to semantic encoding, and the age difference became even smaller in a subsequent experiment in which the semantic encoding instruction was combined with testing by recognition rather than recall. It seems that, left to their own devices, older people tend to both encode less richly and retrieve less effectively than younger people, so it is hardly surprising that they remember less.

It is of course possible to train older subjects to use more effective learning strategies. Paul Baltes in Berlin carried out an extensive series of studies in which both older and younger subjects were taught mnemonic strategies for learning word lists. He found that both groups improved substantially when given mnemonic techniques, with older subjects performing better than untrained younger subjects. However, it is unlikely that an old person will ever become quite as adept as a young person who has had an equivalent amount of practice or training. Good strategies help, but they will not give a 70-year-old the memory of a 20-year-old.

There are, however, some conditions of learning in which differences between the old and the young are very small. This is certainly the case with remembering *self-performed tasks,* tasks which require one to interact with the items to be remembered (*matchbox* — pick up a matchbox and shake it; *pencil* — pick up a pencil and write with it; *cup* — turn a cup upside down). On self-performed tasks memory differences between young and old may even be non-existent. It was initially thought that this might reflect some special kind of auto-matically encoded memory, but subsequent research suggests that recall is good because the information is multiply encoded — through vision, verbal labelling and action. Multiple encoding, encoding the material to be remembered as richly and in as many modalities as possible, therefore becomes a strategy for enhancing memory. This is a relatively recent discovery, which to the best of my knowledge has not been turned into a practical mnemonic aid yet. A promising line for further applied research?

Prospective memory

When the Rivermead Behavioral Memory Test was used to assess the memory of the over-60s, the component that appeared to be most sensitive to the effects of age was prospective memory. This finding was confirmed using a newly developed test of prospective memory which involved reading a passage of prose with a series of instructions embedded in it. For example, the subject might be told 'Place a cross in the box at the end of each paragraph', 'Underline the word *fox* when you next encounter it', or 'In three minutes' time place a tick in the margin indicating how far you have got in the test.' When younger and older subjects took the test, the older subjects fared consistently worse. Age deficits have also been reported on an ingenious computer-based test which simulates the task of cooking breakfast; subjects are required to lay the table while starting various dishes that take different times to cook. Elderly subjects were consistently more likely to burn the computerized toast!

There is therefore good evidence that prospective memory deteriorates with age. On the other hand questionnaires asking young and old subjects about the frequency of memory lapses show that it is the young who consistently report forgetting appointments and failing to do things on time. Is it simply that older people forget how often they forget? Apparently not. A number of studies have tested prospective memory by requiring people to make telephone calls at specified times over a period of days or weeks. In general, the young forget to call significantly more often than the old, even when a financial inducement is given for good performance. This does not simply indicate a lack of other more engrossing activities in retired people, since pre-retired middle-aged subjects are also better than the young. The good level of performance in older subjects seems much more likely to stem from their more skilful and consistent use of external memory aids such as diaries and 'to do' lists.

Semantic memory

Whether the news is good or bad for semantic memory depends on which measure you use. There is no doubt that speed and fluency of access to memory stores diminish as we get older. The bar graph overleaf shows the results of a study on word-finding in young and old subjects with and without cues. Subjects were given definitions of target words and asked to produce the target words as rapidly as possible. For example, if the target word was *unicorn,* the definition might be 'A mythical animal with one straight horn on its head'. Alternatively, subjects were given the definition and asked to produce the target word with the help of cues; in the case of *unicorn* just the initial letters *(uni——)* might be given, or a word with a similar structure *(uniform),* or a semantically unrelated word *(candle),* or a semantically related word *(dragon).* Words similar in structure tended to improve access to the correct word, while similar meaning had little effect on access. Cues tended to be less helpful to older subjects. As we get older, it seems, we become less able to find the appropriate word and more likely to be put off our stride when the wrong word pops up. As we shall see later, one of the major problems of old age may be failure to inhibit irrelevant material rather than failure to access what is relevant.

Young and old subjects are equally good at matching definitions to target words when both are given. When given the definition and asked for the word, the elderly are less likely to succeed than the young, except when the first few letters are provided as a hint. (Poon, Rubin and Wilson, 1989)

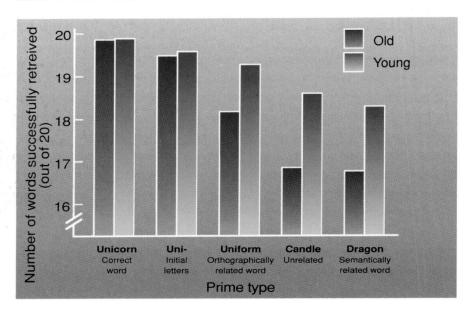

However, this is tempered by the fact that our store of knowledge continues to grow as we get older. In many traditional societies the old are valued for their accumulated knowledge, for their wisdom. It would be nice to have a test for wisdom. Sadly the current world is changing so fast that growth in wisdom is often obscured by the demands of adaptation.

Implicit learning

The evidence in this area appears to be somewhat mixed. The elderly do appear to show comparatively normal effects of priming (earlier presentation of the word *crocodile,* for example, makes it easier to find a word fitting the letter pattern *c-o-o-i-e*). There is some suggestion, however, that procedural learning, as indicated by rate of acquisition of new motor skills, is impaired in the elderly. Post-retirement is probably not the ideal time to acquire acrobatic skills. Indeed, in the case of female Olympic gymnasts old age appears to begin at about 12.

Biological influences on learning and memory

Whether we like it or not, as we get older our physiology gradually changes. Some of those changes have implications for learning and memory. Over the years my wife has become great friends with an elderly neighbor. During the week our neighbor is provided with lunch through a voluntary service called Meals on Wheels, which delivers around noon. On Sundays, if we are at home, my wife takes lunch to her at around 1.30 pm. She recently noticed that her old friend's memory seemed to be substantially worse on Sundays. Was this because she had gone too long without food? A mid-morning snack seemed to help. In a recent study of the effects of blood sugar level on memory in the elderly, subjects were asked to skip breakfast and turn up for testing in the laboratory, where they were given a drink containing glucose or a sugar-free placebo containing saccharine. There was a significant tendency for the glucose drink to lead to better performance on two long-term verbal memory tasks, one involving learning lists of words, the other requiring retention of a prose paragraph. Measurement of serum glucose levels revealed that subjects showing the greatest increase after the glucose drink also showed the most long-term memory improvement. No equivalent effect was found in young subjects — they appeared to be able to maintain fasting blood sugar levels much better than older subjects. This suggests that elderly people should eat a little and often rather than larger quantities once or twice a day.

In all age groups moderate and regular exercise helps to promote cardio-vascular fitness and control blood sugar levels. It also relieves stress.

A second biological factor concerns the effects of competition stress on performance. This was studied by two Swedish psychologists, Thomas Bäckman and Bo Molander, both enthusiasts of miniature golf, a game that is played competitively in Sweden. Miniature golf is a good sport to study experimentally, since each hole always presents the same challenge to each competitor, with the effects of factors such as weather being minimal, or indeed non-existent if, like Bäckman and Molander, you set up your course indoors. They were interested in the effects of age on performance under stress, and compared young and middle-aged golfers (in their 50s) under practice conditions and in competition. They found that if an older and a younger player did equally well in practice, in competition the younger player tended to maintain his level of performance, while the middle-aged player tended to deteriorate.

It is possible to measure attentional concentration indirectly by measuring heart rate. When a golfer concentrates on making a crucial shot, the heart tends to slow down during the preparation period; after the shot has been made it speeds up. Under competition conditions young players continued to show this pattern, but older players did not. In another study, in which the two groups attempted to ignore distracting information, the young players did so more effectively than the middle-aged. When it came to recounting their various shots, the middle-aged players found that recollection of irrelevant material tended to get in the way of detailed recall. Bäckman and Molander concluded that advancing years make it harder to concentrate, harder to inhibit potentially distracting influences, particularly under conditions of stress.

Nevertheless Bäckman and Molander found wide individual differences in the effects of age on resistance to stress. Top-class athletes such as the great American football quarterback, Joe Montana, continue to be successful well after the average age of retirement in their sport. It is of course possible to develop techniques for relaxation and for handling stress. Such techniques often feature in programs designed to help the elderly cope with some of the limitations of an aging memory system.

Individual differences in the effects of aging

Using it rather than losing it! Skills and capacities that are not used show more deterioration with age.

Virtually all studies of aging have shown that as people become older, the differences between individuals become larger. This may be due in part to associated factors such as declining health, which tend to be linked to impaired cognitive performance. However, even in healthy elderly people there is a very wide range in cognitive decline, making it particularly unwise to make predictions about individuals.

Do different mental capacities decline at different rates within a given individual? Or, to echo Patrick Rabbitt, 'Does it all go together when it goes?' The Seattle study mentioned at the beginning of this chapter throws some light on this question. The two graphs on page 249 show the likelihood of decline in one, two, three, four, or five of the functions measured by Schaie over successive seven-year periods. Decline is by no means uniform. As the lower of the two graphs shows, typically only one or two functions show marked decline.

To what extent can one predict when decline will occur in a particular individual? In order to answer this question Schaie has applied a number of techniques originally developed by insurance assessors. It seems that the average age at which intellectual decline is likely to be first detectable is about 65, meaning that performance at 65 will typically be detectably poorer than at 58. However, the decline is likely to be influenced by other factors. If you are female, the decline is not likely to be detectable uintil you are about 70. If you have a higher than average education, then noticeable decline will probably be delayed by one year for each year of education above the average. If you have been more than averagely successful in life, then decline may be delayed by another three years. But if you have started to become more rigid in your behavior, the downward path may start six years earlier.

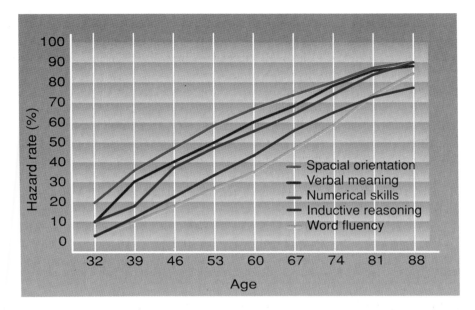

This graph shows how five separate abilities —understanding words, spatial orientation, numerical skills, inductive reasoning, word fluency—decline with age. (Schaie, 1989)

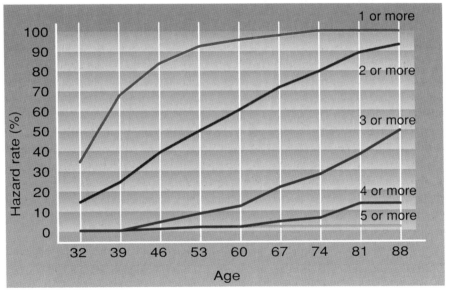

This graph shows how likely it is for just one, or two, or three, or four or all of these abilities to be affected as the years go by. So, the answer to the question 'Does it all go together when it goes?' is a resounding 'No'. (Schaie, 1989)

Can we do anything to delay the process of intellectual decline? Changing sex would probably not work, and by the time one starts to become aware of cognitive deterioration it is probably too late to worry about the number of years of education one has had. It helps to be successful — 'Unto him that hath shall more be given.' About the only thing one might try to change is behavior; it is obviously a bad thing to be too set in one's ways, either in terms of habits or attitudes. One should try to remain flexible for as long as possible. Schaie himself is fairly optimistic. He mentions a number of training programs which have had some degree of success; in one study, for example, some 40 per cent of participants who had shown some decline over a period of 14 years were able to return to their earlier level of functioning, not only on the specific tasks that were trained, but also on others which had not been directly practised. In general, the precept of 'Use it or lose it' seems to be a sensible one. There are a growing number of memory groups and workshops being set up for the elderly, and they appear to have a certain amount of success. One of these is described in the next chapter.

Alzheimer's disease

Not only do our sensory and cognitive skills lose their sharpness as we get older, but we are also more likely to suffer from one or more pathologies. Some of these, such as cardiovascular disease, may have more or less marked secondary effects on brain function and quite possibly on memory. Others, such as the dementias, have a much more direct and progressive effect on the efficiency with which we learn and remember. There are many different dementias, most of them fortunately rare.

This ex-soldier, demonstrating for invalid servicemen's rights in South Korea, obviously has no intention of rusting in peace. Many retired people are ardent protesters about all sorts of things. Perhaps rebellion keeps their faculties sharp?

Others are less rare, including Huntington's disease, progressive degeneration of the brain which causes disordered movement (uncontrollable writhing) and gradual mental deterioration; the condition is inherited, which means that those at risk are likely to know this from an early age and must learn to face the possibility of its onset as they grow older. Multi-infarct dementia is a condition in which the effect of a number of minor strokes cumulates, each one reducing the efficiency of the brain; this can be treated to some extent by drugs which reduce the likelihood of stroke. By far the most common dementia, however, is Alzheimer's disease (AD). It accounts for over 50 per cent of cases of dementia in the elderly, occurring in about 10 per cent of the population over the age of 65 and increasing in likelihood with age.

Alzheimer's disease is difficult to diagnose reliably, other than at post-mortem, when the patient's brain is found to contain characteristic plaques and neuro-fibrillary tangles. Since such physical signs are not readily detectable in the living patient, it is necessary to rely on behavioral and psychological evidence, coupled with careful exclusion of other possible causes of dementia. The exact form of the psychological impairment can vary from patient to patient, particularly during the early stages, with the result that no single symptom is regarded as crucial. Instead, the diagnosis depends upon the patient performing at a level below the bottom 5 per cent of the population in two or more areas of the following eight aspects of cognition:

1   Orientation in time and place
2   Memory
3   Language
4   Praxis (control of movement and action)
5   Attention
6   Visual perception
7   Problem solving
8   Social functioning.

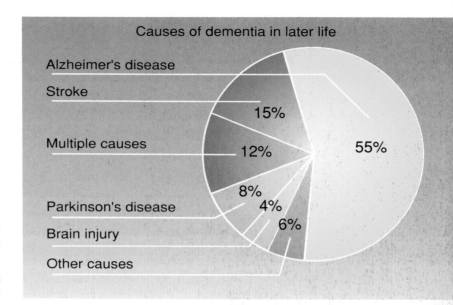

Causes of dementia in later life

Alzheimer's disease
Stroke   15%
Multiple causes   12%   55%
                8%
Parkinson's disease   4%
                    6%
Brain injury

Other causes

As there are no generally accepted normative tests for these eight areas, diagnosis remains a problem. A patient who underperforms in two or more of these areas is likely to be provisionally categorized as 'possible AD'. The diagnosis would not be confirmed unless the decrement proved to be progressive on retesting a few months later. Using the best available methods, a research-oriented clinic with a special interest in AD is likely to be correct about 90 per cent of the time (when diagnosis is checked against post-mortem). In general clinical practice the accuracy of diagnosis is almost certainly lower than this.

Most research is carried out on patients with a mild or moderate degree of AD, since severly impaired patients are likely to be unable to follow instructions or maintain attention sufficiently well to take part in tests. Patients suffering from mild AD may function quite well in their own home, although they may need some help with finances and possibly with household chores. They may or may not be aware of their cognitive decline, but will probably need to retire from work if they have not already done so, particularly if they have a demanding job (although I know of an American detective and an Italian judge, both diagnosed as suffering from AD, who continued in their jobs, largely supported by their colleagues).

AD patients often tend to withdraw from earlier social activities. They also become dependent upon others for transport, partly due to problems of getting lost. The aforementioned judge, who liked to drive, solved this problem by having his chauffeur drive a car ahead of him, following in his own car. As the disease progresses, and lapses of memory and judgement lead to problems in cooking and cleaning and failure to take medication, patients are likely to need the help of carers. Although the disease may begin with one or two relatively isolated areas of deficit, as it progresses it becomes more general, ultimately leaving the person in a condition of general cognitive decline, often unable to recognize his or her family or regular carers.

Given the commonness of AD, and the problem of early diagnosis, there

Dementia among the elderly has many causes, but Alzheimer's disease is the commonest. The percentages in this diagram are based on studies done in the United States and described by Selkoe (1992).

·has been a good deal of research on characterizing the cognitive deficits found in AD patients. Memory problems are often the first sign of the disease, and continue to feature prominently as it progresses. However, as we have just seen, a deteriorating memory is characteristic of perfectly normal aging, and even a disproportionate memory deficit is by no means necessarily a sign of AD. For that reason there is continuing interest in trying to categorize the memory deficit in AD more precisely, both to avoid false diagnosis and because treatment is likely to be most effective during the early stages of the disease.

Long-term memory in AD

The clearest and most obvious deficit in AD tends to be in long-term episodic memory, whether this is tested by a standard task such as paired-associate learning or the recall of a prose paragraph, or by more ecologically oriented tests such as the Rivermead Behavioral Memory Test. AD patients tend to do badly on these tests, but then of course so do patients with brain damage due to other causes, making it extremely important to test the patient over a period of time to assess whether the deterioration is progressive. In the meantime there are other measures that can be made that will contribute to a correct diagnosis. One characteristic of AD that differentiates it from the more classic amnesic syndrome is the impaired operation of semantic memory. A sensitive test of this is verbal fluency, where the patient is asked to produce as many examples of a particular semantic category as possible in 60 seconds. AD patients are also very slow at performing the Silly Sentences test (see page 142) and inclined to make a rather high proportion of errors.

As the dementia progresses, problems with semantic memory increase, moving from simple word-finding problems to misidentification of objects to a complete loss of particular concepts. While the early stages might well reflect perceptual and word-finding problems, the fact that specific concepts become consistently inaccessible over time suggests that the actual storage of the representation might itself be eventually eroded by the disease. Autobiographical memory also deteriorates. One study probed AD patients' recall of facts about their lives and events from different periods in their lives. These were subsequently checked with relatives. The pattern found was one of marked impairment of memory for facts and events throughout the lifespan, but with a gradient indicating that more recent experiences were particularly vulnerable to the disease, even though they occurred before the onset of the disease itself.

Implicit learning in AD

The pattern of results for implicit learning and memory in AD sufferers is somewhat complex. Some AD patients appear to show normal implicit memory. For example, in one study subjects were required to decide as rapidly as possible whether a string of letters represented a real word or a nonword; both AD patients and controls showed a substantial advantage when an item was repeated. In another study subjects were required to press four buttons in response to the illumination of four lights on a computer screen. Unbeknown to the subjects, the sequence of lights was not random, but repeated after each sequence of ten. Both AD patients and controls speeded up with practice, and were equally slowed down when the repeating sequence was changed. However, the AD patients differed from the controls in not apparently noticing the repetition, although their performance indicated that they had certainly learned it implicitly.

Set against this, however, there are a number of demonstrations of failure to show implicit learning, notably in tasks involving word stem completion (for example, the word *metal* is presented and the subject is required to produce a word beginning *met—*). One suggestion is that AD patients do not adequately process words when they are initially presented. This may also partly explain a second failure to show implicit learning; AD subjects presented with a line drawing of an object and then shown a fragment of the original object and asked to identify it, failed to show priming. Once again, their perceptual problems may have prevented them from adequately encoding the figure in the first place.

Working memory in AD

It has been known for some years that AD patients tend to have reduced digit span. They also perform poorly on the Corsi Block Tapping test, the visuo-spatial equivalent of the digit span test in which the experimenter taps a series of locations and the subject has to copy the sequence of taps. Performance is measured by the maximum length of sequence correctly reproduced. A third traditional measure of short-term memory is the recency effect in free recall, where subjects are presented with a string of unrelated words and asked to recall them in any order. The tendency for the last few words to be well recalled is comparatively preserved in AD, although recall of earlier words is clearly impaired.

One interpretation of this pattern of data is that it reflects a deficit in the central executive component of working memory, which indirectly influences performance on the two span tests but is minimally involved in the recency effect. Further evidence for this comes from studies of immediate verbal memory span in AD patients. These indicate that although overall performance is reduced, AD groups show standard effects of both phonological similarity and word length. This suggests that they are using the phonological loop in the normal way, that is encoding words in terms of their sound and maintaining them by subvocal rehearsal.

My Italian colleagues and I decided to try to test the central executive hypothesis more directly. We asked a group of AD patients, a group of normal elderly subjects and a group of normal young subjects to perform a task that involved doing two things at once. The first task was visuo-spatial tracking; the subject had to keep a stylus in contact with a moving spot of light (the speed of

The deficiency that progressively tears the fabric of memory in Alzheimer's disease is neurochemical. Perhaps the saddest loss of all is the loss of autobiographical memory, first of recent events, then of more distant ones.

movement of the light was adjusted so that the overall level of performance was equivalent for the three groups). The purpose of this task was to load the visuo-spatial sketch pad. The second task, digit span, was chosen in order to load the phonological loop. Again we adjusted difficulty level to a point at which the performance of the three groups in terms of errors was equivalent, although the AD patients were of course remembering shorter sequences than either of the two control groups. The third stage of the experiment involved requiring all three groups to perform both tasks at the same time. Under these conditions the AD patients made a greater number of errors on the digit span task than either of the control groups, and also performed significantly less well on the tracking task. Performance of both the elderly and young control groups decreased very slightly under the two-task condition, but not nearly as much as that of the AD group,

In a later experiment we studied the same patients three times over a period of a year. We found that their capacity to perform the tracking and digit span tasks separately showed no deterioration; however, performance on the combined task showed a marked and systematic decline as the disease progressed. A second task, in which only difficulty was varied, showed no greater rate of deterioration for the hard than the easy condition, suggesting that coordination rather than simple level of difficulty is the crucial factor. We are continuing to investigate this test, since it seems sensitive to the deficits of AD while apparently being unaffected by the processes of normal aging.

Treating Alzheimer's disease

Can AD be cured? At present, the answer has to be 'No'. Because of the importance and extent of the problem, there is a pressing need to identify the neurophysiological or neurochemical deficits responsible, and to use that knowledge to provide treatment. There appears to be good evidence that AD patients are deficient in the neurotransmitter substance acetylcholine, which is thought to play an important role in learning and memory. This discovery initially led to high hopes of treatment; patients were fed with the missing substance, a procedure that was subsequently described as equivalent to tackling a fuel crisis in a country by flying over it and pouring the missing gasoline from cans. Alas, the jibe was all too appropriate since the only effect of feeding choline to patients is to make them smell of bad fish. The next stage involved administering lecithin, a precursor of choline. Although odor-free, lecithin therapy fared little better. It now seems that choline may be only one of a number of neurochemical deficiencies in AD. Treatment is unlikely to be as straightforward as administering a single 'missing' substance, but in the long run some form of neuropharmacological treatment would seem to be the most likely solution.

Tissue implantation, which involves implanting fetal brain tissue in order to remedy neurochemical deficits, is a potential alternative to medication. At present the method is principally being targeted at Parkinson's disease, in which the neurotransmitter dopamine is known to be depleted, and for which drug treatment has proved at least partially successful. Preliminary results are encouraging, but the method is still some way from being viable as a routine clinical treatment for human patients, and researchers are further away still from developing an equivalent treatment for Alzheimer's disease.

In the meantime, all the therapist can do is to try to help patients and carers to manage the disease. Unfortunately the memory improvement strategies outlined in the next chapter are less suitable for AD patients than for normal subjects because of the progressive nature of the deficit in AD. On the other hand, external aids can be used quite productively, particularly if they are introduced during the early stages when the patient is most capable of learning to use them. Even relatively simple strategies can be helpful if appropriately targeted. Moffat, who has had considerable experience with elderly and demented patients, describes one patient who continually lost his pipe and spectacles around the house, much to his frustration. He was helped by the very simple expedient of encouraging him to keep the errant objects in a bright orange bag. Once he had acquired this habit, the bag was easily detected, and the spectacles or pipe readily found. Another patient became very disturbed when left alone, being unable to remember where the carers had gone or when they would be back. The problem was solved by putting up a bulletin board on which the carers always left a message saying when they had gone and when they would return. The patient was taught to use the board, and became much less worried about being left alone. Such strategies can never be more than minor palliatives, but if appropriately targeted they can reduce at least some of the stress and frustration caused by AD.

Fortunately, for most of us, the fallibility of our memory is far less than that encountered by the AD patient, and the supporting cognitive skills are commensurately greater. We are in a much better position to improve the functioning of our memories, provided we identify the problem correctly and are prepared to put the necessary effort and ingenuity into solving it.

14 Improving your memory

We all tend to complain about our memories. Despite the elegance of the human memory system it is not infallible, and we have to learn to live with that fallibility. It seems to be socially much more acceptable to complain of a poor memory, and much more acceptable to blame a social lapse on 'a terrible memory', than to attribute it to stupidity or insensitivity. But how much do we know about our own memories? Obviously we need to remember our memory lapses in order to know just how bad our memories are. One of the most amnesic patients I have ever tested was a lady suffering from Korsakoff's syndrome, memory loss following chronic alcoholism. The test involved presenting her with lists of words; after each list she would comment with surprise on her inability to recall the words, saying: 'I pride myself on my memory!' She appeared to have forgotten just how bad her memory was.

One of the main problems in trying to evaluate one's own memory is that in doing so one is implicitly comparing it with the memories of other people. Typically we do not really know how good or bad other people's memories are, so it is very easy to have a distorted view of our own.

Everyday remembering

Studying for exams requires some sort of memory strategy. Generally speaking, it is a mistake to pigeonhole information too tightly; memorizing things in a particular order may not always be helpful either.

In recent years there has been a considerable growth of interest in the problem of assessing everyday memory as a whole. Clearly it is very difficult to obtain an objective measure of memory in everyday life since memory pervades so many tasks and depends so much on the lifestyle of the person concerned. However, there have been attempts to make assessments using memory questionnaires. One such questionnaire, designed by my colleagues John Harris and Alan Sunderland, appears in adapted form on the next page. I suggest you attempt to complete it, scoring yourself on each question in the boxes provided. When you have finished, ask a close friend, preferably someone who lives with you, to give his or her estimate of your memory, using the same questionnaire. How does your estimate compare with that of your friend, and with the average scores obtained by Harris and Sunderland? Let us suppose that there are discrepancies between your estimate of your memory and that given by your companion. Whose estimate is likely to be correct? Clearly the answer to this depends on the particular item being judged. You yourself are likely to have a much better idea of whether you have difficulty following the plots of plays and films since, unless you complain about such a difficulty, others are unlikely to be aware of it. However, forgetting appointments and losing things around the house may well be something that is as obvious to your companion as it is to you.

MEMORY QUESTIONNAIRE

This questionnaire was developed by John Harris and Alan Sunderland to test lapses in everyday memory. Work through the questionnaire below, scoring in the spaces provided. Give yourself a score of 1 to 9 on each of the questions below, then total all your scores. Score your answer to each question as follows:

1 Not at all in the last six months
2 About once in the last six months
3 More than once but less than once a month

4 About once a week
5 More than once a month but less than once a week
6 About once a week

7 More than once a week but less than once a day
8 About once a day
9 More than once a day

	Questions	Self-scoring	Independent scoring	Average scores*
1	Do you forget where you have put things? Lose things around the house?	9		5
2	Do you fail to recognize places that you are told you have often been to before?	1		1
3	Do you find television stories difficult to follow?	2		2
4	Have you forgotten a change in your daily routine, such as a change in the place where something is kept, or a change in the time something happens? Have you followed your old routine by mistake?	2		2
5	Have you had to go back to check whether you have done something that you meant to do?	4		4
6	Have you forgotten when something happened? For example, whether something happened yesterday or last week?	3		3
7	Have you completely forgotten to take things with you, or left things behind and had to go back and fetch them?	3		3
8	Have you forgotten that you were told something yesterday or a few days ago, and had to be reminded about it?	5		3
9	Have you started to read something (a book or an article in a newspaper/magazine) without realizing you have read it before?	3		1
10	Have you let yourself ramble on about unimportant or irrelevant things?	8		2
11	Have you failed to recognize, by sight, close relatives or friends that you meet frequently?	1		1
12	Have you had difficulty picking up a new skill? For example, learning a new game or operating a new gadget after you have practised once or twice?	2		1
13	Have you found that a word is 'on the tip of your tongue'? You know what it is but cannot quite find it.	4		4

	Questions	Self-scoring	Independent scoring	Average scores*
	14	4		2
	15	1		1
	16	7		3
	17	6		1
	18	6		2
	19	1		1
	20	6		2
	21	6		2
	22	1		2
	23	2		2
	24	2		2
	25a	1		1
	25b	3		2
	26	2		1
	27	2		2
Total		99		58

14 Have you completely forgotten to do things you said you would do, and things you planned to do?

15 Have you forgotten important details of what you did or what happened to you the day before?

16 When talking to someone, have you forgotten what you have just said? Maybe saying 'What was I talking about?' or 'Where was I?'

17 When reading a newspaper or magazine, have you been unable to follow the thread of a story or lost track of what it is about?

18 Have you forgotten to tell somebody something important? Forgotten to pass on a message or remind someone of something?

19 Have you forgotten important details about yourself? For example, your date of birth or where you live?

20 Have you got the details of what someone has told you mixed up and confused?

21 Have you told someone a story or joke that you have told them already?

22 Have you forgotten details of things you do regularly, whether at home or at work? For example, details of what to do, or at what time to do something?

23 Have you found that the faces of famous people, seen on television or in photographs, look unfamiliar?

24 Have you forgotten where things are normally kept or looked for them in the wrong place?

25 (a) Have you got lost or taken a wrong turning on a journey, a walk or in a building where you have OFTEN been before?

   (b) Have you got lost or taken a wrong turning on a journey, a walk or in a building where you have only been ONCE OR TWICE before?

26 Have you done some routine thing twice by mistake? For example, putting two lots of tea in the teapot, or going to brush/comb your hair when you have just done so?

27 Have you repeated to someone what you have just told them or asked them the same question twice?

*Scores obtained by Harris and Sunderland. These averages are not necessarily representative of the population at large.

A total score of 27–58 means that your memory is generally good; 58–116 is average; 116–243 is rather below average. However, do not be alarmed if your score is below average. This may simply mean that you lead a very busy life. Statistically the greater the number of situations in which lapses are possible, the greater the number of lapses you will report overall.

Demands on memory

A complicating factor in evaluating people's estimates of their own memory powers stems from the fact that people lead very different lives. One person might lead an extremely structured and sheltered life, making few demands on memory, while another may live a very active and stressful existence. Given an equal memory capacity, the second person is clearly likely to experience far more memory lapses than the first. A similar explanation probably applies to the observation made by a number of researchers, including ourselves, that the elderly often report fewer memory lapses than the young. This is probably because older people tend to live more structured and ordered lives than the young. Within a family, the mother often acts as a memory not only for her own activities but for those of her husband and children as well. To do this she is likely to have to make more extensive use of memory aids such as calendars or diaries than they do, and is likely to make fewer errors as a result. Such organized habits are likely to continue into old age.

Choosing a memory. Diaries are, on the whole, a very efficient way of reducing demands on memory. Older people tend to be more systematic users of such aids.

John Harris conducted a survey to find out what sort of mnemonic aids people use most frequently. He tested a group of university students and a sample of housewives. His question-naire, in modified form, appears opposite. Try it for yourself, filling in the answer boxes provided. See how your use of mnemonic aids compares with that of Harris's test groups. The figures given are the most frequently chosen categories (in descending order where not equal). Overall, Harris found, his two groups had a similar pattern of mnemonic use, but there were some minor differences; for example, housewives seemed less inclined to write on their hands than students and more inclined to write on calendars!

Virtually everyone in Harris's study showed some use of mnemonic aids, but these were overwhelmingly external aids such as diaries, calendars, lists and timers. Recent years have seen an enormous growth in the availability of commercial memory aids, often based on new developments in micro-electronics; the humble diary or daybook, for example, has become the portable personal computer complete with keyboard and screen. In 1988 Douglas Herrmann and Susan Petro published a paper on the information that they had collected over the years on a total of 74 kinds of commercial memory aid. Unfortunately it proved rather difficult to discover how useful such aids actually are. They did, however, question a small group of people as to what external aids they found most helpful. Some of the most useful proved to be traditional aids such as calendars, appointment books and alarm clocks. Beeping keychains (a lost key can be summoned by clapping the hands) were found to be quite helpful, as were telephone answering machines and watches and calculators with 'reminder' features. To be fair to commercial aids, many of them may well not have been purchased by this relatively small sample of subjects.

How often do you use these memory aids?

Rate your use of each of the memory aids below with a score of 1 to 6, using the scoring system below.

0 Never used	**4** Used three to five times in last 2 weeks
1 Used less than three times in last 6 months	**5** Used six to ten times in last 2 weeks
2 Used less than three times in last 4 weeks	**6** Used eleven or more times in last 2 weeks
3 Used less than three times in last 2 weeks	

Questions	Your rating	Students	Housewives
1		3,2,1	3,4,5
2		1	0,1
3		1,6	6
4		0	0
5		0,1	0,1
6		0	0
7		2,3	4,3,2
8		5,6	1,5,6
9		0,1	4,0
10		0	0
11		0	0
12		0	0
13		1,2 5,6	2,3
14		0	0
15		1	1,0
16		0	6
17		2	3
18		2	3,4 5
19		0	0

1 *Shopping lists*

2 *First-letter memory aids* For example, the first letters of 'Richard Of York Gave Battle In Vain' give the first letters of the colors of the rainbow

3 *Diary*

4 *Rhymes* For example, 'In fourteen hundred and ninety-two Columbus sailed the ocean blue' helps you to remember the date 1492

5 *The place method* Items to be remembered are imagined in a series of familiar places. When recall is required, one 'looks' at the familiar places

6 *Writing on hand* (or any other part of your anatomy or clothing)

7 *The story method* Making up a story which connects items to be remembered in the correct order

8 *Mentally retracing a sequence of events or actions* in order to jog your memory; useful for remembering where you lost or left something, or at what stage something significant happened

9 *Alarm clock* (or other alarm device) for waking up only

10 *Cooker timer* with alarm for cooking only

11 *Alarm clock* (or other alarm devices such as watches, radios, timers, telephones, calculators) used for purposes other than waking up or cooking

12 *The pegword method* 'One is a bun, two is a shoe, three is a tree', etc. as a method of remembering lists of items in correct order (see pages 98–99)

13 *Turning numbers into letters* For remembering telephone numbers, for example

14 *Memos* For example, writing notes-and 'To do' lists for yourself

15 *Face-name associations* Changing people's names into something meaningful and matching them with something unusual about their face. For example, red-bearded Mr Hiles might be imagined with hills growing out of his beard

16 *Alphabetical searching* Going through the alphabet letter by letter to find the initial letter of a name. For example, does a particular person's name begin with A . . . B . . . Ah yes! C! C for Clark . . .

17 *Calendars, wall charts, year planners, display boards, etc.*

18 *Asking other people to remember things for you*

19 *Leaving objects in special or unusual places* so that they act as reminders

Two or more scores indicate large differences between individuals, with each of the numbers being given by a subgroup of those tested.

Very few internal mnemonics of the kind advocated by memory training courses were reported by Harris's subjects. I am referring here to courses of the kind devised by Lorayne and Lucas and described in *Time* magazine as a 'never-fail system to help you remember everything'. What do such systems involve? While the present book does not aim to be a primer for memory training, it would be appropriate to outline at least some of the more popular mnemonic systems before saying something about the general principles of improving your memory.

Visual imagery mnemonics

Mnemonics based on visual imagery have been common at least since classical times. According to Cicero, writing in the first century BC, the first such mnemonic was devised by the Greek poet Simonides in about 500 BC. It appears that a Greek who had won a wrestling victory at the Olympic Games gave a banquet at his house to celebrate. Simonides was invited to attend and to give a recitation in honor of the victor. Shortly after completing his eulogy Simonides was called away . . . luckily for him, because just after he left the floor of the banqueting hall collapsed, killing and mutilating the guests. Many of the bodies were unrecognizable. How were the victims' relatives to identify them and give them a decent burial? Simonides found that he could quite easily remember where most of the guests had been at the time he left, and so was able to identify the bodies. This set him thinking: if his visual memory was so good, could he not use it to help himself recall other material? He therefore devised a system in which he visualized a room in great detail, and then imagined various items in special places in the room. Whenever he needed to remember what these items were he would 'look' at the appropriate location in his mind's eye. The system became popular with classical orators such as Cicero and has continued in use to the present day. The Russian mnemonist Shereshevskii used this system (see page 101). As you will realize if you give it a serious trial, it operates very effectively and easily.

First of all, think of ten locations in your home, choosing them so that the sequence of moving from one to the other is an obvious one — for example, front door to entrance hall to kitchen to bedroom, and so on. Check that you can imagine moving through your ten locations in a consistent order without difficulty. Now think of ten items and imagine them in those locations. If the first item is a pipe, you might imagine it poking out of the letter box in your front door and great clouds of smoke billowing into the street. If the second is a cabbage, you might imagine your hall obstructed by an enormous cabbage, and so on.

Now try to create similarly striking images associating your ten chosen locations with the words in the panel on the right.

shirt
eagle
paperclip
rose
camera
mushroom
crocodile
handkerchief
sausage
mayor

I have used this particular mnemonic technique very often in student laboratory classes and almost invariably it works extrememly well. Although it is much easier to perform with concrete words, such as the names of objects, it is still effective in remembering abstract words such as 'truth', 'hope', 'patriotism' and so on, provided one manages to come up with a satisfactory image. The use of imagery can be prevented either by presenting material very rapidly or, as we saw in the chapter on working memory, by introducing an interfering spatial task, so do not try to use the locations method while skiing down a mountain or driving your car!

The same set of locations can be used repeatedly, as long as only the most recent item in a particular location is remembered; earlier items in that location will suffer from the usual interference effects, unless of course one deliberately links them into a coherent chain. Clearly one can create a system which has many more than ten locations; this is certainly true of classical mnemonic systems and of the complex and somewhat mystical systems developed during the Middle Ages. I suggest you now try to recall the ten items listed two paragraphs ago. No, don't look. Rely on the images you created at various points around you.

There are obvious similarities between the locations method and the pegword method described on pages 98–99. The main difference is that the pegword system uses numbers rather than locations, and bridges the gap between number and image by means of a rhyme: *one is a bun, two is a shoe, three is a tree*, and so on. An intermediate system, developed in Cambridge during the seventeenth century by Henry Herdson, relied on a series of visual images of objects whose shape resembled that of various numbers. Hence 1 might be represented by a candle or a tower, 2 by a swan, 3 by a trident, and so on. The first object would then be imagined interacting with a candle in some way, the second with a swan . . . An elaboration of this system, combining it with a location mnemonic, was used by the late eighteenth-century mnemonist Gregor von Feinaigle.

One of the most extensive current uses of visual imagery mnemonics is in foreign language learning, where the application ranges from teaching imagery mnemonics to students through to development of entire courses concerned with vocabulary and grammar. Michael Gruneberg, a psychologist with a strong interest in the practical application of memory research, has applied visual imagery mnemonics to learning both the vocabulary and grammar of Russian and of seven other European languages. The original programs, for English speakers, were produced as computer software together with audio tapes to assist pronunciation, while later developments have been published in book form. As we saw in reviewing the role of the phonological loop in foreign language learning, visual imagery is good for learning to understand a foreign language, although rote repetition is better for learning to speak the language, suggesting that the audio tape versions, with an emphasis on accurate repetition, may be preferable.

Verbal mnemonics

Although classical mnemonics relied mainly on visual imagery, this was by no means the case in later times. In the sixteenth century, for example, Peter Ramus devised a system in which information was represented in a hierarchical tree, with abstract concepts branching into progressively more concrete instances.

Peter Ramus (Pierre Ramée), 1515-1472, mathematician and inventor of a system of verbal mnemonics.

Supporters of the Ramist system argued that it had the advantage of not requiring the learner to remember as much additional irrelevant information as the location and pegword systems did. The Puritans favored verbal systems for an additional rather curious reason: they regarded images as wicked and liable to give rise to 'depraved carnal affections'!

Verbal mnemonics fitted in well with the Victorian educational tradition of rote learning, with its requirement that the unfortunate pupil should memorize vast numbers of facts, such as the dates of accession of kings and queens. A Yorkshire headmaster, the Reverend Brayshaw, published a book in 1849 entitled *Metrical Mnemonics* containing a selection of rhymes incorporating over 2,000 dates and numerical facts drawn from physics, astronomy, history and geography. The system underlying Brayshaw's mnemonics was a fairly old one, or certainly extant since the seventeenth century. It involved substituting consonants for particular numbers and then using the consonants to create words. This was the code used by Brayshaw:

1	2	3	4	5	6	7	8	9	0	00
B	D	G	J	L	M	P	R	T	W	St
C	F	H	K		N	Q		V	X	
			S			Z				

To turn a number sequence into a word one simply selects one of the appropriate consonants, inserting vowels where necessary. Hence, to represent the year World War I broke out, 1914, one could use the consonants *CTBS*, which could be turned into the words *CAT BASE*. In fact, since all Brayshaw's dates were later than 1000 AD he used to ignore the initial 1000. Here are some examples of his rhymes, which give the dates of English kings.

> By MeN, near Hastings, William gains the crown. 1066
> A RaP in Forest New brings Rufus down. 1087
> Gaul's CoaSt first Henry hates, whose son is drowned. 1100
> Like BeaGLe Stephen fights with Maud renoun'd. 1135

The vital information about a date is always given in the second or second and third word in the line, and the line is completed by incorporating the name of the monarch and some striking feature about him. Fortunately, rote memorization of dates is no longer a central part of history teaching. However, the system can be adapted for other purposes. For instance, Ernest Wombaugh of California has modified it to allow him to provide chapter and verse for 1,200 selected quotations from the Bible (well, it makes a change from the first 2,000 decimal places of *pi*). Perhaps it might also be worth adapting for learning the plethora of telephone numbers, PIN numbers and zip codes that seem to be an ever increasing feature of modern life.

There are many other situations in which mnemonics are useful and still widely used. Take, for example, the colors of the spectrum, where a whole range of mnemonics can be created from the simple acronym, *ROYGBIV* (red, orange, yellow, green, blue, indigo, violet) to pieces of Brayshaw-like doggerel, such as *Richard Of York Gains Battles In Vain*. Medical students learning anatomy sometimes seem to be required to perform as much rote learning as Brayshaw's pupils, and still buy books of mnemonics to help them. One of the best-known anatomy mnemonics refers to the names of the cranial nerves: *On Old Olympia's*

Towering Top A Finn And German Vault And Hop (olfactory, optic, oculomotor, trochlear, trigeminal, abducens, facial, auditory, glossopharyngeal, vagus, accessory and hypoglossal). The assumption is that one knows the particular names but cannot reliably retrieve them, or retrieve them in the appropriate order; the rhythmic and relatively meaningful verse, with its first letter retrieval cues, is quite easily remembered.

A well-known mnemonic of a different kind, which I have never been able to dispense with, is that for remembering the number of days in a month. It starts: *Thirty days hath September, April, June and November, all the rest have thirty-one except that* . . . I always forget the rest but remember that it has something to do with February and leap years.

This problem of remembering how many days there are in each month, and how different cultures tackle it, is excellently discussed by Hunter. It appears that Italy, France and the Netherlands have a rhyme which is similar in form and function to the English verse. Greece, Finland, Russia, China, Tibet and most of South America apparently use a system based on knuckle counting. Clench your fist and count off the months alternately on the knuckles and on the hollows between the knuckles. January is on a knuckle and is therefore long, February is on a gap between knuckles and is therefore short, March is long, April short, May long, June short and July long. This takes you to the end of one set of knuckles. Continue by returning to the beginning of the fist again. This gives you August as long, September short, and so forth.

Other cultures have yet other ways of solving the problem. The Iranian calendar has 31 days for each of the first six months of the year and 30 days for the next five, with the last month of the year having 29 days except in leap years. Thailand has a calendar similar to our own, but the months have suffixes which indicate the number of days; months with 31 days end in *om* (January is *Magarakom*, March *Minakom*, etc.), and months with 30 end in *on* (September is *Kanyayon*, November *Prusjikayon*, etc.), while February has the special suffix *an*, *Kumpapan*. In short, the months are a problem in many cultures and mnemonics are routinely used as a way of remembering their unequal lengths.

Before moving away from verbal mnemonics, it is perhaps worth citing one cautionary tale. While writing about mnemonics in a previous book, I remembered a mnemonic told to me by an old friend which enables one to perform the rather useless task of remembering the value of *pi* to the first 20 decimal places.

PIE

I wish I could remember pi
Eureka cried the great inventor
Christmas pudding
Christmas pie
Is the problem's very center

Unfortunately, I simply could not remember how on earth one got from the rhyme to the appropriate numbers! I rang my friend, and he explained that one simply counts the number of letters in each word to give 3.14159265358979323846. When the book was duly published I pointed out the section to him, only to be told that I had got it wrong — the second line should be 'I wish I could *determine* pi', making the fifth decimal place 9, not 8. As he pointed out, psychologists remember (or misremember) but mathematicians determine!

A folk tale woven into a Qashqa'i rug from Fars, southern Iran.

Ritual and oral tradition

While mnemonics are certainly useful in contemporary Western society, the role they play is comparatively minor. The reason is simple: important information is usually written down, or indeed recorded on film or magnetic tape. In non-literate societies, however, tradition is crucially dependent on memory, and hence devices to preserve and communicate traditions assume vital importance. One means of achieving this preservation is to use ritual. Hunter describes the ritual involved in making a traditional Japanese ceremonial sword; each step in the complex process is marked by a ritual act. Religious ritual often has a similar purpose; it reminds the participants of some aspect of their faith. Here is a description of the Jewish Passover feast by Paul Levy, writing in the *Observer* a few years ago.

'The table (and the stage for the retelling of the Passover story) is set with three matzot . . . They represent not only the unleavened bread of the Israelites' journey but also "the poverty they suffered both in Egypt and in the desert".

'A roasted lamb bone is on the table "to commemorate the paschal sacrifice which every family brought to the Temple in ancient times". Boiled eggs are on the table as "symbolic of the festival sacrifice which was always additional to the paschal lamb".

'Bitter herbs, usually horseradish, are eaten to remind the Seder participants that the lives of the slaves in Egypt were bitter. A mixture of nuts, apples, sweet wine and spices, *charoset*, commemorates the mortar used by Jews at forced labor to build the Egyptian "treasure cities".

'Green herbs such as parsley and watercress are eaten to symbolize the return of spring and the renewal of life; but they are dipped into salt water in memory of the tears shed by the enslaved Hebrews.

'The best part of the evening is the compulsory four glasses of wine — of which even the youngest member of the party takes a sip. An extra place is laid at the table for the Prophet Elijah, who is supposed to visit every Jewish home during the Seder. And his glass of wine is always poured out too.

'In addition to ensuring that the feast is a jolly one, the wine plays its symbolic part in the proceedings. At one point in the ceremony ten drops of wine are poured out to represent the Ten Plagues suffered by the Egyptians before they would agree to Moses leading away the children of Israel. I well remember the look of malicious pleasure on my grandfather's face as he conducted the ceremony, and visited locusts and boils on the Egyptians. It was just after the war, and even the children knew that the "Egyptians" he had in mind were German.'

Non-literate societies depend heavily on oral tradition, enshrining important or significant information in some form of verse or song which is passed

Mursi tribesmen (Ethiopia) listen to a storyteller. Traditional stories are part of the communal 'memory' and have an important social function; through stories the tribe reminds itself of its identity, its place in the scheme of things.

down from father to son. Such societies often have a specific person who is responsible for remembering such information. The Rwanda of Central Africa, for example, have four specialized remembrancers. The task of the first (*Abacurabwenge*) is to remember the lists of kings and queen mothers; the second (*Abateekerezi*) is required to remember the most important events in the various reigns; the third (*Abasizi*) celebrates the deeds and qualities of the kings; and the fourth (*Abiiru*) must preserve the secrets of the dynasty.

This kind of information is highly important to a society, and there is evidence to suggest that when a society changes, remembered legend changes with it. Goody and Watt give a good example of a changed legend in the state of Gonja in Northern Ghana, which was ruled by several chieftains. It was the custom that certain of these chieftains took turns to rule the whole state. The precedent for this is contained in a legend which tells how the state was founded by a man who had seven sons. He allocated a territory to each of his sons, and commanded them to rule the state in turn. This legend was initially recorded around 1900. But since that time the number of territories has been reduced from seven to five; now the original founder is said to have had only five sons.

In communities which have a strong oral tradition, memory is frequently supplemented by rhythm and music. Drums are used as a mnemonic aid throughout most of Africa. In many African languages the pitch of speech sounds is an important feature, enabling much information to be conveyed using a set rhythm and tone. Hunter discusses at some length the use of singing and epic poetry as a means of preserving oral tradition. He points out, however, that the bard or poet does not rely on rote learning alone; his art is much more sophisticated. Every time he tells a story or a legend he recreates it, but within a constrained yet flexible poetic system (flamenco and jazz share this characteristic). The storyteller adheres to a highly stylized set of characters and events, and to specific rhythms, but is free to combine them somewhat differently on each occasion. In order to allow him to fit his theme to the appropriate rhythm, a number of stylistic devices are available. For example, in Homeric verse it was customary to refer to a ship as *equal, curved around* or *dark-prowed,* but the exact choice of adjective depended entirely on whether the verse required two, two and a half, or two and three-quarter units of metre.

Most of the external memory aids listed in John Harris's questionnaire depend either on literacy (calendars, diaries, and so on) or on technology (watches or alarms, for example), but there are many other possibilities. The Incas used knotted cords (*quipu*) as memory aids, and I myself often use the related but more primitive mnemonic of tying a knot in my handkerchief. That was effective at first, but after a while I began to discover that I had a handkerchief full of knots and no memory for what they meant. I now combine knotting with an imagery mnemonic, imagining the person or object being carefully tied within the knot, and find that it seems to work reasonably well.

Australian aborigines used notched-sticks or tallies to help them remember messages. Although they lived in small nomadic groups, an important part of their social and cultural identity depended on occasional intertribal ceremonies. The decision to hold a ceremony would be taken by the elders of the tribe, who would also decide which groups and which members of those groups should be invited. The actual invitation would be delivered by one of the younger men carrying a message stick. He would look on while the head man of the group made marks on the stick, a notch at one end indicating the sender, and a large notch for each tribal group invited to attend. If all the people were invited, then the stick would be notched along the edge from end to end; if only a few were invited, then only a portion of the stick would be notched; if very few, then a notch would be made for each individual, who would be named to the messenger. Once the head man had completed the message on the stick, he would hand it to the elder nearest to him, who would inspect it and add any necessary further instructions before passing it to the other elders present. The messenger would then take the stick to the group to be invited and relate the message, referring as he did so to the marks on the stick. The marks did not represent a written language, in that the messenger was not able to 'read' messages he had not heard, but they were retrieval cues for an oral message.

Memory aids

A society where few people can read and write must rely heavily on memory, and will rightly value the capacity to remember large amounts of information in great detail. But in a society such as our own we are not obliged to commit everything to memory. Indeed in very important matters it would not be sensible to do so. That is why committees have minutes, companies have company reports, and lawyers put agreements in writing. These are obvious precautions against the distortions and deletions to which human memory is heir. Even for the purposes of shopping I must confess that once the list of items gets beyond three or four I do not imagine my house festooned with them but simply write a shopping list. It's more convenient, just as a diary is more convenient, and relieves one from worrying about not remembering something. However, there are situations in which such obvious aids as diaries and shopping lists are inappropriate.

What the particular problems are will vary from person to person, and just as the problems will vary, so will the solutions. There is no alternative to tackling each problem in its own right, using as much good sense and ingenuity as possible. Although there are no simple rules for improving your memory, there are a number of general principles that will help you make the most of your memory.

Improving your memory

As I hope the previous chapters have demonstrated, human memory is a remarkably effective system for storing and retrieving information. Nonetheless we all find that our memory lets us down occasionally, particularly as we get older. Our lapses are often rather trivial and easily remedied — describing an incident involving a mutual friend and forgetting his name, for example. Other memory failures can be more serious, however; a missed appointment may sour a potentially important working relationship or lose a valuable contract. If you are a student, you need to remember information for exams; if you have a job dealing with people, you need to remember faces and names.

In one sense we cannot change our memory. By this I mean that I know of no way in which the neural systems underlying memory can be systematically enhanced. What we can do, however, is use the system we have more effectively.

First of all, it is important to accept that your memory is not a system, like your heart and lungs, for which simple 'fitness' exercises can be prescribed. This particular fallacy used to be common among nineteenth-century educationists and is still sneakingly believed today. For example, it is not uncommon for speech therapists to try to help patients with memory problems by giving them practice at Kim's Game (a trayful of objects is shown to the patient and then covered while the patient tries to remember as many of the objects on the tray as possible). Well-meaning though this may be, the chances of it actually helping the patient are rather slight.

Ian Hunter, whose excellent book on memory has two very useful chapters on improving memory performance, cites an experiment published by W. G. Sleight in 1911 in which 84 12-year-old schoolgirls were tested on their ability to memorize the dates of historical events, lists of nonsense syllables, verses of poetry, passages of prose, lists of names, the position of towns and rivers on a map, an array of visual forms, and a sequence of letters of the alphabet. The girls were then split into four groups, three of which were given memory practice for half an hour a day, four days a week, over a six-week period, making 12 hours of practice in all. One group practised memorizing poetry, a second memorized quantitative facts such as scientific formulae and geographical distances, while the third was given passages of prose about geographical, historical and scientific subjects, and required to reproduce the content of these passages from memory. The fourth group acted as a control and had no practice. All four groups were then retested using material similar to that used at the beginning of the experiment. Did practice in memorizing a particular type of material enhance later performance on the same type of material? Sleight's results were unequivocal: the control group, which had no training at all, performed just as well as the three other groups, which showed virtually no difference in performance as a result of their intervening training.

Similar negative results have emerged from a number of other studies. One of the most interesting was a study by Daniel Wagner of the memory capacity of rural Moroccan students attending a Koranic school. Although a great deal of their schooling involved memorizing verses from the Koran, their performance on memory tests involving other material was relatively poor compared with that of other Moroccans or American students. They also showed little use of mnemonics.

In contrast to this Hunter cites an experiment by Woodrow, published in 1927, involving 182 university students. They were tested initially on a range of memory tasks involving remembering poetry and prose, learning the English

Everything in its place and a place for everything? Although the neural basis of memory is probably not susceptible to alteration by conscious effort, the ways in which we catalog incoming information and link it to existing information can usually be improved.

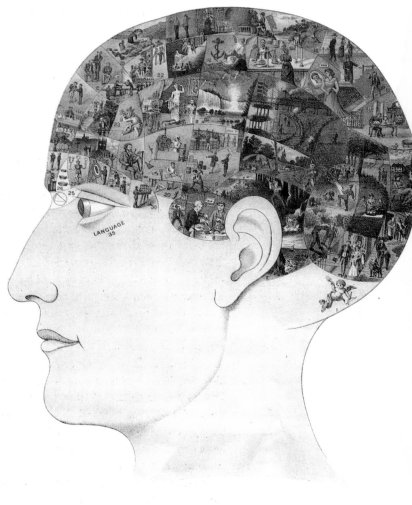

meaning of Turkish words, the dates of historical events, and a memory span test using consonants. One group spent a total of three hours distributed over a four-week period memorizing poems and nonsense syllables. A second group spent the same amount of time being instructed in memorization techniques for poetry and nonsense syllables. A third group served as a control and was given no memory training. When retested at the end of the four-week period, the first group performed no better or worse than the control group. The second group, the memory training group, however, did consistently better than either of the other groups on all the tests, including some which were quite different from those used during the training period; the techniques they had learned stood them in good stead.

Memory improvement in the elderly

There has been renewed interest in recent years in programs to improve memory utilization in the normal elderly and in patients who have brain damage. One such program is described by McEvoy and Moon, who worked with a group of 34 subjects in Florida who were, on average, 68 years old at the time of taking the memory improvement course. A number of areas were targeted.

Names and faces Subjects were taught how to use imagery mnemonics to link a face to a name; these included linking the new name to someone who was already known, together with techniques such as expanded rehearsal, where subjects test themselves initially rather frequently, gradually extending the interval between successive tests.

Appointments The use of external aids such as calendars and diaries was stressed, together with the importance of regularly reviewing forthcoming commitments.

Routine tasks This aimed to improve the reliability with which subjects carried out such routine activities as taking medicine and watering plants. Again the use of external aids such as diaries and automatic pillboxes was discussed, as was the importance of building up consistent habits and attempting to link a necessary activity with a consistent event, such as always taking pills after breakfast.

Spatial orientation This was concerned with problems such as forgetting where the car has been parked, or becoming lost in unfamiliar department stores or new towns. Subjects were encouraged to use both visual and verbal coding, paying attention to landmarks and ensuring that they looked back on the outward route, so as to be familiar with the return route. These skills were practised while walking through unfamiliar building complexes.

Locating objects Difficulty remembering where things are is a common problem with a number of causes. Sometimes it happens because the object is placed without thought in some unusual or unintended place, or because it is put in different locations on different occasions, causing confusion between where it is now and where it used to be. A third problem, may be that the object is in its proper place and one simply fails to see it. To cope with this problem one has to learn to store things consistently in an appropriate place, and avoid putting them down without thinking. The problem of failing to see something can sometimes be helped by marking the item to make it more visible or making one's search more careful and systematic.

Concentration The need to maintain concentration when listening to information or reading was emphasized, and strategies for checking and reviewing material were practised.

An attempt to evaluate the success of the course was made by requiring subjects to complete a questionnaire before starting the course, and two weeks after completing it. The questionnaire concerned the six areas covered in the training, together with four that were not. There was a clear tendency for improvement in most of the areas that had been trained, although not in the areas of concentration or of losing objects; no improvement was found in the four areas that had not been taught. In general this result is modestly encouraging, as indeed are some of the reports from studies in which brain-damaged patients with memory problems are encouraged to take part in memory groups which teach them helpful strategies and techniques. Improvements are not dramatic, but they do appear to be genuine when measured objectively, and to be valued by the participants.

Will the informal application of such principles help you? The answer is that they, and other principles like them, will help you to help yourself provided you are prepared to tackle the task of improving your memory with initiative and persistence. You will have to develop new habits, and these cannot be acquired without a fair amount of effort, so the first question to ask is whether you have a serious need to improve your memory and, if so, which aspect of it.

If you are worried about your memory, keep a diary and jot down your memory lapses. This has two advantages: first it usually reveals that your memory problem is not nearly as dramatic as you imagine, and second it pinpoints those situations which are giving most trouble.

Attention and interest

It should be clear from previous chapters that nothing is likely to get into long-term memory unless you attend to it. As we saw in the case of the BBC saturation advertising campaign, even presenting the same information a thousand times over will not make it stick if the listener does not pay attention and process it actively. This is almost certainly the failing which underlies the common difficulty of remembering people's names on first meeting. On being introduced to someone new, one's attention tends to focus on looking at them and making whatever initial remarks are appropriate, with the result that the name often 'goes in one ear and out of the other'. If you want to improve your memory for people's names on first meeting, you have no option but to make sure you consciously attend to them, if necessary asking for the name to be repeated. Socially it is much less embarrassing to ask for someone's name to be repeated immediately you are introduced to them than to have to confess to having forgotten it later; asking for a repetition implies interest, whereas forgetting implies that perhaps you were not sufficiently interested in the other person to notice or retain his or her name. Similarly, it makes sense to look directly at people when you are being introduced; to show interest in the appearance of someone you have just met is likely to seem much more flattering than staring at them on a subsequent meeting, racking your brains to think whether you really have met them before and, if so, what their name is. Having learned the name, check from time to time that you can recall it. Check after a short delay at first, gradually increasing the interval between checks. The process of recall will of itself help you learn the name.

The same principle applies if you want to remember the contents of a book you are reading. If you skim through with one eye on the book and the other on the television, you cannot expect to absorb very much of the content of either. One reason why top chess players have a phenomenal memory for chess games, or football fans for the teams of yesteryear, is that they have an intense interest in the topic and avidly attend to incoming information about it.

The relationship between interest, expertise and memory is of course not limited to Western culture. Sir Frederick Bartlett reported an attempt he made to check out a claim that the Swazi of South Africa had remarkable memory capacities. He began by asking a Swazi boy to take a message to the other end of the village. The message contained ten elements and the journey took about two minutes. The boy made two major errors, about what one might expect from an English boy of the same age. A similar conclusion followed the testing of Swazi adults on a range of memory tests. Then a white farmer suggested that one of his herdsmen should be tested on his memory for cattle. The man was sent for and asked to give a list of the cattle bought by a former employer a year previously, together with any details he could remember. He squatted on the ground and rapidly recited a list of nine transactions, of which the following two are typical: 'From Mbimbimaseko, one young black ox with a white bush to its tail, for £2; from Ndoda Kedeli, one young red heifer, the calf of a red cow, and with a white belly, for £1.' The nine transactions were checked against the sales list from the farmer's records and all nine were found to be accurate, with small exceptions —one price was out by 10 shillings and the color of one animal was discrepant. The reason for this remarkable memory for stock transactions, none of which the herdsman had conducted himself, lies in the fact that cattle were of enormous interest to the Swazi, since they played a very important role in their social structure.

In the case of new material (sets of facts, a foreign language), the way in which it can best be organized for learning is obviously crucially dependent on the material itself and on the level of interest of the learner. In general, it helps to relate new material to yourself and to your own circumstances as richly and elaborately as possible in the time available. A good example of this comes from a study by Chase and Ericsson in which an individual was given the unpromising task of improving his performance on the digit span task; in all he practised for more than 200 hours, spread over a period of 18 months, and was simply encouraged to do whatever he could to increase his capacity for repeating back a sequence of digits, each time a different sequence, presented at a rate of one digit per second. By the end of 18 months he was able to repeat back sequences of more than 70 digits (as you will recall most people can manage six or seven digits, but ten or more is rather exceptional). How did he do it?

For the first four hours of practice Chase and Ericsson's subject, SF, showed very little improvement, but on the fifth day his span jumped from eight to ten digits. From then on his span continued to increase at the rate of about one digit per week. What happened on the crucial fifth session was that SF hit on a strategy for coding the digits he was presented with. He was, as it happened, a keen and accomplished middle- and long-distance runner, with a detailed know-ledge of times for various distances and standards. What he did was to recode number sequences as running times: hence 3 4 9 2 would become *3 minutes 49.2 seconds, a near world record for the mile.* He has 11 major categories of running

Sports quiz freaks do not have special multi-megabyte memories. They are simply intensely interested in their subject.

times at his disposal, ranging from the half-mile to the marathon, and within each category he has lots of sub-categories.

People in jobs with a heavy memory load often develop their own mnemonics. Ericsson describes the case of a waiter who used a complex range of different strategies to remember orders, ranging from semantic encoding, based on his assessment of customers and their likely tastes, through visual imagery mnemonics to remember the extent to which they wished their steaks to be rare or well done, to sequences of initial letters for salad dressings. Another approach taken by a school for barmen studied by the American psychologist King Beach encouraged trainees to utilize the fact that different cocktails come in glasses of different shapes and sizes, and in different associated colors, as a means of facilitating memory for orders. When required to mix cocktails in identical black glasses, experienced barmen began to make errors, but identical glasses had little effect on the novices, who based their rather less reliable retention on subvocal rehearsal.

The general conclusion to be drawn from these various examples is that good memory demands attention and organization, and this can be developed for even the most unpromising material. So, if you are a student following a set curriculum, what can you do to boost your attention to material which may be, by any standards, rather tedious and boring?

You should begin by selecting a working environment that does not have too many distractions. People vary in the kind of environment they find most conducive to work, some preferring complete seclusion and silence, others claiming to work best against a background of quite loud music. I myself find that if a task is very demanding, an atmosphere with occasional distractions is sometimes more productive than complete peace. Once you have found a good environment for your work, use it regularly; with practice, you will find it increasingly easy to adopt the habit of studying there.

Try to read whatever you are reading as *actively* as you can — not in the spirit of someone trying to commit it to memory, but of someone questioning the author. Try to relate what he or she says to what you already know. If you find the material very unsympathetic, why not attempt to pinpoint your dissatisfaction, and imagine how the author might reply to your criticisms? You may well find that this gives you a greater understanding of what is

Complete peace and quiet is not always the best environment in which to absorb new information. Many people find a certain amount of background noise helps their concentration.

being said, even if you move no closer to the writer's viewpoint.

This may be all very well if you are reading a text on history or biology, but what if you are learning a foreign language? Once again, the same broad principles apply. If you are learning the language in order to be able to hold a conversation, it is essential that you do not confine your attention to the rote learning of grammar and vocabulary, but actively use the words and phrases as you acquire them. Imagine yourself in various situations and attempt to produce the necessary requests and replies. It is obviously much easier if you have colleagues who are also learning the language, 'or better still have already acquired it. Some students find it helpful to use visual imagery mnemonics to acquire some of the rote-learned aspects of a language, such as vocabulary. But if you wish to use the language, there is no alternative to practising speaking it. Pay attention to the sound and rhythm of word sequences as well as to their meaning. Finally, try to bear in mind the range of tasks you will have to perform in the language; bear in mind your own purpose in learning the language and try to gear your practice to that purpose.

Organization

Back in 1891 the great American psychologist William James suggested that all improvement of memory consists in the improvement of one's habitual methods of recording facts. Needless to say, this remains true. As mentioned earlier, long-term memory is like an enormous library. Unless the information stored in it is organized in a systematic way, it is unlikely to be retrievable when required. Organization helps in two ways: it structures what is being learnt, so that recalling a fragment of information is likely to make the rest accessible; and it relates newly learnt material to what has gone before, which means that the richer your existing knowledge structure the easier it is to comprehend and remember new material. A student beginning a new subject finds research papers extremely laborious and difficult to understand, but an experienced researcher in the field is likely to be able to skim the same papers very rapidly, extracting the essentials in a fraction of the time.

How should you organize new material? Obviously a lot depends on the nature of the material you are trying to commit to memory. In general, however, it helps to relate the new material to yourself and your own interests as richly and elaborately as possible in the available time. Suppose, for example, that I wanted to memorize my office postal code, *CB2 2EF*. What associations does it conjure up? The first two letters are easy — they are shorthand for CamBridge, the town where I live — or I might possibly have remembered them as the standard abbreviation for 'Confined to Barracks', imagining myself confined to my office. The *22* I might remember as the number of yards in a cricket pitch, so I could imagine myself confined to barracks and barred from playing cricket. As for the *EF*, I could perhaps remember that they are the fifth and sixth letters in the alphabet and also the fifth and sixth letters in the code.

Practice

But no matter how ingenious your techniques for committing information to memory, you cannot escape the effects of the total time hypothesis, which states that the amount you learn depends on the time you spend learning. This is true whether you are trying to learn the name of someone you have just met, trying to commit a telephone number to memory, or trying to master a difficult concept in physics. Nevertheless it is important to organize your practice time sensibly. Massing all your practice together into a few marathon learning sessions is not an efficient way of learning. A little and often is a better strategy.

The novelist Arnold Bennett once wrote a short book entitled *How to Live on 24 Hours a Day,* which I remember reading as a student. The main theme of the book, at least as I remember it, is that there are far more things to do, to read, to learn, and to think about than one can ever find time for. And yet most of our lives are filled with intervals — intervals waiting for a bus, washing up, walking across town — when we simply let our mind freewheel. Bennett argued that these unoccupied interludes can and should be used productively to think about and plan new projects, work out solutions to current problems, or rehearse material we are trying to learn. As a student who did not want to give up too much of his social life to revising for exams, I adopted the policy of writing very brief but systematic summaries of the topics I needed to revise and carrying them around with me in a small notebook. I found I could use the odd few minutes spent waiting for a train or bus very productively.

If you know you are going to need to use newly acquired material in a wide range of contexts, try varying the way in which you rehearse it. To use an academic example, examiners often expect students to answer questions in ways which go beyond mere regurgitation of curriculum facts; they are looking for the rather rarer ability to apply concepts in different ways, or to crosslink concepts previously treated separately. If you concentrate on merely committing material to memory without thinking more deeply and widely about it, you are likely to find later manipulation of that material very difficult; all your new thinking will have to be done during the examination itself. But if, as you revise, you think fairly broadly about the topics concerned, interrelate them, and imagine their application to problems you yourself have encountered, you are likely to do better in the examination and also retain more of what you have learned.

This point is discussed in some detail by John Bransford, who lays great emphasis on what he calls *transfer-appropriate processing.* By this he means that you should ensure that what you do during learning will enable you to apply what you have learned when the need arises. He refers to the case of a graduate student learning statistics who was quite sure he understood each chapter and could do the exercises; however, once the order of the exercises was switched, he found great difficulty. This is not uncommon with statistics where it is easy to become preoccupied with the mechanics of performing a particular test while neglecting to learn which statistical test one should apply in what situation. It is important

Waiting for trains and buses and planes, waiting in shops and cafes and queues . . . Why not convert some of those idle moments into learning time?

therefore to continue to monitor your learning, and be alert to the danger of being too easily satisfied. It is tempting to move on when you can *recognize* the right answer, but not *produce* it. It is often said that the best way to learn a subject is to teach it; to convey the necessary information to someone else, you must be able to produce it, not just recognize it.

Conclusion

The human memory system is remarkably efficient, but it is of course extremely fallible. That being so, it makes sense to take full advantage of memory aids to minimize the disruption caused by such lapses. If external aids are used, it is sensible to use them consistently and systematically — always put appointments in your diary, always add wanted items to a shopping list, and so on. If you use internal aids such as mnemonics, you must be prepared to invest a reasonable amount of time in mastering them and practising them. Mnemonics are like tools — they cannot be used until forged. Overall, however, as William James pointed out (the italics are mine): 'Of two men with the same outward experiences and the same amount of mere native tenacity, *the one who thinks over his experiences most and weaves them into systematic relations with each other will be the one with the best memory.*'

Bibliography

Chapter 1

Atkinson, R.C. & Shiffrin, R. M. (1971). 'The control of short-term memory'. *Scientific American, 225*, 82-90.

Bartlett, F. (1932). *Remembering*. Cambridge: Cambridge University Press, pp. 59-61, reprinted 1972.

Conrad, R. & Hull, A.J. (1964). 'Information, acoustic confusion and memory span'. *British Journal of Psychology, 55*, 429-432.

Di Vesta, F.J., Ingersoll, G., & Sunshine, P. (1971). 'A factor analysis of imagery tests'. *Journal of Verbal Learning and Verbal Behavior, 10*, 471-479.

Galton, F. (1883). 'Inquiries into Human Faculty and its Development'. London: Dent, Everyman Edition, pp. 57-78.

Squire, L.R. (1992). 'Declarative and non-declarative memory: Multiple brain systems supporting learning and memory'. *Journal of Cognitive Neuroscience, 4*, 232-243.

Tulving, E. (1972). 'Episodic and semantic memory'. *In* E. Tulving and W. Donaldson (Eds.), *Organization of Memory*. New York: Academic Press, pp. 381-403.

Chapter 2

Atkinson, R.C. & Shiffrin, R.M. (1968). 'Human memory: A proposed system and its control processes'. *In* K.W. Spence (Ed.), *The Psychology of Learning and Motivation: Advances in Research and Theory* Vol. 2. New York: Academic Press, pp. 89-195.

Baddeley, A.D. (1966). 'Short-term memory for word sequences as a function of acoustic, semantic and formal similarity'. *Quarterly Journal of Experimental Psychology, 18*, 362-365.

Baddeley, A.D., Conrad, R., & Thomson, W.E. (1960). 'Letter structure of the English language'. *Nature, 186*, 414-416.

Brown, J. (1958). 'Some tests of the decay theory of immediate memory'. *Quarterly Journal of Experimental Psychology, 10*, 12-21.

Conrad, R. (1964). 'Acoustic confusion in immediate memory'. *British Journal of Psychology, 55*, 75-84.

Craik, F.I.M. & Lockhart, R.S. (1972). 'Levels of processing: A framework for memory research'. *Journal of Verbal Learning and Verbal Behavior, 11*, 671-684.

Craik, F.I.M. & Watkins, M.J. (1973). "The role of rehearsal in short-term memory'. *Journal of Verbal Learning and Verbal Behavior, 12*, 599-607.

Galton, F. (1883). 'Inquiries into Human Faculty and its Development'. London: Dent, Everyman Edition, p. 146.

Hamilton, W. (1859). *Lectures on Metaphysics and Logic*, Vol.1. Edinburgh: Blackwood.

Hunter, I.M.L. (1977). 'An exceptional memory'. *British Journal of Psychology, 68*, 155-164.

Jacobs, J. (1887). 'Experiments in "prehension"'. *Mind, 12*, 75-79.

James, W. (1890). *The Principles of Psychology*. New York: Holt, Rinehart and Winston.

Melton, A.W. (1963). 'Implications of short-term memory for a general theory of memory'. *Journal of Verbal Learning and Verbal Behavior, 2*, 1-21.

Murdock, B.B. Jr. (1961). 'The retention of individual items'. *Journal of Experimental Psychology, 62*, 618-625.

Peterson, L.R. & Peterson, M.J. (1959). Short-term retention of individual verbal items'. *Journal of Experimental Psychology, 58*, 193-198.

Sachs, J.S. (1967). 'Recognition memory for syntactic and semantic aspects of connected discourse'. *Perception and Psychophysics, 2*, 437-442.

Wagner, D. (1978). Memories of Morocco: The influence of age, schooling and environment on memory'. *Cognitive Psychology, 10*, 1-28.

Wickens, D.D. (1970). 'Encoding categories of words: An empirical approach to meaning'. *Psychological Review, 77*, 1-15.

Chapter 3

Baddeley, A.D. (1968). 'A 3-min reasoning test based on grammatical transformation'. *Psychonomic Science, 10*, 341-342.

Baddeley, A.D. & Hitch, G. (1974). 'Working memory. *In* G.A. Bower (Ed.), *The Psychology of Learning and Motivation*, Vol. 8. New York: Academic Press, pp. 47-89.

Baddeley, A.D., Grant, S., Wight, E., & Thomson, N. (1973). 'Imagery and visual working memory'. *In* P.M.A. Rabbitt and S. Dornic (Eds.), *Attention and Performance V*. London: Academic Press, pp. 205-217.

Baddeley, A.D. & Lewis, V.J. (1981). 'Inner active processes in reading: The inner voice, the inner ear and the inner eye'. *In* A.M. Lesgold and C.A. Perfetti (Eds.), *Interactive Processes in Reading*. Hillsdale, N.J.: Lawrence Erlbaum, pp. 107-129.

Baddeley, A.D. & Lieberman, K. (1980). 'Spatial working memory'. *In* R.S. Nickerson (Ed.), *Attention and Performance VIII*. Hillsdale, N.J.: Lawrence Erlbaum Associates, pp. 521-539.

Baddeley, A.D., Papagno, C., & Vallar, G. (1988). 'When long-term learning depends on short-term storage'. *Journal of Memory and Language, 27*, 586-595.

Baddeley, A D., Thomson, N., & Buchanan, M. (1975). 'Word length and the structure of short-term memory'. *Journal of Verbal Learning and Verbal Behavior, 14*, 575-589.

Brooks, L.R. (1968). 'Spatial and verbal components in the act of recall'. *Canadian Journal of Psychology, 22*, 349-368.

Daneman, M. & Carpenter, P.A. (1980). 'Individual differences in working memory and reading'. *Journal of Verbal Learning and Verbal Behavior, 19*, 450-466.

Daneman, M. & Carpenter, P.A. (1983). 'Individual differences in integrating information between and within sentences'. *Journal of Experimental Psychology: Learning, Memory, and Cognition, 9*, 561-584.

Ellis, N.C. & Beaton, A. (in press). 'Factors affecting the learning of foreign language vocabulary II: Psycholinguistic determinants'. *Quarterly Journal of Experimental Psychology*.

Ellis, N.C. & Hennelley, R.A. (1980). 'A bilingual word-length effect: Implications for intelligence testing and the relative ease of mental calculation in Welsh and English'. *British Journal of Psychology, 71*, 43-52.

Farah, M.J. (1988). 'Is visual memory really visual? Overlooked evidence from neuropsychology'. *Psychological Review, 95*, 307-317.

Gathercole, S. & Baddeley, A.D. (1990). 'Phonological memory deficits in language-disordered children: Is there a causal connection?' *Journal of Memory and Language, 29*, 336-360.

Gathercole, S. & Baddeley, A.D. (1990). 'The role of phonological memory in vocabulary acquisition: A study of young children learning new names'. *British Journal of Psychology, 81*, 439-454.

Geiselman, R.E. & Bjork, R.A. (1980). 'Primary versus secondary rehearsal in imagined voices: differential effects on recognition'. *Cognitive Psychology, 12*, 185-205.

Goldman-Rakic, P.W. (1988). 'Topography of cognition: Parallel distributed networks in primate association cortex.' *Annual Review of Neuroscience, 11*, 137-156.

Kosslyn, S.M. & Shwartz, S.P. (1981). 'Empirical constraints on theories of visual mental imagery'. *In* J. Long and A.D. Baddeley (Eds.), *Attention and Performance IX*. Hillsdale, N.J: Erlbaum, pp. 241-260.

Kyllonen, P.C. & Christal, R.E. (1990). 'Reasoning ability is (little more than) working-memory capacity'. *Intelligence, 14*, 389-433.

Norman, D.A. (1970). *Models of Human Memory*. New York: Academic Press.

Oakhill, J.V., Yuill, N., & Parkin, C. (1988). 'Memory and inference in skilled and less-skilled comprehenders'. *In* M.M. Gruneberg, P.E. Morris and R.N. Sykes (Eds.), *Practical Aspects of Memory: Current Research and Issues, Vol. 2. Clinical and Educational Implications*. Chichester: John Wiley, pp. 315-320.

Paulesu, E., Frith, C.D. and Frackoviak, R. S J. 'The neural correlates of the verbal component of working memory'. *Nature, 362 pp342-345.*

Service, E. (1992). 'Phonology, working memory, and foreign-language learning'. *Quarterly Journal of Experimental Psychology, 45A,* 21-50.

Shepard, R.N. & Feng, C. (1972). 'A chronometric study of mental paper-folding'. *Cognitive Psychology, 3,* 228-243.

Shepard, N. & Metzler, J. (1971). 'Mental rotation of three-dimensional objects'. *Science, 171,* 701-703.

Wason, P.C. & Johnson-Laird, P.N. (1972). *Psychology of Reasoning: Structure and Content.* London: Batsford.

Chapter 4

Baddeley, A.D. (1976). *The Psychology of Memory.* New York: Basic Books, p. 307.

Baddeley, A.D. & Longman, D.J.A. (1978). 'The influence of length and frequency of training sessions on the rate of learning to type'. *Ergonomics, 21,* 627-635.

Bekerian, D.A. & Baddeley, A.D. (1980). 'Saturation advertising and the repetition effect'. *Journal of Verbal Learning and Verbal Behavior, 19,* 17-25.

Brooks, D.N. & Baddeley, A.D. (1976). 'What can amnesic patients learn?' *Neuropsychologia, 14,* 111-122.

Claparède, E. (1911). *Récognition et moiïte.* Archives Psychologiques Genève, *11,* 79-90.

Ebbinghaus, H. (1885). *Über das Gedächtnis.* Leipzig: Dunker. Translation by H. Ruyer and C. E. Bussenius, *Memory.* New York: Teachers College, Columbia University, 1913.

Folkard, S., Monk, T.H., Bradbury, R., & Rosenthall, J. (1977). 'Time of day effects in school children's immediate and delayed recall of meaningful material'. *British Journal of Psychology, 68,* 45-50.

Ghoneim, M.M. & Block, R.I. (1992). 'Learning and consciousness during general anaesthesia'. *Anaesthesiology, 76,* 279-305.

Jacoby, L.L., Woloshyn, V., & Kelley, C.M. (1989). 'Becoming famous without being recognised: Unconscious influences of memory produced by dividing attention'. *Journal of Experimental Psychology: General, 118,* 115-125.

Johnson, M.K., Kim, J.K., & Risse, G. (1985). 'Do alcoholic Korsakoff's syndrome patients acquire affective reactions?' *Journal of Experimental Psychology: Learning, Memory, and Cognition, 11,* 22-36.

Kleinsmith, L.J. & Kaplan, S. (1963). 'Paired associated learning as a function of arousal and interpolated interval'. *Journal of Experimental Psychology, 65,* 190-193.

Landauer, T.K. & Bjork, R.A. (1978). 'Optimum rehearsal patterns and name learning'. *In* M.M. Gruneberg, P.E. Morris and R.N. Sykes (Eds.), *Practical Aspects of Memory.* London: Academic Press, pp. 625-632.

Nilsson, L.-G. (1987). 'Motivated memory: Dissociation between performance data and subjective reports'. *Psychological Research, 49,* 183-188.

Schacter, D.L. (1992). 'Priming and multiple memory systems: Perceptual mechanisms of implicit memory'. *Journal of Cognitive Neuroscience, 4,* 244-256.

Stewart, E.W., Shimp, T.A., & Engle, R.W. (1987). 'Classical conditioning of consumer attitudes: Four experiments in an advertising context'. *Journal of Consumer Research, 14,* 334-349.

Taylor, W.L. (1953). '"Cloze Procedure" a new tool for measuring readability'. *Journalism Quarterly, 30,* 415-433.

Chapter 5

Bartlett, F. (1932). *Remembering.* Cambridge: Cambridge University Press (reprinted 1972).

Bower, G. H. (1970). 'Analysis of a mnemonic device'. *American Scientist, 58,* 496-510.

De Groot, A.D. (1966). 'Perception and memory versus thought: Some old ideas and recent findings'. *In* B. Kleinmuntz (Ed.), *Problem Solving.* New York: Wiley.

Ericsson, K.A., Chase, W.G., & Falloon, S. (1980). 'Acquisition of a memory skill'. *Science, 208,* 1181-1182.

Hastorf, A.A. & Cantril, H. (1954). 'They saw a game: A case study'. *Journal of Abnormal and Social Psychology, 97,* 399-401.

Luria, A.R. (1968). *The Mind of a Mnemonist.* New York: BasicBooks.

Thompson, C.P., Cowan, P., Frieman, J., Mahadevan, R.S., Vogl, R.J., & Frieman, J. (in press). 'Rajan: A study of a memorist'. *Journal of Memory and Language.*

Chapter 6

Ausubel, D.P., Stager, M., & Gaite, A.J.H. (1968). 'Retroactive facilitation in meaningful verbal learning'. *Journal of Educational Psychology, 59,* 250-256.

Baddeley, A.D. & Hitch, G. (1977). 'Recency re-examined'. *In* S. Dornic (Ed.), *Attention and Performance VI.* Hillsdale, N.J.: Lawrence Erlbaum Associates, pp. 647-667.

Bahrick, H.P., Bahrick, P.O., & Wittlinger, R.P. (1975). 'Fifty years of memory for names and faces: A cross-sectional approach'. *Journal of Experimental Psychology: General, 104,* 54-75.

Bahrick, P. & Phelphs, E. (1987). 'Retention of Spanish vocabulary over eight years'. *Journal of Experimental Psychology: Learning, Memory and Cognition, 13,* 344-349.

Blakemore, C. (1977). 'The unsolved marvel of memory'. *The New York Times Magazine,* 6 February 1977, p. 88. (Reprinted in *Readings in Psychology, 78/79.* Guildford, Connecticut: Annual Editions, Dushkin Publishing Group, 1979.)

Conway, M.A., Cohen, G., & Stanhope, N.M. (1991). 'On the very long-term retention of knowledge'. *Journal of Experimental Psychology: General, 120,* 395-409.

Costa Pinto, A. & Baddeley, A.D. (1991). 'Where did you park your car? Analysis of a naturalistic long-term recency effect'. *European Journal of Cognitive Psychology, 3,* 297-313.

Crouse, J.H. (1971). 'Retroactive interference in reading prose materials'. *Journal of Educational Psychology, 62,* 39-44.

Ebbinghaus, H. (1885). *Über das Gedächtnis.* Leipzig: Dunker. Translation by H. Ruyer and C.E. Bussenius, *Memory.* New York: Teachers College, Columbia University, 1913.

Gunter, B., Berry, C., & Clifford, B.R. (1981). 'Proactive interference effects with television news items: Further evidence'. *Journal of Experimental Psychology: Human Learning and Memory, 7,* 480-487.

Gittens, D. (1979). 'Oral history, reliability and recollection'. *In* L. Moss and H. Goldstein (Eds.), *The Recall Method in Social Surveys.* London: University of London Institute of Education, Studies in Education, 9, pp. 85-86.

Linton, M. (1978). 'Real world memory after six years: An in vivo study of very long-term memory'. *In* M.M. Gruneberg, P.E. Morris and R.N. Sykes (Eds.), *Practical Aspects of Memory.* London: Academic Press, pp. 69-76.

McGeoch, J.A. & MacDonald, W.T. (1931). 'Meaningful relation and retroactive inhibition'. *American Journal of Psychology, 43,* 579-588.

McKenna, S.P. & Glendon, A.I. (1985). 'Occupational first aid training: Decay in cardiopulmonary resuscitation (CPR) skills'. *Journal of Occupational Psychology, 58,* 109-117.

Minami, H. & Dallenbach, K.M. (1946). 'The effect of activity upon learning and retention in the cockroach'. *American Journal of Psychology, 59,* 1-58.

Slamecka, N.J. (1960). 'Retroactive inhibition of connected discourse as a function of practice level'. *Journal of Experimental Psychology, 59,* 104-108.

Squire, L.R. & Slater, P.C. (1975). 'Forgetting in very long-term memory as assessed by an improved questionnaire technique'. *Journal of Experimental Psychology: Human Learning and Memory, 104,* 50-54.

Underwood, B.J. (1957). 'Interference and forgetting. *Psychological Review, 64,* 49-60.

Warrington, E.K. & Sanders, H.I. (1971). 'The fate of old memories'. *Quarterly Journal of Experimental Psychology, 23,* 432-442.

Chapter 7

Baker, R.A. (1992). *Hidden Memories.* Buffalo: Prometheus Books.

Bass, E. & Davis, L. (1988). *The Courage to Heal.* New York: Harper & Row.

Bower, G.H. (1981). 'Mood and memory'. *American Psychologist, 36,* 129-148.

Bradley, B.P. & Baddeley, A.D. (1990). 'Emotional factors in forgetting'. *Psychological Medicine, 20,* 351-355.

Freud, S. (1904). 'Psychopathology of everyday life'. *In* A.A. Brill (Ed.), *The Writings of Sigmund Freud.* New York: Modern Library, 1938.

Hester, M.E. & Fricke, W.C. (1990). Brief of Appellant. State of Washington v. Paul Ingram. Division 2 of the Court of Appeals.

Hunter, I.M.L. (1957). *Memory: Facts and Fallacies*. Baltimore: Penguin, p. 270.

Janet, P. Cited in Hunter, op cit, pp. 233-234.

Levinger, G. & Clark, J. (1961). 'Emotional factors in the forgetting of word associations'. *Journal of Abnormal and Social Psychology*, *62*, 99-105.

Loftus, E.F. (1992). 'The reality of repressed memories'. The PsiChi/Frederick Howell Lewis Distinguished Lecture presented at the Centennial meeting of the American Psychological Association, Washington D.C., August 1992.

Malmquist, C.P. (1986). 'Children who witness parental murder: Post-traumatic aspects'. *Journal of American Academy of Child Psychiatry*, *25*, 320-325.

Siegan, R.S. (1992, March 11th). Personal communication cited in Loftus (1992).

Smith, M. & Pazder, L. (1980). *Michelle Remembers*. New York: Congdon & Lattes.

Thigpen, C.H. & Cleckley, H. (1957). *The Three Faces of Eve*. London: Secker and Warburg.

Zeller, A.F. (1951). 'An experimental analogue of repression: III. The effect of induced failure and success on memory measured by recall'. *Journal of Experimental Psychology*, *42*, 32-38.

Chapter 8

Bartlett, F. (1932). *Remembering*. Cambridge: Cambridge University Press (reprinted 1972).

Bransford, J.D. & Johnson, M.K. (1972). 'Contextual prerequisites for understanding: Some investigations of comprehension and recall'. *Journal of Verbal Learning and Verbal Behavior*, *11*, 717-726.

Bransford, J.D. & Nitsch, K.E. (1978). 'Coming to understand things we could not previously understand'. *In* J. F. Kavanagh and W. Strange (Eds.), *Speech and Language in the Laboratory, School and Clinic*. Cambridge, Mass: MIT Press.

Brown, R.W. & Lenneberg, E.H. (1954). 'A study in language and cognition'. *Journal of Abnormal and Social Psychology*, *49*, 454-462.

Bruce, D.J. (1958). 'The effect of listeners' anticipations on the intelligibility of heard speech'. *Language and Speech*, *1*, 79-97.

Collins, A.M. & Quillian, M.R. (1972). 'Experiments on semantic memory and language comprehension'. *In* L. W. Gregg (Ed.), *Cognition in Learning and Memory*. New York: Wiley.

Freedman, J.L. & Loftus, E.F. (1971). 'Retrieval of words from long-term memory'. *Journal of Verbal Learning and Verbal Behavior*, *10*, 107-115.

Hart, J. Jr., Berndt, R.S., & Caramazza, A. (1985). 'Category-specific naming deficit following cerebral infarction'. *Nature*, *316*, 439-440.

Heidbreder, E. (1946). 'The attainment of concepts: I. Terminology and methodology'. *Journal of General Psychology*, *35*, 173-189.

Johnson-Laird, P.N., Herrmann, D.J., & Chaffin, R. (1984). 'Only connections: A critique of semantic networks'. *Psychological Bulletin*, *96*, 292-315.

Lissauer, H.(1988). 'A case of visual agnosia with a contribution to theory'. Original 1888, translation published in *Cognitive Neuropsychology*, *5*, 157-192.

Loftus, E.F. & Loftus, G.R. (1974). 'Changes in memory structure and retrieval over the course of instruction'. *Journal of Educational Psychology*, *66*, 315-318.

Moar, I.T. (1978). 'Mental triangulation and the nature of internal representations of space'. Unpublished PhD thesis, University of Cambridge.

Potter, M.C. & Faulconer, B.A. (1975). 'Time to understand pictures and words'. *Nature*, *253*, 437-438.

Rosch, E. (1977). 'Human categorisation'. *In* N. Warren (Ed.), *Advances in Cross Cultural Psychology* Vol. 1. London: Academic Press.

Rosch-Heider, E. (1972). 'Universals in color naming and memory'. *Journal of Experimental Psychology*, *93*, 10-20.

Schank, R.C. (1982). *Dynamic Memory*. New York: Cambridge University Press.

Shallice, T. & Jackson, M. (1988). 'Lissauer on Agnosia'. *Cognitive Neuropsychology*, *5*, 153-192.

Warrington, E.K. & Taylor, A.M. (1978). 'Two categorical stages of object recognition'. *Perception*, *7*, 695-705.

Whorf, B.L. (1956). *Language, Thought and Reality*. Cambridge: Technology Press.

Chapter 9

Brown, J., Lewis, V. J., & Monk, A.F. (1977). 'Memorability, word frequency and negative recognition'. *Quarterly Journal of Experimental Psychology*, *29*, 461-473.

Brown, R. & McNeill, D. (1966). 'The "tip of the tongue" phenomenon'. *Journal of Verbal Learning and Verbal Behavior*, *5*, 325-337.

Burgess, A. (1991). *You've Had Your Time*. Harmondsworth, Middlesex: Penguin Books, p. 97.

Camp, J.C., Lachman, J.L., & Lachman, R. (1980). 'Evidence for object-access and inferential retrieval in question answering'. *Journal of Verbal Learning and Verbal Behavior*, *19*, 583-596.

Craik, F.I.M. & Lockhart, R.S. (1972). 'Levels of processing: A framework for memory research'. *Journal of Verbal Learning and Verbal Behavior*, *11*, 671-684.

Eich, J.E. (1980). 'The cue-dependent nature of state-dependent retrieval'. *Memory and Cognition*, *8*, 157-173.

Engen, T., Kuisma, J.E., & Eimas, P.D. (1973). Short-term memory of odors'. *Journal of Experimental Psychology*, *99*, 222-225.

Godden, D. & Baddeley, A.D. (1975). 'Context-dependent memory in two natural environments: on land and under water'. *British Journal of Psychology*, *66*, 325-331.

Godden, D. & Baddeley, A.D. (1980). 'When does context influence recognition memory?' *British Journal of Psychology*, *71*, 99-104.

Locke, J. (1690). *An Essay Concerning Human Understanding*. London: Dent, Everyman Edition, 1961.

McClelland, J.L. (1981).'Retrieving general and specific knowledge from stored knowledge of specifics. *In* Proceedings of the Third Annual Conference of the Cognitive Science Society, Berkeley, California.

Sternberg, S. (1966). 'High-speed scanning in human memory'. *Science*, *153*, 652-654.

Clark, D.M. & Teasdale, J.D. (1982). 'Diurnal variation in clinical depression and accessibility of memories of positive and negative experiences'. *Journal of Abnormal Psychology*, *91*, 87-95.

Tulving, E. (1966). 'Subjective organization and effects of repetition in multi-trial free-recall learning.' *Journal of Verbal Learning and Verbal Behavior*, *5*, 193-197.

Tulving, E. & Osler, S. (1968). 'Effectiveness of retrieval cues in memory for words'. *Journal of Experimental Psychology*, *77*, 593-601.

Tulving, E. & Thomson, D.M. (1973). 'Encoding specificity and retrieval processes in episodic memory'. *Psychological Review*, *80*, 352-373.

Velten, E. (1968). 'A laboratory task for induction of mood states'. *Behavioural Research and Therapy*, *6*, 473-482.

Wallace, W.T. & Rubin, D.C. (1988). 'Memory of a ballad singer. *In* M.M. Gruneberg, P. E. Morris and R. N. Sykes (Eds.), *Practical Aspects of Memory: Current Research and Issues, Vol.1: Memory in Everyday Life*. Chichester: Wiley, pp. 257-262.

Chapter 10

Baddeley, A.D. & Woodhead, M. (1983). 'Improving face recognition ability'. *In* S.M.A. Lloyd-Bostock and B.R. Clifford (Eds.), *Evaluating Witness Evidence*. Chichester: John Wiley & Sons, pp.125-136.

Bekerian, D.A. & Bowers, J.M. (1983). 'Eyewitness testimony: Were we misled?' *Journal of Experimental Psychology: Human Learning and Memory*, *9*, 139-145.

Bekerian, D.A. & Dennett, J.L. (in press). 'The cognitive interview technique: Reviving the issues'. *Applied Cognitive Psychology*.

Cattell, J.M. (1895). 'Measurement of the accuracy of recollection'. *Science*, *20*, 761-776.

Davis, G., Ellis, H., & Shepherd, J. (1978). 'Face recognition accuracy as a function of mode of representation'. *Journal of Applied Psychology*, *63*, 180-187.

Devlin, P. (1976). Report to the Secretary of State for the Home Department Committee on Evidence of Identification in Criminal Cases. London: HMSO.

Fisher, R.P. & Geiselman, R.E. (1988). 'Enhancing eyewitness memory with the cognitive interview'. *In* M.M. Gruneberg, P.E. Morris and R.N. Sykes (Eds.), *Practical Aspects of Memory: Current Research and Issues, Vol. 1: Memory in Everyday Life.* Chichester: John Wiley & Sons, pp. 34-39.

Jones, G.V. & Martin, M. (1992). 'Misremembering a familiar object: Mnemonic illusion, not drawing bias.' *Memory and Cognition, 20,* 211-213.

Jones, G.V. (1988). 'Images, predicates, and retrieval cues'. *In* M. Denis, J. Engelkamp and J.T.E. Richardson (Eds.), *Cognitive and Neuropsychological Approaches to Mental Imagery.* Dordrecht: Martinus Nijhoff, pp. 89-98.

Lindsay, R.C., Lea, J.A., Nosworthy, G.J., & Fulford, J.A. (1991). 'Biased line-ups: Sequential presentation reduces the problem'. *Journal of Applied Psychology, 76,* 796-802.

Loftus, E.F. (1977). 'Shifting human color memory'. *Memory and Cognition, 5,* 696-699.

Loftus, E. F. (1979). *Eyewitness Testimony.* Cambridge, Mass: Harvard University Press, pp. 118-120.

Loftus, op cit, pp. 62-63.

Loftus, E.F. & Palmer, J.C. (1974). 'Reconstruction of automobile destruction: An example of the interaction between language and memory'. *Journal of Verbal Learning and Verbal Behavior, 13,* 585-589.

McCloskey, M. & Zaragoza, M. (1985). 'Misleading post-event information and memory for events: Arguments and evidence against memory impairment hypotheses'. *Journal of Experimental Psychology: General, 114,* 1-16.

Nickerson, R.S. & Adams, M.J. (1979). 'Long-term memory for a common object'. *Cognitive Psychology, 11,* 287-307.

Orne, M.T., Soskis, D.A., Dinges, D.F., & Orne, E.C. (1984). 'Hypnotically-induced testimony. *In* G.L. Wells and E.F. Loftus (Eds.), *Eyewitness Testimony: Psychological Perspectives.* New York: Cambridge University Press.

Patterson, K.E. & Baddeley, A.D. (1977). 'When face recognition fails'. *Journal of Experimental Psychology: Human Learning and Memory, 3,* 406-417.

Thomson, D.M. (1983). 'Person identification: Influencing the outcome'. *Australian and New Zealand Journal of Criminology.*

da Vinci, L. (1962). 'Trattato della Pittura'. After the edition by H. Ludwig, Vienna, 1882, cited in E.H. Gombrich, *Art and Illusion.* London: Phaidon Press, page 294.

Woodhead, M.M., & Baddeley, A.D. (1981). 'Individual differences and memory for faces, pictures and words'. *Memory and Cognition, 9,* 368-370.

Woodhead, M.M., Baddeley, A.D., & Simmonds, D.C.V. (1979). 'On training people to recognize faces'. *Ergonomics, 22,* 333-343.

Yin, R. (1970). 'Face recognition by brain-injured patients: A dissociable ability?' *Neuropsychologia, 8,* 395-402.

Chapter 11

Brooks, D.N. & Baddeley, A.D. (1976). 'What can amnesic patients learn?' *Neuropsychologia, 14,* 111-122.

Butters, N. & Cermak, L.S. (1986). 'A study of the forgetting of autobiographical knowledge: Implications for the study of retrograde amnesia'. *In* D. Rubin (Ed.), *Autobiographical Memory.* Cambridge: Cambridge University Press, pp. 253-272.

Claparede, E. (1911). *Récognition et moiite.* Archives Psychologiques Geneve, 11, 79-90.

Glisky, E.L., Schacter, D., & Tulving, E. (1986). 'Computer learning by memory impaired patients: Acquisition and retention of complex knowledge'. *Neuropsychologia, 24,* 313-328.

Johnson, M.K., Kim, J. K., & Risse, G. (1985). 'Do alcoholic Korsakoff's syndrome patients acquire affective reactions?' *Journal of Experimental Psychology: Learning, Memory, and Cognition, 11,* 22-36.

Meltzer, M.L. (1983). 'Poor memory: A case report'. *Journal of Clinical Psychology, 39,* 3-10.

Milner, B. (1966). 'Amnesia following operation on the temporal lobes'. *In* C.W.M. Whitty and O.L. Zangwill (Eds.), *Amnesia.* London: Butterworths, pp. 109-133.

Russell, W.R. (1959). *Brain, Memory, Learning: A Neurologist's View.* London: Oxford University Press.

Sunderland, A., Harris, J.E., & Baddeley, A.D. (1983). 'Do laboratory tests predict everyday memory?' *Journal of Verbal Learning and Verbal Behavior, 22,* 341-357.

Tulving, E. & Schacter, D.L. (1990). 'Priming and human memory systems'. *Science, 247,* 301-306.

Wilson, B. A., Cockburn, J., Baddeley, A. D., & Hiorns, R. (1989). 'The development and validation of a test battery for detecting and monitoring everyday memory problems'. *Journal of Clinical and Experimental Neuropsychology, 11,* 855-870.

Wilson, B.A. (1986). *Rehabilitation of Memory.* New York: Guilford Press.

Wilson, B.A. (1991). 'Long term prognosis of patients with severe memory disorders'. *Neuropsychological Rehabilitation, 1,* 117-134.

Yarnell, P.R. & Lynch, S. (1970). 'Retrograde memory immediately after concussion'. *Lancet, 1,* 863-865.

Chapter 12

Bradley, L. & Bryant, P.E. (1983). 'Categorising sounds and learning to read: A causal connection'. *Nature, 301,* 419-421.

Case, R.D., Kurland, D.M., & Goldberg, J. (1982). 'Operational efficiency and the growth of short-term memory span'. *Journal of Experimental Child Psychology, 33,* 386-404.

Ceci, S.J., Baker, J.E., & Bronfenbrenner, U. (1988). 'Prospective remembering, temporal calibration, and context'. *In* M.M. Gruneberg, P.E. Morris and R.N. Sykes (Eds.), *Practical Aspects of Memory: Current Research and Issues, Vol. 1: Memory in Everyday Life.* Chichester: Wiley, pp. 360-365.

Flavell, J.H., Beach, D.H., & Chinsky, J.M. (1966). 'Spontaneous verbal rehearsal in a memory task as a function of age'. *Child Development, 37,* 283-299.

Flin, R., Boon, J., Knox, A., & Bull, R. (1992). 'The effect of a five-month delay on children's and adult's eyewitness memory'. *British Journal of Psychology, 83,* 323-336.

Hitch, G.J., Halliday, M.S., & Littler, J. (1984). 'Memory span and the speed of mental operations'. Paper presented at the joint Experimental Psychology Society/Netherlands Psychonomic Foundation Meeting, Amsterdam.

Hudson, J.A. & Fivush, R. (1991). As time goes by: Sixth graders remember a kindergarten experience'. *Applied Cognitive Psychology, 5,* 347-360.

McCloskey, M. & Zaragoza, M. (1985). 'Misleading post-event information and memory for events: Arguments and evidence against memory impairment hypotheses'. *Journal of Experimental Psychology: General, 114,* 1-16.

Rovee-Collier, C. (1989). 'The joy of kicking: Memories, motives and mobiles'. *In* P.R. Soloman, G.R. Goethals, C.M. Kelley and B.R. Stephens (Eds.), *Memory: Interdisciplinary Approaches.* New York: Springer-Verlag, pp. 151-180.

Perris, E.E., Myers, N.A., & Clifton, R.K. (1990). 'Long-term memory for a single infancy experience'. *Child Development, 61,* 1796-1807.

Schacter, D.L. & Moscovitch, M. (1984). 'Infants, amnesics and dissociable memory systems'. *In* M. Moscovitch (Ed.), Infant Memory. New York: Plenum Press, pp. 173-216.

Sheingold, K., & Tenney, Y.J. (1982). 'Memory for a salient childhood event'. *In* U. Neisser (Ed.), *Memory in its Natural Context.* San Francisco: Freeman.

Chapter 13

Baddeley, A.D., Emslie, H., & Nimmo-Smith, I. (in preparation). *The Doors and People Test.* Flempton, Bury St Edmunds, England: Thames Valley Test Company.

Baddeley, A.D., Emslie, H., & Nimmo-Smith, I. (1993). 'The spot-the-word test: A robust estimate of verbal intelligence based on lexical decision'. *British Journal of Clinical Psychology, 32,* pp 55-65.

Baddeley, A.D., Bressi, S., Della Sala, S., Logie, R. & Spinnler, H. (1991). 'The decline of working memory in Alzheimer's Disease: A longitudinal study'. *Brain, 114,* 2521-2542.

Baddeley, A. D., Logie, R., Bressi, S., Della Sala, S., & Spinnler, H. (1986). 'Dementia and working memory'. *Quarterly Journal of Experimental Psychology, 38A,* 603-618.

Backman, L. & Molander, B. (1986). 'Adult age differences in the ability to cope with situations of high arousal in a precision sport'. *Psychology and Aging, 1,* 133-139.

Backman, L. & Molander, B. (in press). 'The relationship between level of arousal and cognitive operations during motor behavior in young and older adults'. *In* A.C. Ostrow (Ed.), *Aging and Motor Behavior.* Indianapolis: Benchmark Press.

Backman, L. & Nilsson, L-G. (1985). 'Prerequisites for lack of age differences in memory performance'. *Experimental Ageing Research, 11,* 67-73.

Baltes, P.B., & Kliegl, R. (1992).'Further testing of limits of cognitive plasticity: Negative age differences in a mnemonic skill are robust'. *Developmental Psychology, 28,* 121-125.

Charness, N. (1985). 'Ageing and problem-solving performance'. *In* N. Charness (Ed.), *Ageing and Human Performance.* Chichester: John Wiley & Sons, pp. 225-260.

Craik, F.I.M. (1992). 'Working memory and ageing'. Paper presented at the International Congress of Psychology, Brussels.

Evans, J., Wilson, B.A., Baddeley, A.D. (in preparation). 'A new test of prospective memory'.

Heindel, W.C., Salmon, D.P., Schults, C.W., Walicke, P.A., & Butters, N. (1989). 'Neuropsychological evidence for multiple implicit memory systems: A comparison of Alzheimer's, Huntington's, and Parkinson's disease patients'. *Journal of Neuroscience, 9,* 582-587.

Kemper, S. (1990). 'Adults' diaries: Changes made to written narratives across the life-span'. *Discourse Processes, 13,* 207-223.

Kirasic, K.C. & Allen, G.L. (1985). 'Ageing, spatial performance and spatial competence'. *In* N. Charness (Ed.), *Ageing and Human Performance.* Chichester: John Wiley & Sons, pp. 191-224.

Kopelman, M.D. (1985). 'Rates of forgetting in Alzheimer-type dementia and Korsakoff's syndrome'. *Neuropsychologia, 23,* 623-638.

Manning, C.A., Hall, J.L., & Gold, P.E. (1990). 'Glucose effects on memory and other neuropsychological tests in elderly humans'. *Psychological Science, 1,* 307-311.

Moffat, N. (1989). 'Home-based cognitive rehabilitation with the elderly'. *In* L. Poon, D. Rubin, and B.A. Wilson (Eds.), *Everyday Cognition in Adult and Later Life.* Cambridge: Cambridge University Press, pp. 659-680.

Molander, B. & Bachman, L. (1989). 'Adult age differences in heart rate patterns during concentration in a precision sport: Implications for attentional functioning'. *Journal of Gerontology: Psychological Sciences, 44,* 80-87.

Morris, R.G. (1984). 'Dementia and the functioning of the articulatory loop system'. *Cognitive Neuropsychology, 1,* 143-157.

Moscovitch, M. (1982). 'A neuropsychological approach to memory and perception'. In F.I.M. Craik and S. Trehub (Eds.), *Aging and Cognitive Processes.* New York: Plenum Press, pp. 55-78.

Nebes, R.D., Brady, C.B., & Jackson, S.T. (1989). 'The effect of semantic and syntactic structure on verbal memory in Alzheimer's Disease'. *Brain and Language, 36,* 301-313.

Poon, L., Rubin, D., and Wilson, B.A. (1989). *Everyday Cognition in Adult and Later Life.* New York: Cambridge University Press.

Rabbitt, P.M.A. (1989). 'Inner-city decay? Age changes in structure and process in recall of familiar topographical information'. *In* L. Poon, D. Rubin, and B.A. Wilson (Eds.), *Everyday Cognition in Adult and Later Life.* Cambridge: Cambridge University Press, pp. 284-299.

Salthouse, T. A. (1992). *Mechanisms of Age-cognition Relations in Adulthood.* Hillsdale, N.J: Lawrence Erlbaum Associates.

Schaie, K.W. 'The hazards of cognitive ageing.' *The Gerontologist, 29,* 484-493.

Schaie, K.W. (1980). 'Cognitive development in ageing'. *In* L.K. Obler and M.L. Albert (Eds.), *Language and Communication in the Elderly: Clinical, Therapeutic and Experimental Issues.* Lexington, Mass.: Lexington Books.

Selkoe, D. J. (1992). 'Aging brain, aging mind'. *Scientific American, 267,* 96-103.

Chapter 14

Baddeley, A.D. (1976). *The Psychology of Memory.* New York: Basic Books.

Bartlett, F. (1932). *Remembering.* Cambridge: Cambridge University Press, reprinted 1972.

Beach, K.D. (1988). 'The role of external mnemonic symbols in acquiring an occupation'. *In* M.M. Gruneberg, P.E. Morris and R.N. Sykes (Eds.), *Practical Aspects of Memory: Current Research and Issues, Vol. 1: Memory in Everyday Life.* Chichester: Wiley, pp. 342-346.

Bransford, J.D. (1979). *Human Cognition: Learning, Understanding and Remembering.* Belmont, California: Wadsworth Publishing Company, pp. 205-245.

Chase, W.G., Lyon, D.R., & Ericsson, K.A. (1981). 'Individual differences in memory span'. *In* M.P. Friedman, J.P. Das and N. O'Connor (Eds.), *Intelligence and Learning.* New York: Plenum Press, pp. 157-162.

Glisky, E.L., Schacter, D., & Tulving, E. (1986). 'Computer learning by memory impaired patients: Acquisition and retention of complex knowledge'. *Neuropsychologia, 24,* 313-328.

Goody, J. & Watt, I. (1968). 'The consequences of literacy'. *In* J. Goody (Ed.), *Literacy in Traditional Societies.* Cambridge: Cambridge University Press.

Harris, J.E. (1980). 'Memory aids people use: Two interview studies'. *Memory and Cognition, 8,* 31-38.

Herrmann, D.J., & Petro, S. J. (1988). 'Commercial memory aids'. *Applied Cognitive Psychology, 4,* 439-450.

Hunter, I.M.L. (1957). *Memory: Facts and Fallacies.* London: Penguin, pp. 306-310.

Hunter, I.M.L. (1979). 'Memory in everyday life'. *In* M. M. Gruneberg and P.E. Morris (Eds.), *Applied Problems in Memory.* London: Academic Press, pp. 1-24.

James, W. (1890). *The Principles of Psychology.* New York: Holt, Rinehart and Winston.

McEvoy, C.L. & Moon, J.R. (1988). 'Assessment and treatment of everyday memory problems in the elderly'. *In* M.M. Gruneberg, P.E. Morris and R.N. Sykes (Eds.), *Practical Aspects of Memory: Current Research and Issues, Vol. 2.* Chichester: Wiley, pp.155-160.

Sleight, W.G. (1911). Cited in Hunter, *Memory: Facts and Fallacies,* pp. 306-310.

Sunderland, A., Harris, J.E., & Gleave, J. (1984). 'Memory failures in everyday life following severe head injury'. *Journal of Clinical Neuropsychology, 6,* 127-142.

Vansina, J. (1973). *Oral Tradition.* Harmondsworth, England: Penguin University Books, page 32.

Wagner, D. (1978). 'Memories of Morocco: The influence of age, schooling and environment on memory'. *Cognitive Psychology, 10,* 1-28.

Wilson, B.A. (1987). *Rehabilitation of Memory.* New York: Guilford Press.

Index

Illustration credits

The author and publishers are grateful for permission to reproduce the graphs which appear in this book. Details of the relevant publications are given in the Bibliography.

Andes Press Agency, London Carlos Reyes 242 • **Associated Press, London** 250 • **Alan Baddeley** 54, 227, 243 • **David Black Oriental Carpets, London** 267 • **CNRI** 206 • **Camera Press, London** 48 • **J. Allan Cash Photolibrary, London** 30, 40, 162, 170 top • **Anne Cope** 222, 226 top • **Edito-Service, Geneva** 103 • **Mary Evans Picture Library, London** 27, 44, 64, 113, 180, 271 Sigmund Freud copyright 125 • Kornak 195 left, 195 centre left • **Hulton Deutsch Collection, London** 107, 225 • **Hutchison Library, London** 268 Kobal Collection, London 129, 196 right • **Kirsty McLaren** 10, 18, 29, 46, 132 left, 132 right, 175, 204, 219, 247 • **Hansell Collection, London** 139 • **Metropolitan Police Service, London** 202 • **Multimedia Books** 73, 119, 126 right, 145, 207, 211, 214, 241, 260 Ron Isaak 126 left, 189, 238 M. Koren 126 centre, 172, 209 • **Oxford Medical Illustration** 155 • **Pictures for Print,** 68, 90, 97, 109, 111, 157, 160, 230, 234, 239, 248, 276 • **Paul Popper, Overstone** 96, 196 left, 275 • **Rex Features, London** 106,. 196 centre • **C. Rovee-Collier** 224 • **Scala, Antella** 195 centre right, 195 right • **Science Photo Library, London** 78, 80, 117 • **Frank Spooner Pictures, London** 135 • **Still Pictures, London** Adrian Arbib 148 • © **University of Newscastle upon Tyne** 14, 72, • **John Walmsley, Albury Heath** 233 • **Wellcome Institute Library, London** 264 • **Janine Wiedel, London** 21, 23, 220 • **ZEFA Picture Library (UK), London** 13, 20 left, 20 right, 22, 25 right, 26, 37, 43, 56 left, 56 centre, 56 right, 60, 70, 77, 83, 88, 92, 100, 104, 123, 136, 147, 152, 158, 168 left, 168 centre, 168 right, 170 bottom, 174, 184, 193 left, 193 centre, 193 right, 201 left, 201 centre, 201 right, 212, 217, 254, 256, 279, front jacket, back jacket left, back jacket right.

The illustration on page 8 is *Trace of Memory* by Elie Abrahami, water colour on paper. Collection Daniel L. Schacter and Susan McGlynn. Reprinted with the permission of the Pucker Gallery, Boston, Massachusetts. The illustration on page 124 is *The Scream* by Edvard Munch, 1983, 91cm x 73cm, oil on canvas. Nasjonalgalleriet, Oslo © Munch Museum, Oslo 1993. Photo J. Lathion.

Multimedia Books have endeavored to observe the legal requirements with regard to the rights of suppliers of photographic material.